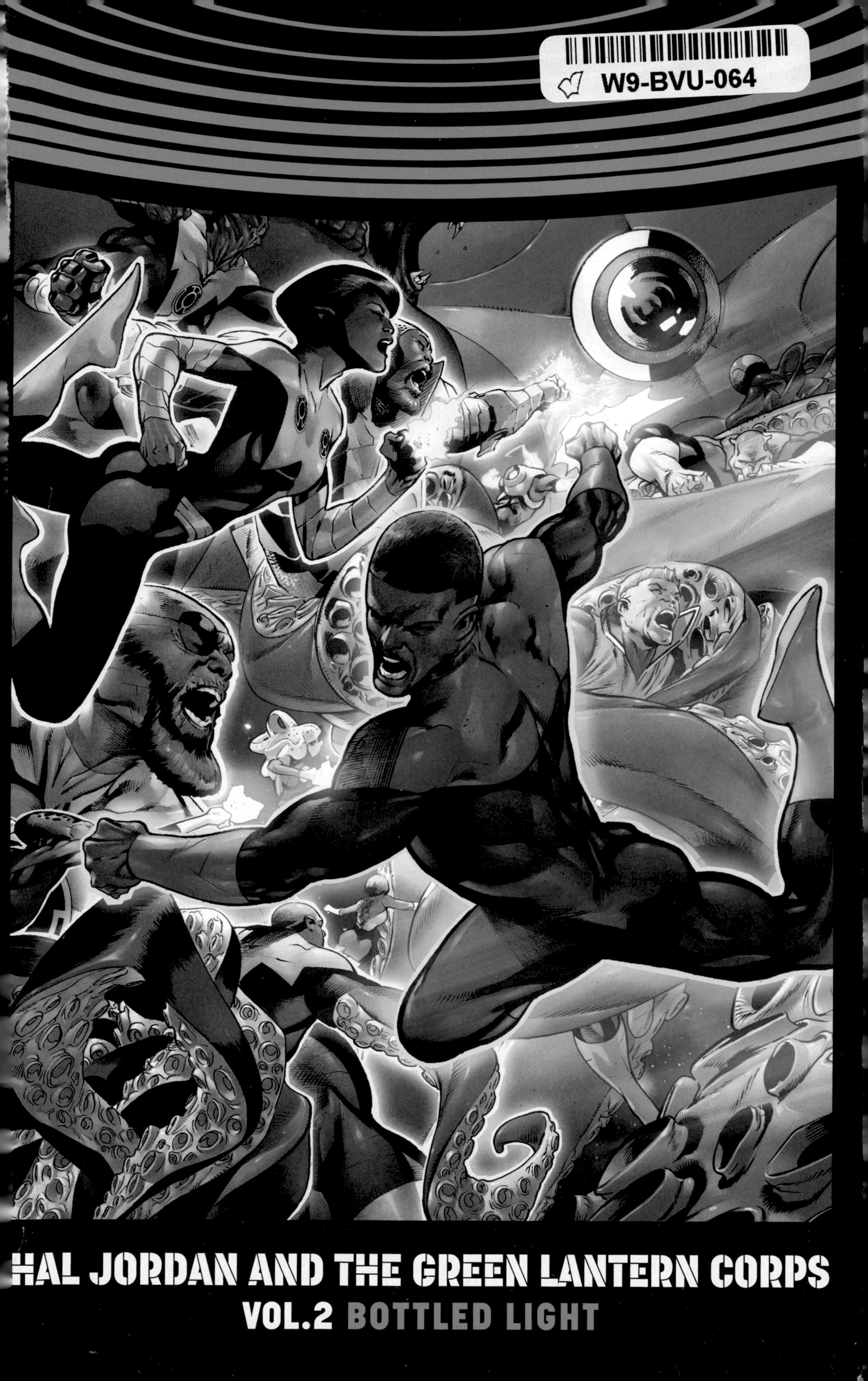

HAL JORDAN AND THE GREEN LANTERN CORPS

VOL.2 BOTTLED LIGHT

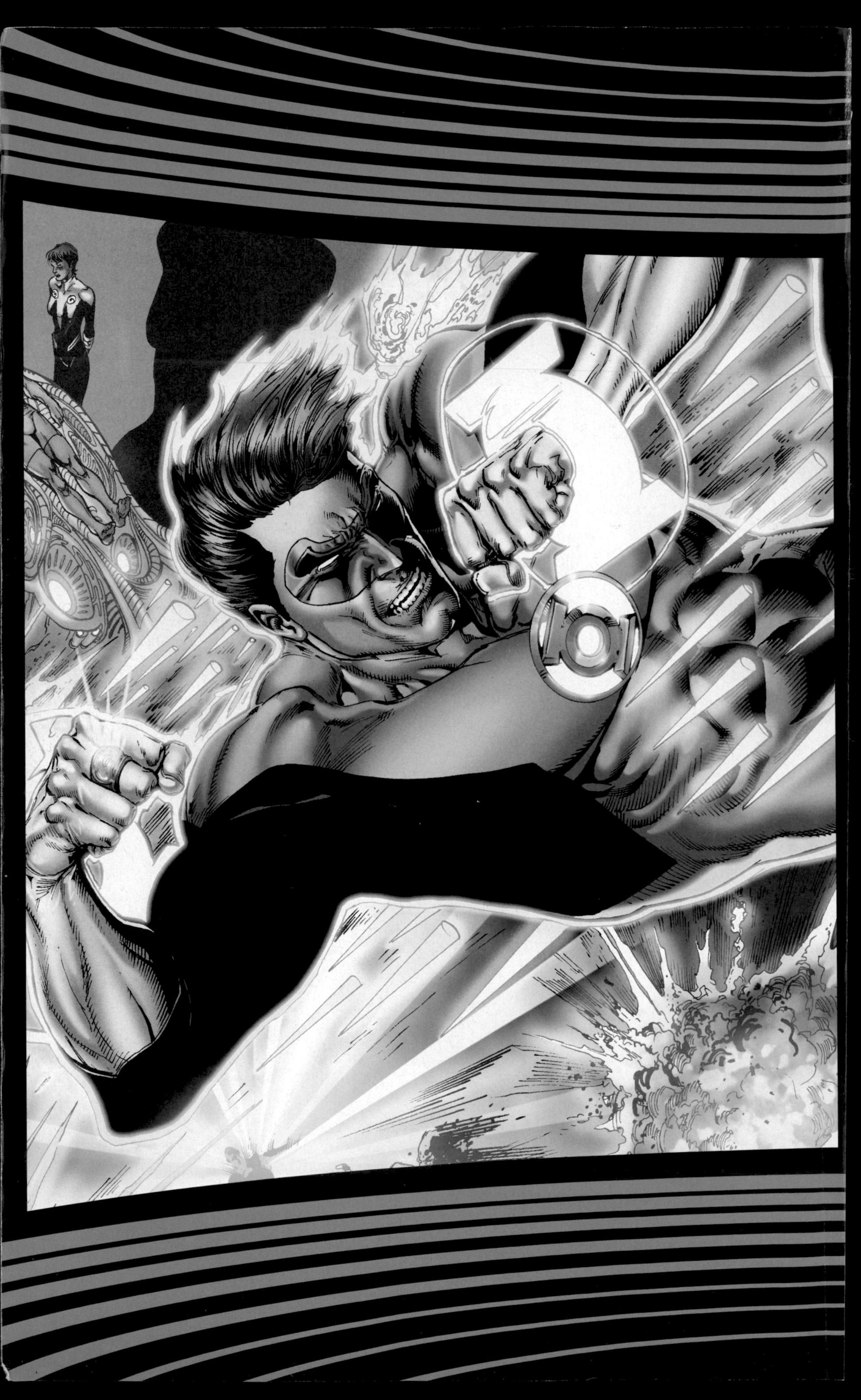

HAL JORDAN AND THE GREEN LANTERN CORPS
VOL.2 BOTTLED LIGHT

ROBERT VENDITTI
writer

ETHAN VAN SCIVER * **RAFA SANDOVAL** * **JORDI TARRAGONA**
ED BENES * **V KEN MARION** * **PAUL NEARY** * **DEXTER VINES**
artists

JASON WRIGHT * **TOMEU MOREY** * **ALEX SOLLAZZO**
colorists

DAVE SHARPE
letterer

ETHAN VAN SCIVER and **JASON WRIGHT**
collection cover artists

MIKE COTTON Editor - Original Series ✴ **ANDREW MARINO** Assistant Editor - Original Series
JEB WOODARD Group Editor - Collected Editions ✴ **PAUL SANTOS** Editor - Collected Edition
STEVE COOK Design Director - Books ✴ **MONIQUE GRUSPE** Publication Design

BOB HARRAS Senior VP - Editor-in-Chief, DC Comics

DIANE NELSON President ✴ **DAN DiDIO** Publisher ✴ **JIM LEE** Publisher ✴ **GEOFF JOHNS** President & Chief Creative Officer
AMIT DESAI Executive VP - Business & Marketing Strategy, Direct to Consumer & Global Franchise Management
SAM ADES Senior VP - Direct to Consumer ✴ **BOBBIE CHASE** VP - Talent Development ✴ **MARK CHIARELLO** Senior VP - Art, Design & Collected Editions
JOHN CUNNINGHAM Senior VP - Sales & Trade Marketing ✴ **ANNE DePIES** Senior VP - Business Strategy, Finance & Administration
DON FALLETTI VP - Manufacturing Operations ✴ **LAWRENCE GANEM** VP - Editorial Administration & Talent Relations
ALISON GILL Senior VP - Manufacturing & Operations ✴ **HANK KANALZ** Senior VP - Editorial Strategy & Administration
JAY KOGAN VP - Legal Affairs ✴ **THOMAS LOFTUS** VP - Business Affairs ✴ **JACK MAHAN** VP - Business Affairs
NICK J. NAPOLITANO VP - Manufacturing Administration ✴ **EDDIE SCANNELL** VP - Consumer Marketing
COURTNEY SIMMONS Senior VP - Publicity & Communications ✴ **JIM (SKI) SOKOLOWSKI** VP - Comic Book Specialty Sales & Trade Marketing
NANCY SPEARS VP - Mass, Book, Digital Sales & Trade Marketing

HAL JORDAN AND THE GREEN LANTERN CORPS VOLUME 2: BOTTLED LIGHT

DC Comics, 2900 West Alameda Ave., Burbank, CA 91505
Printed by LSC Communications, Salem, VA, USA. 4/25/17. First Printing.
ISBN: 978-1-4012-6913-5

Library of Congress Cataloging-in-Publication Data is available.

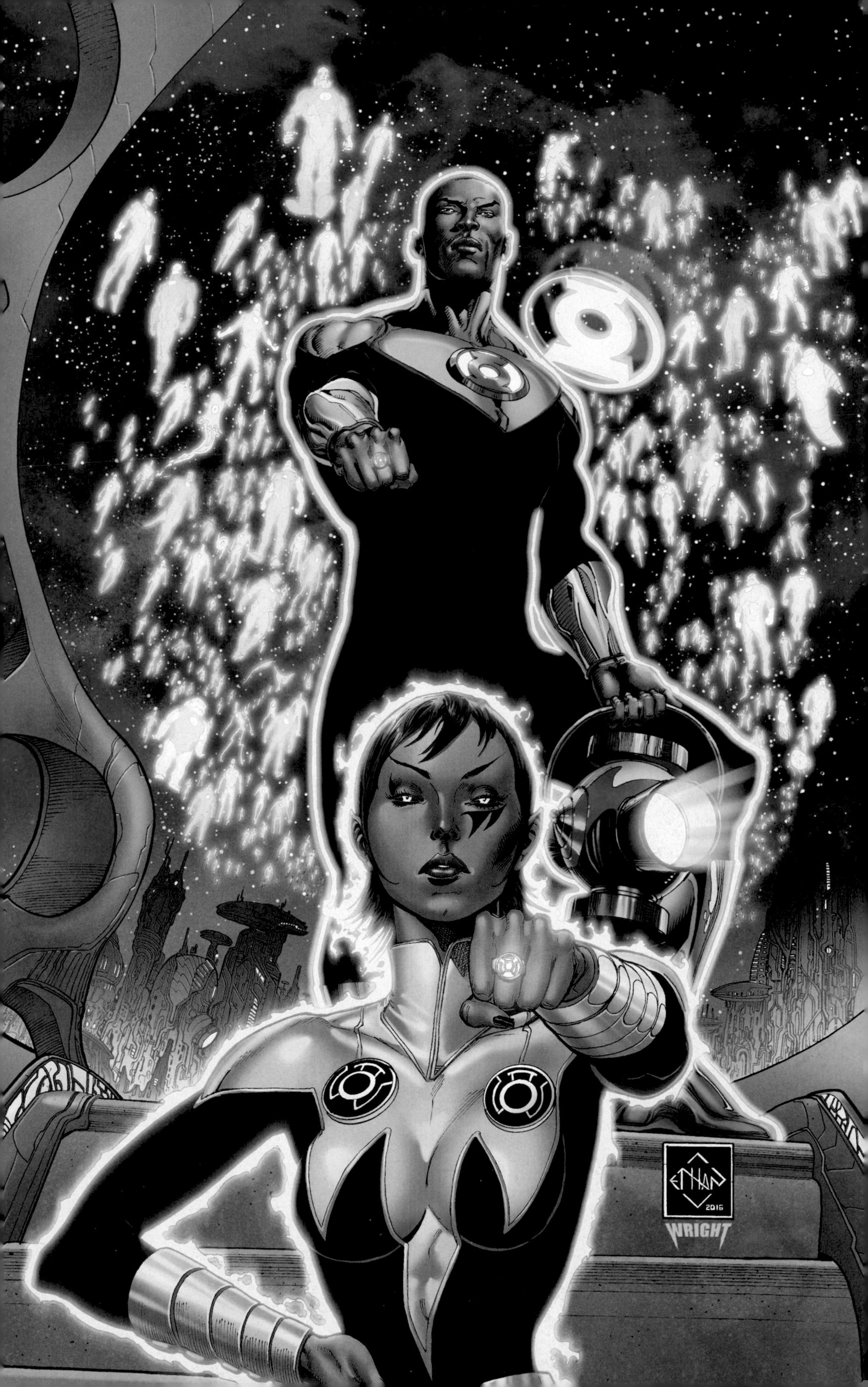
ETHAN
2016
WRIGHT

"BOTTLED LIGHT PART 1: DUTY CALLS"

ETHAN VAN SCIVER artist * JASON WRIGHT colorist

ETHAN VAN SCIVER and JASON WRIGHT cover artists

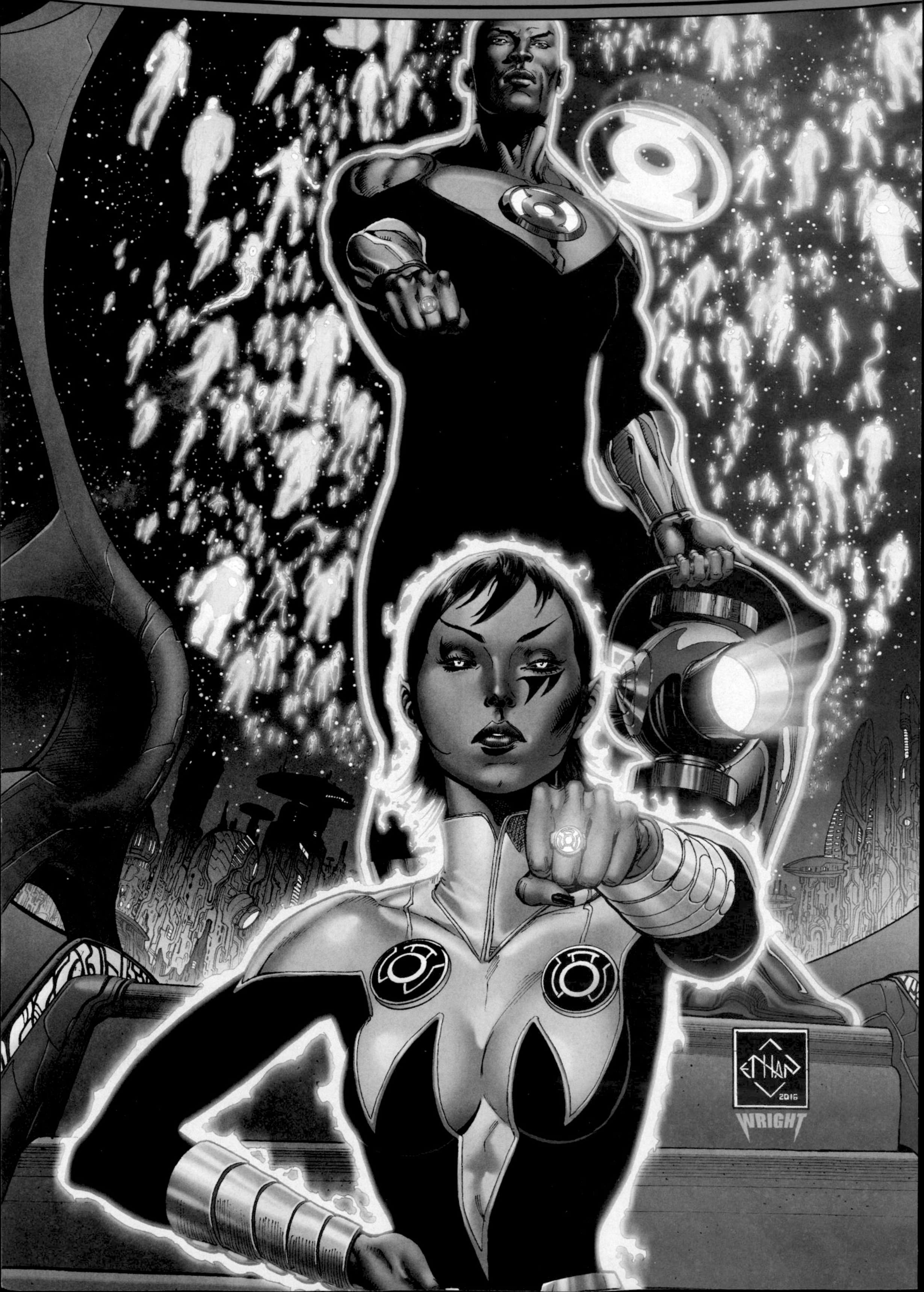

ETHAN 2016
WRIGHT

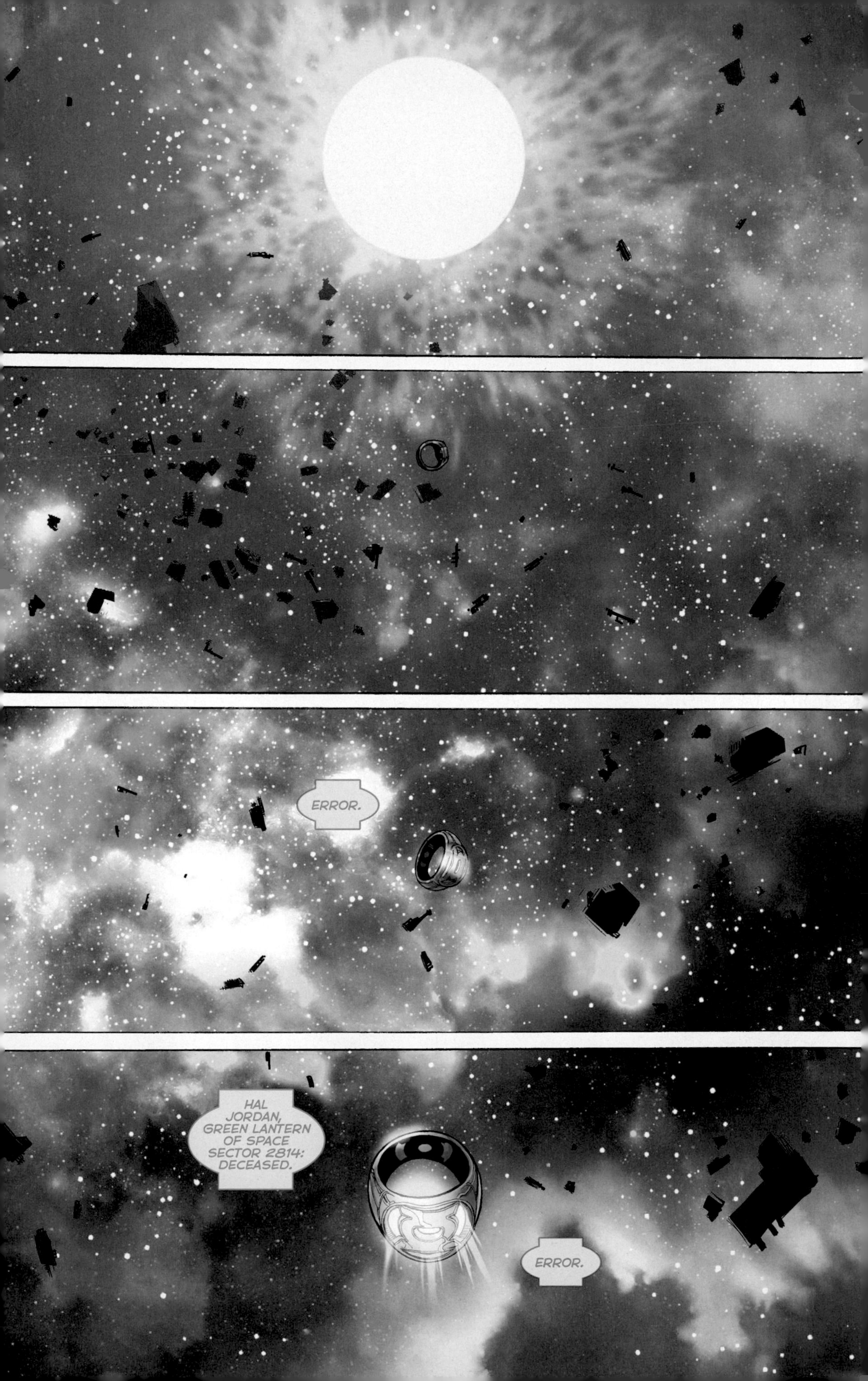
ERROR.
HAL JORDAN, GREEN LANTERN OF SPACE SECTOR 2814: DECEASED.
ERROR.

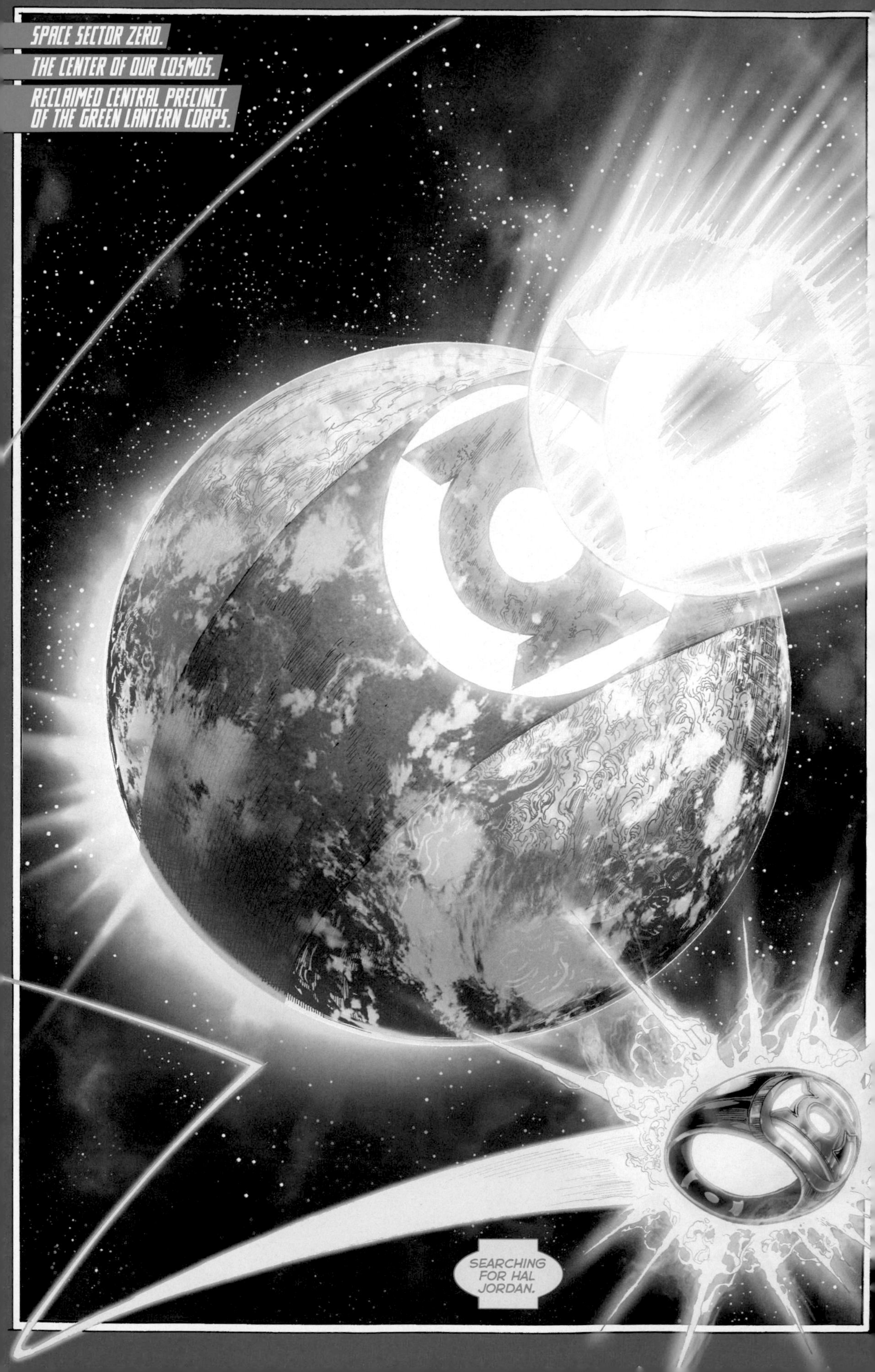
SPACE SECTOR ZERO.
THE CENTER OF OUR COSMOS.
RECLAIMED CENTRAL PRECINCT OF THE GREEN LANTERN CORPS.
SEARCHING FOR HAL JORDAN.

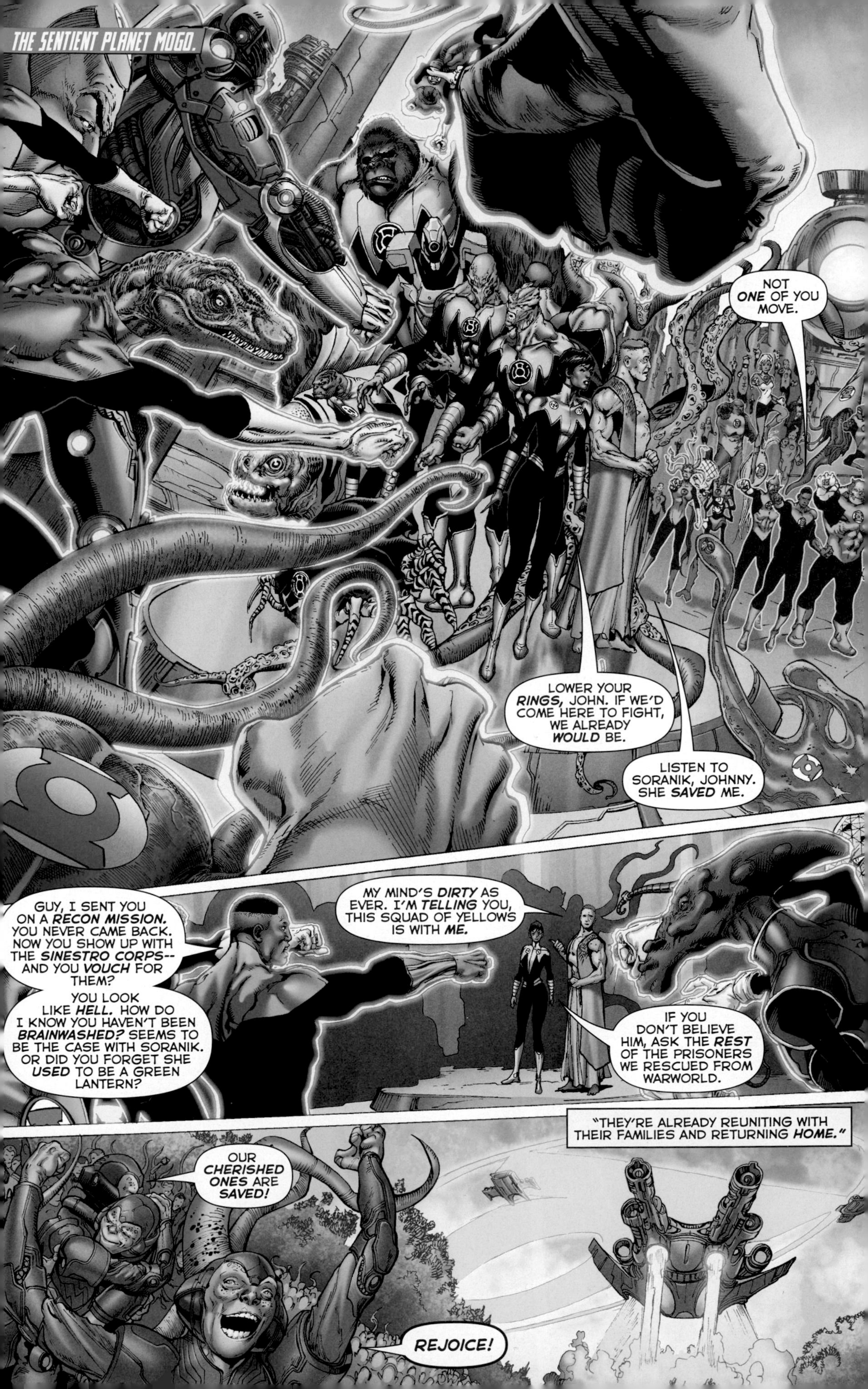
THE SENTIENT PLANET MOGO.
NOT ONE OF YOU MOVE.
LOWER YOUR RINGS, JOHN. IF WE'D COME HERE TO FIGHT, WE ALREADY WOULD BE.
LISTEN TO SORANIK, JOHNNY. SHE SAVED ME.
GUY, I SENT YOU ON A RECON MISSION. YOU NEVER CAME BACK. NOW YOU SHOW UP WITH THE SINESTRO CORPS-- AND YOU VOUCH FOR THEM?
YOU LOOK LIKE HELL. HOW DO I KNOW YOU HAVEN'T BEEN BRAINWASHED? SEEMS TO BE THE CASE WITH SORANIK. OR DID YOU FORGET SHE USED TO BE A GREEN LANTERN?
MY MIND'S DIRTY AS EVER. I'M TELLING YOU, THIS SQUAD OF YELLOWS IS WITH ME.
IF YOU DON'T BELIEVE HIM, ASK THE REST OF THE PRISONERS WE RESCUED FROM WARWORLD.
"THEY'RE ALREADY REUNITING WITH THEIR FAMILIES AND RETURNING HOME."
OUR CHERISHED ONES ARE SAVED!
REJOICE!

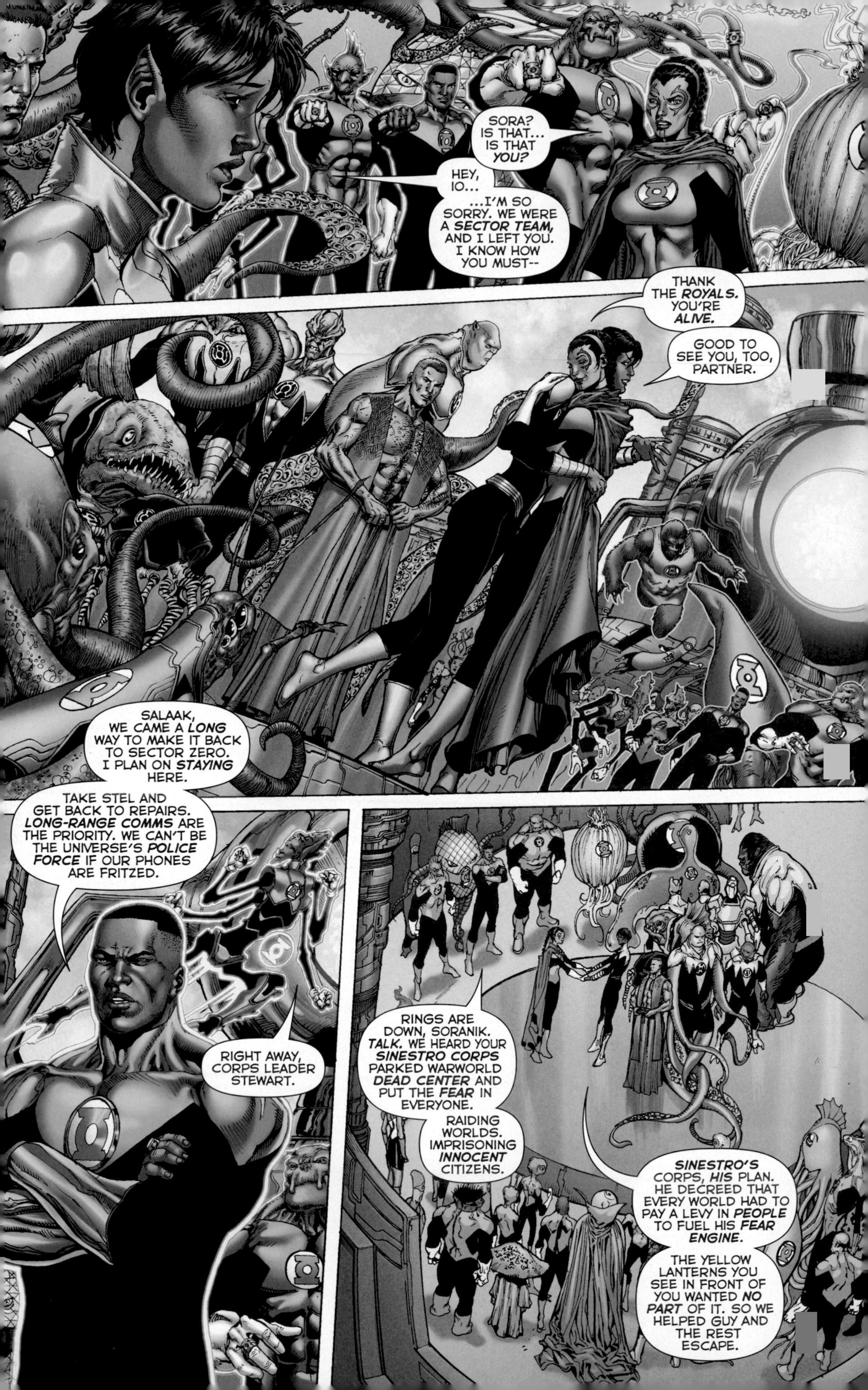
SORA? IS THAT... IS THAT YOU?
HEY, IO...
...I'M SO SORRY. WE WERE A SECTOR TEAM, AND I LEFT YOU. I KNOW HOW YOU MUST--
THANK THE ROYALS. YOU'RE ALIVE.
GOOD TO SEE YOU, TOO, PARTNER.
SALAAK, WE CAME A LONG WAY TO MAKE IT BACK TO SECTOR ZERO. I PLAN ON STAYING HERE.
TAKE STEL AND GET BACK TO REPAIRS. LONG-RANGE COMMS ARE THE PRIORITY. WE CAN'T BE THE UNIVERSE'S POLICE FORCE IF OUR PHONES ARE FRITZED.
RIGHT AWAY, CORPS LEADER STEWART.
RINGS ARE DOWN, SORANIK. TALK. WE HEARD YOUR SINESTRO CORPS PARKED WARWORLD DEAD CENTER AND PUT THE FEAR IN EVERYONE.
RAIDING WORLDS. IMPRISONING INNOCENT CITIZENS.
SINESTRO'S CORPS, HIS PLAN. HE DECREED THAT EVERY WORLD HAD TO PAY A LEVY IN PEOPLE TO FUEL HIS FEAR ENGINE.
THE YELLOW LANTERNS YOU SEE IN FRONT OF YOU WANTED NO PART OF IT. SO WE HELPED GUY AND THE REST ESCAPE.

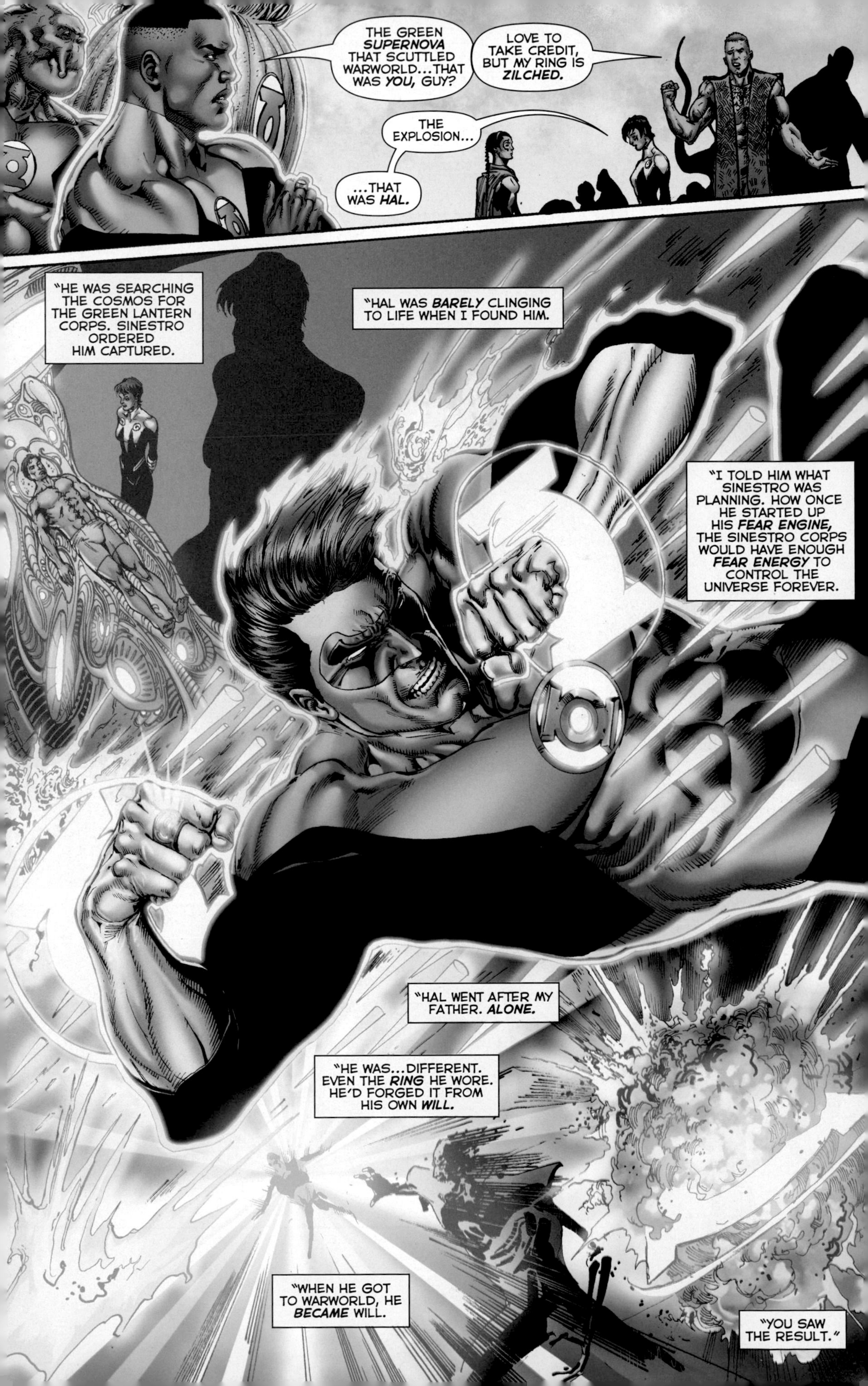
THE GREEN SUPERNOVA THAT SCUTTLED WARWORLD...THAT WAS YOU, GUY?
LOVE TO TAKE CREDIT, BUT MY RING IS ZILCHED.
THE EXPLOSION...
...THAT WAS HAL.
"HE WAS SEARCHING THE COSMOS FOR THE GREEN LANTERN CORPS. SINESTRO ORDERED HIM CAPTURED.
"HAL WAS BARELY CLINGING TO LIFE WHEN I FOUND HIM.
"I TOLD HIM WHAT SINESTRO WAS PLANNING. HOW ONCE HE STARTED UP HIS FEAR ENGINE, THE SINESTRO CORPS WOULD HAVE ENOUGH FEAR ENERGY TO CONTROL THE UNIVERSE FOREVER.
"HAL WENT AFTER MY FATHER. ALONE.
"HE WAS...DIFFERENT. EVEN THE RING HE WORE. HE'D FORGED IT FROM HIS OWN WILL.
"WHEN HE GOT TO WARWORLD, HE BECAME WILL.
"YOU SAW THE RESULT."

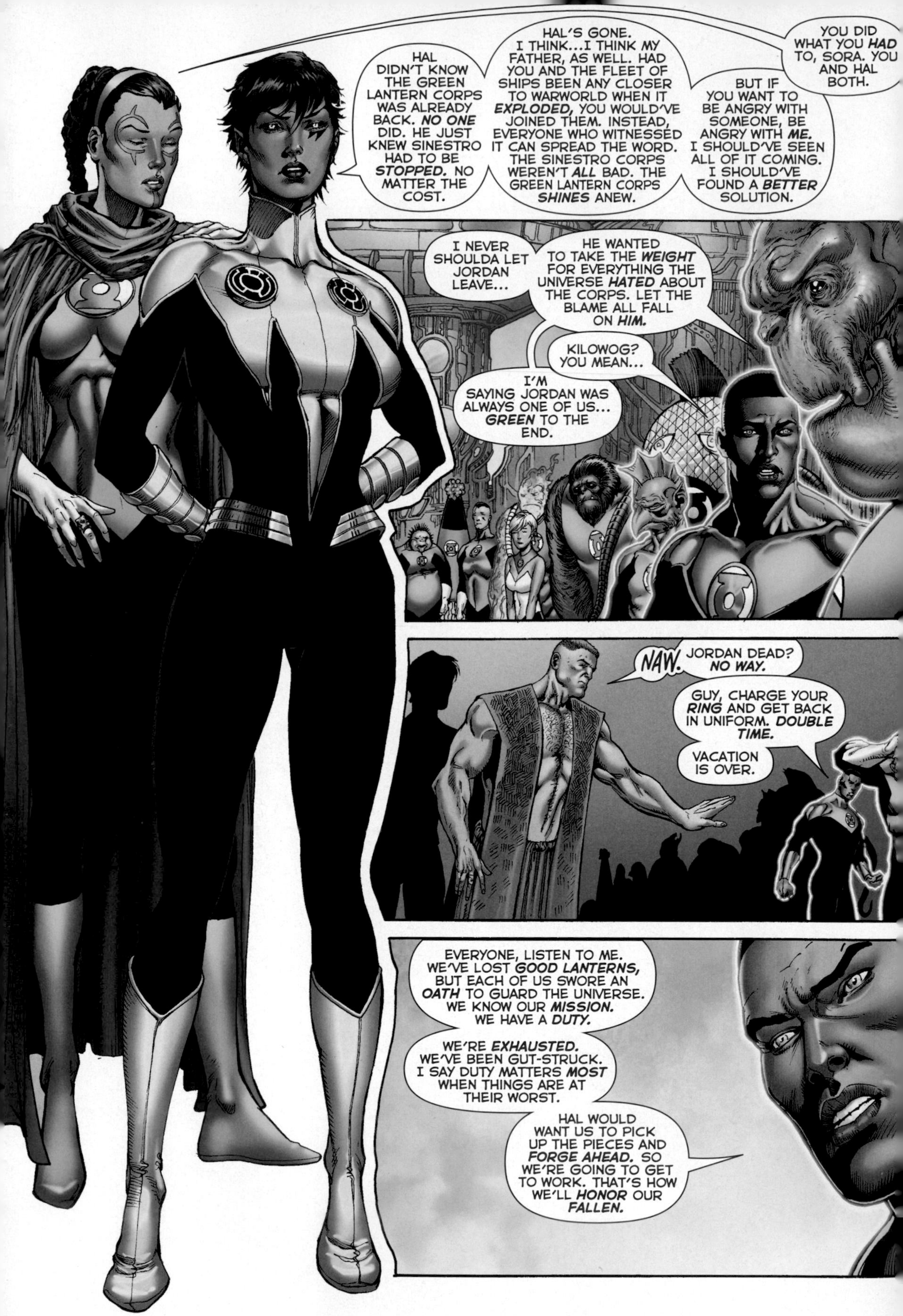
HAL DIDN'T KNOW THE GREEN LANTERN CORPS WAS ALREADY BACK. NO ONE DID. HE JUST KNEW SINESTRO HAD TO BE STOPPED. NO MATTER THE COST.
HAL'S GONE. I THINK...I THINK MY FATHER, AS WELL. HAD YOU AND THE FLEET OF SHIPS BEEN ANY CLOSER TO WARWORLD WHEN IT EXPLODED, YOU WOULD'VE JOINED THEM. INSTEAD, EVERYONE WHO WITNESSED IT CAN SPREAD THE WORD. THE SINESTRO CORPS WEREN'T ALL BAD. THE GREEN LANTERN CORPS SHINES ANEW.
YOU DID WHAT YOU HAD TO, SORA. YOU AND HAL BOTH.
BUT IF YOU WANT TO BE ANGRY WITH SOMEONE, BE ANGRY WITH ME. I SHOULD'VE SEEN ALL OF IT COMING. I SHOULD'VE FOUND A BETTER SOLUTION.
I NEVER SHOULDA LET JORDAN LEAVE...
HE WANTED TO TAKE THE WEIGHT FOR EVERYTHING THE UNIVERSE HATED ABOUT THE CORPS. LET THE BLAME ALL FALL ON HIM.
KILOWOG? YOU MEAN...
I'M SAYING JORDAN WAS ALWAYS ONE OF US... GREEN TO THE END.
NAW. JORDAN DEAD? NO WAY.
GUY, CHARGE YOUR RING AND GET BACK IN UNIFORM. DOUBLE TIME.
VACATION IS OVER.
EVERYONE, LISTEN TO ME. WE'VE LOST GOOD LANTERNS, BUT EACH OF US SWORE AN OATH TO GUARD THE UNIVERSE. WE KNOW OUR MISSION. WE HAVE A DUTY.
WE'RE EXHAUSTED. WE'VE BEEN GUT-STRUCK. I SAY DUTY MATTERS MOST WHEN THINGS ARE AT THEIR WORST.
HAL WOULD WANT US TO PICK UP THE PIECES AND FORGE AHEAD. SO WE'RE GOING TO GET TO WORK. THAT'S HOW WE'LL HONOR OUR FALLEN.

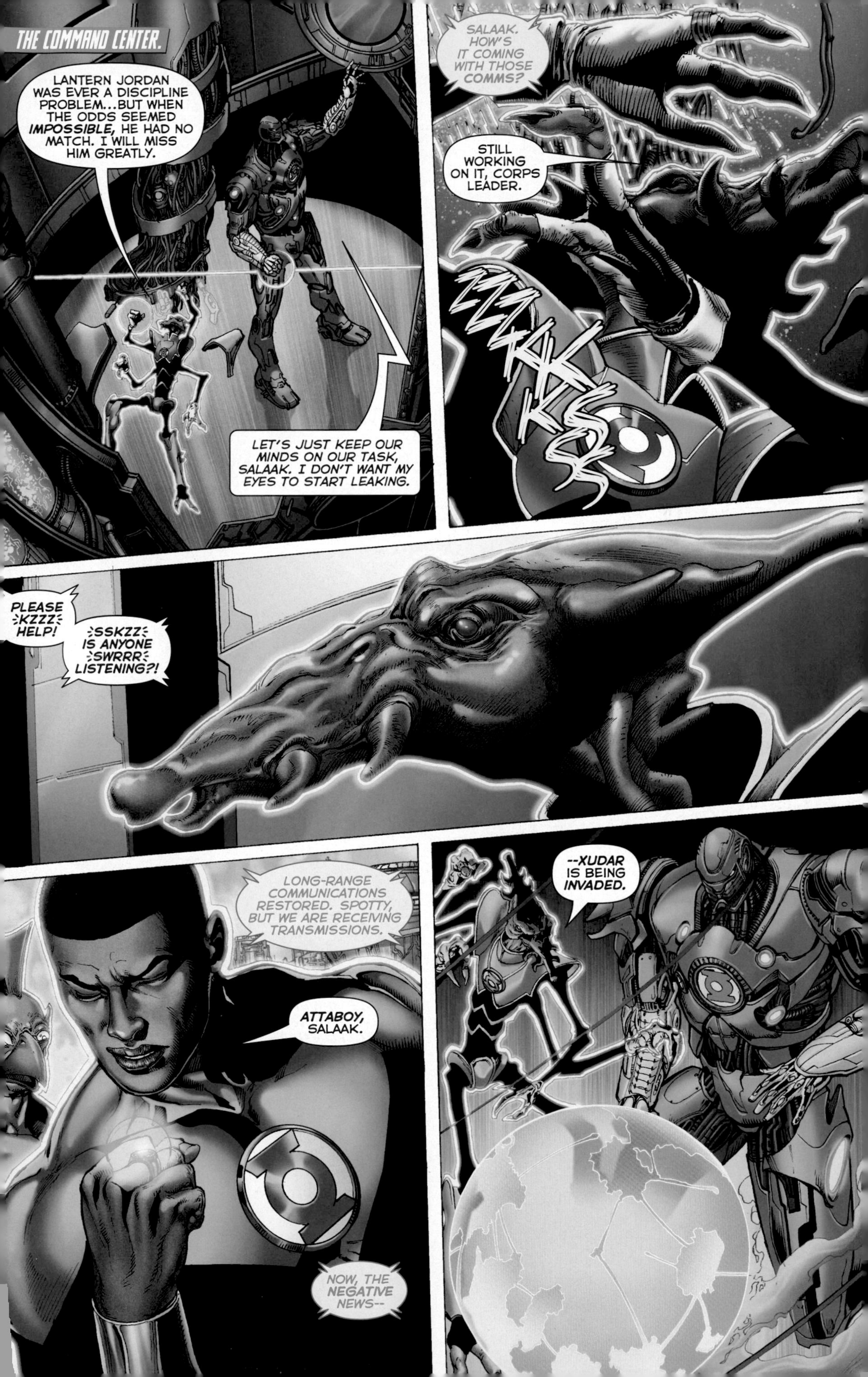
THE COMMAND CENTER.
LANTERN JORDAN WAS EVER A DISCIPLINE PROBLEM...BUT WHEN THE ODDS SEEMED IMPOSSIBLE, HE HAD NO MATCH. I WILL MISS HIM GREATLY.
LET'S JUST KEEP OUR MINDS ON OUR TASK, SALAAK. I DON'T WANT MY EYES TO START LEAKING.
SALAAK. HOW'S IT COMING WITH THOSE COMMS?
STILL WORKING ON IT, CORPS LEADER.
ZZZAKKKKSSSS
PLEASE KZZZ HELP!
SSKZZ IS ANYONE SWRRR LISTENING?!
LONG-RANGE COMMUNICATIONS RESTORED. SPOTTY, BUT WE ARE RECEIVING TRANSMISSIONS.
ATTABOY, SALAAK.
NOW, THE NEGATIVE NEWS--
--XUDAR IS BEING INVADED.

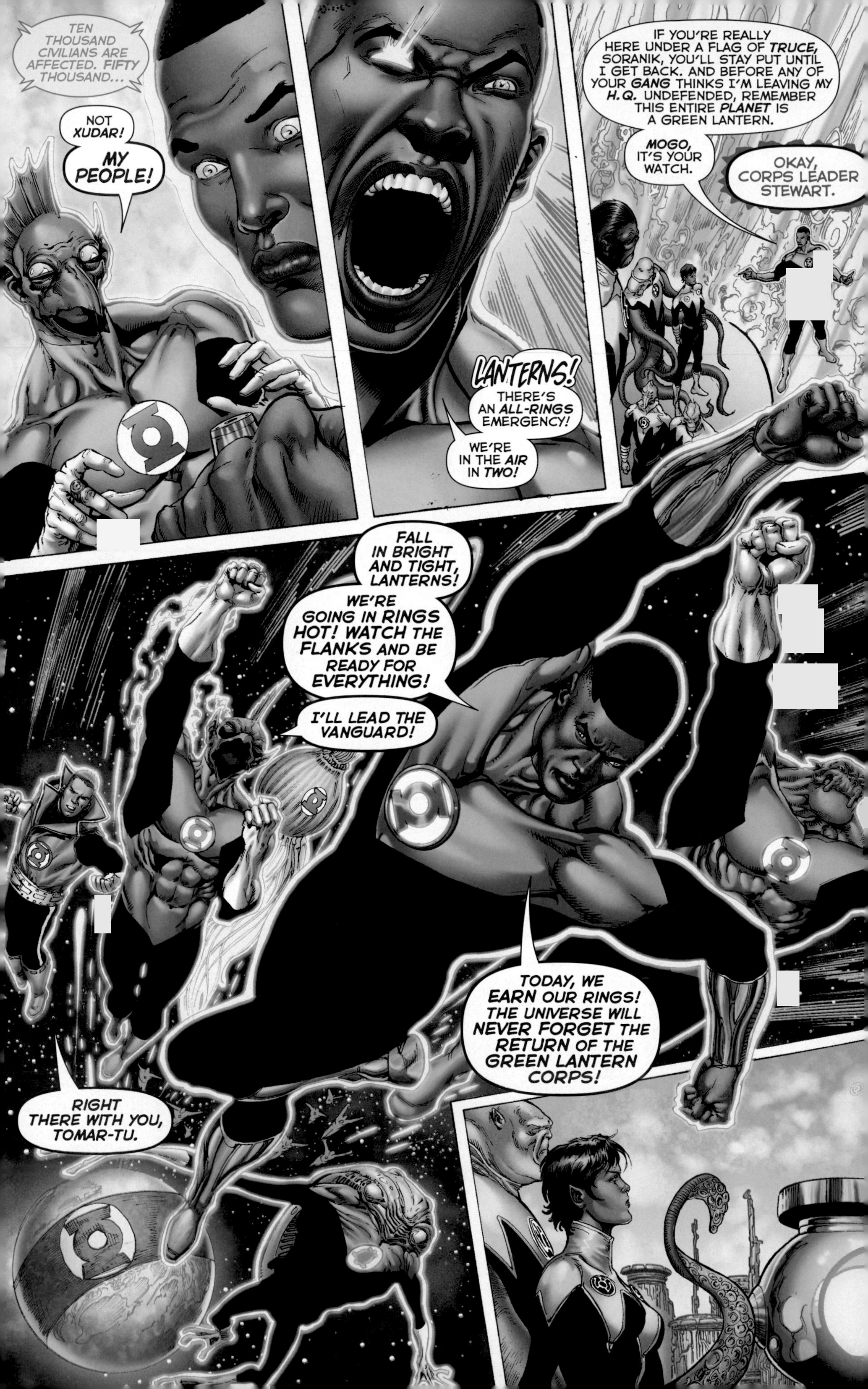
TEN THOUSAND CIVILIANS ARE AFFECTED. FIFTY THOUSAND...
NOT XUDAR!
MY PEOPLE!
LANTERNS!
THERE'S AN ALL-RINGS EMERGENCY!
WE'RE IN THE AIR IN TWO!
IF YOU'RE REALLY HERE UNDER A FLAG OF TRUCE, SORANIK, YOU'LL STAY PUT UNTIL I GET BACK. AND BEFORE ANY OF YOUR GANG THINKS I'M LEAVING MY H.Q. UNDEFENDED, REMEMBER THIS ENTIRE PLANET IS A GREEN LANTERN.
MOGO, IT'S YOUR WATCH.
OKAY, CORPS LEADER STEWART.
FALL IN BRIGHT AND TIGHT, LANTERNS!
WE'RE GOING IN RINGS HOT! WATCH THE FLANKS AND BE READY FOR EVERYTHING!
I'LL LEAD THE VANGUARD!
TODAY, WE EARN OUR RINGS! THE UNIVERSE WILL NEVER FORGET THE RETURN OF THE GREEN LANTERN CORPS!
RIGHT THERE WITH YOU, TOMAR-TU.

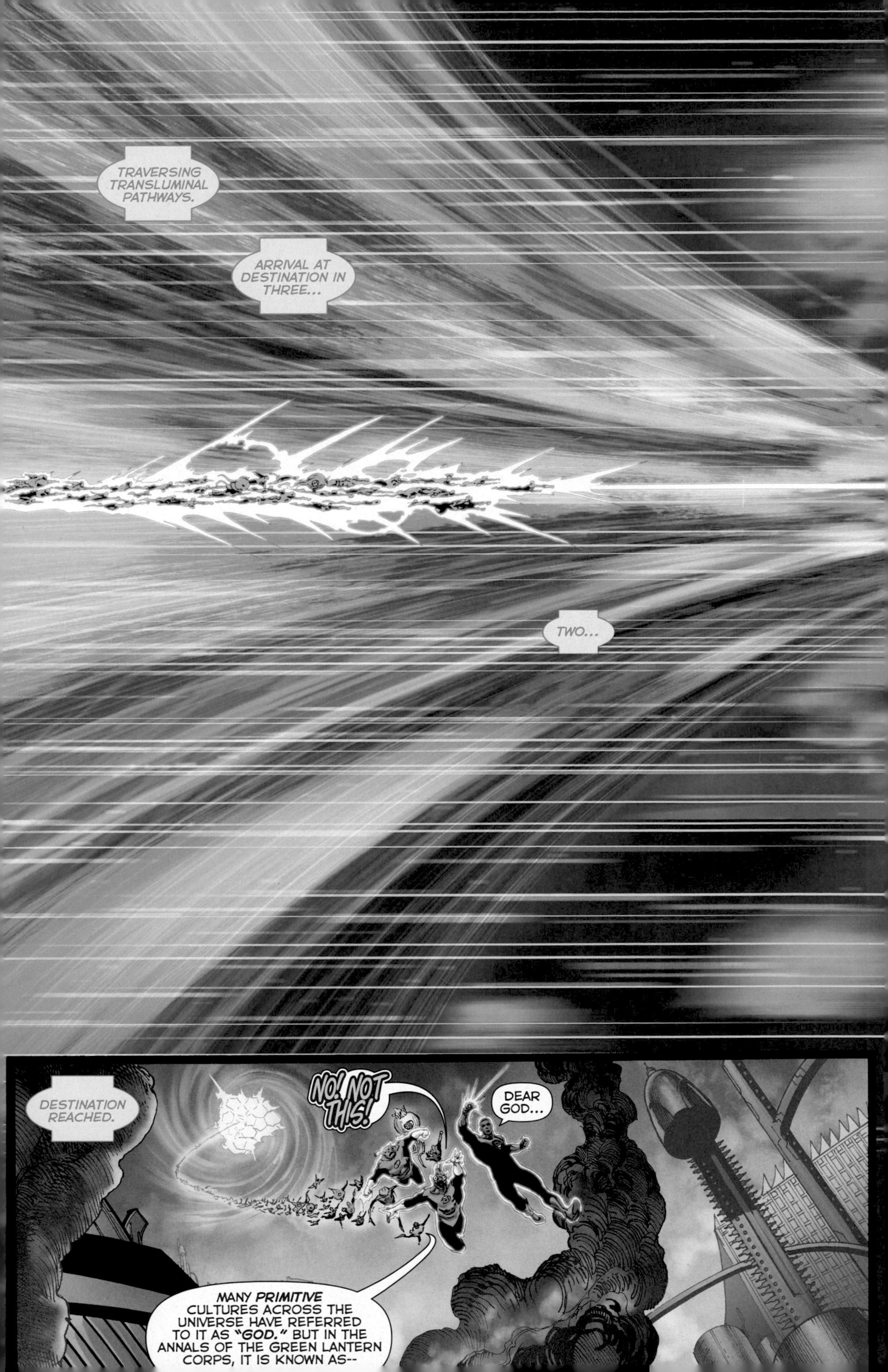
TRAVERSING TRANSLUMINAL PATHWAYS.
ARRIVAL AT DESTINATION IN THREE...
TWO...
DESTINATION REACHED.
NO! NOT THIS!
DEAR GOD...
MANY PRIMITIVE CULTURES ACROSS THE UNIVERSE HAVE REFERRED TO IT AS "GOD." BUT IN THE ANNALS OF THE GREEN LANTERN CORPS, IT IS KNOWN AS--

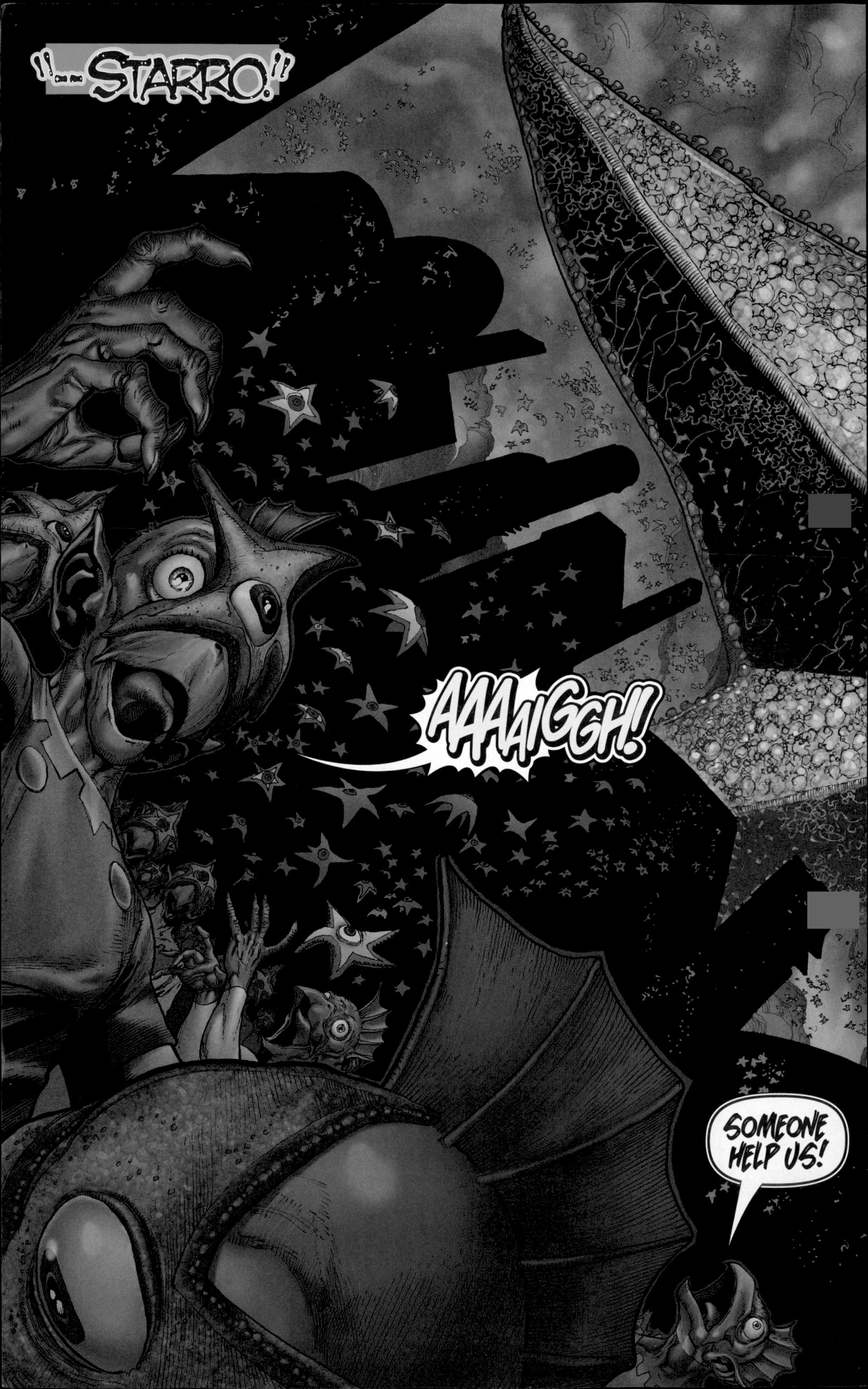
"...STARRO!"
AAAAIGGH!
SOMEONE HELP US!

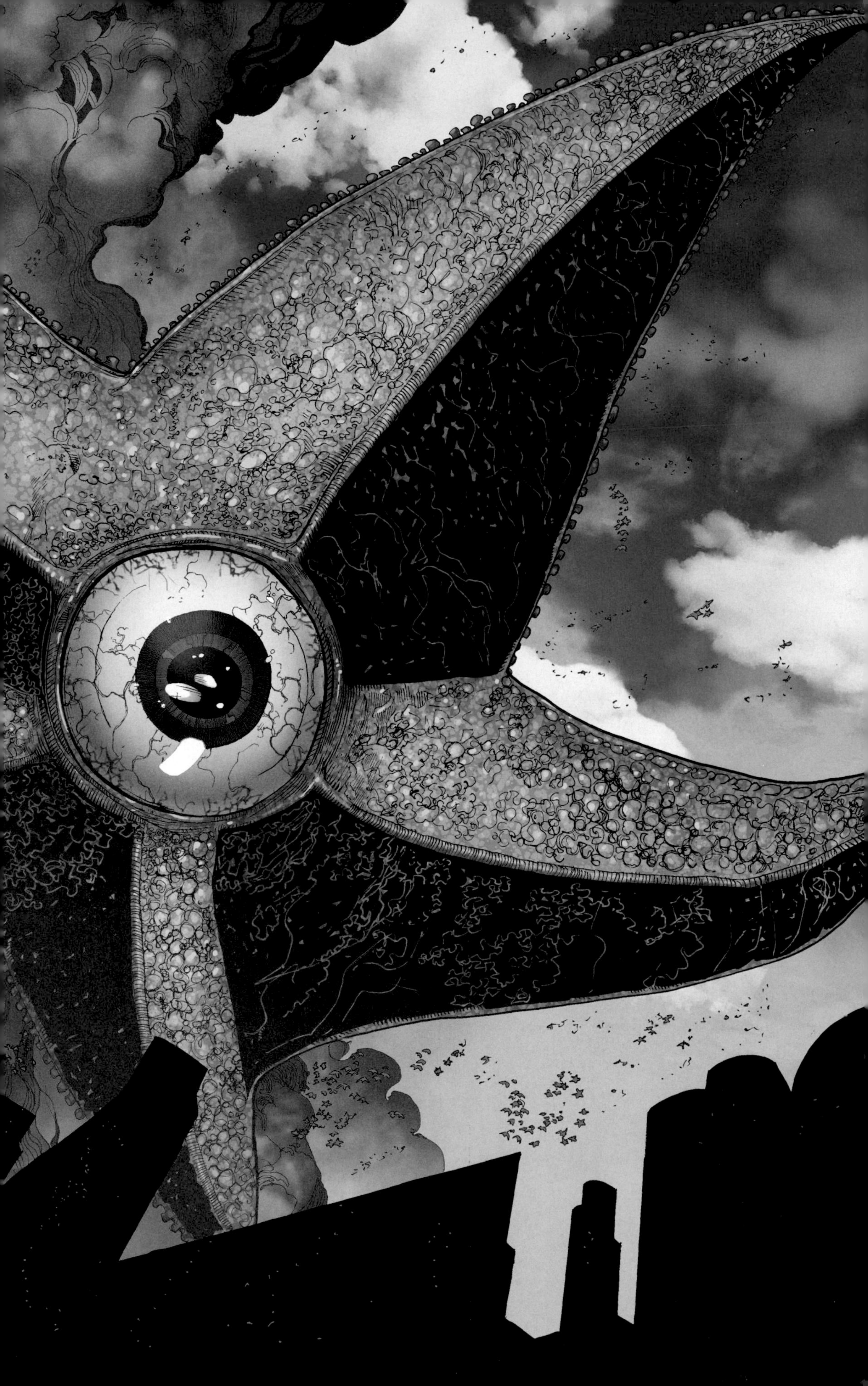

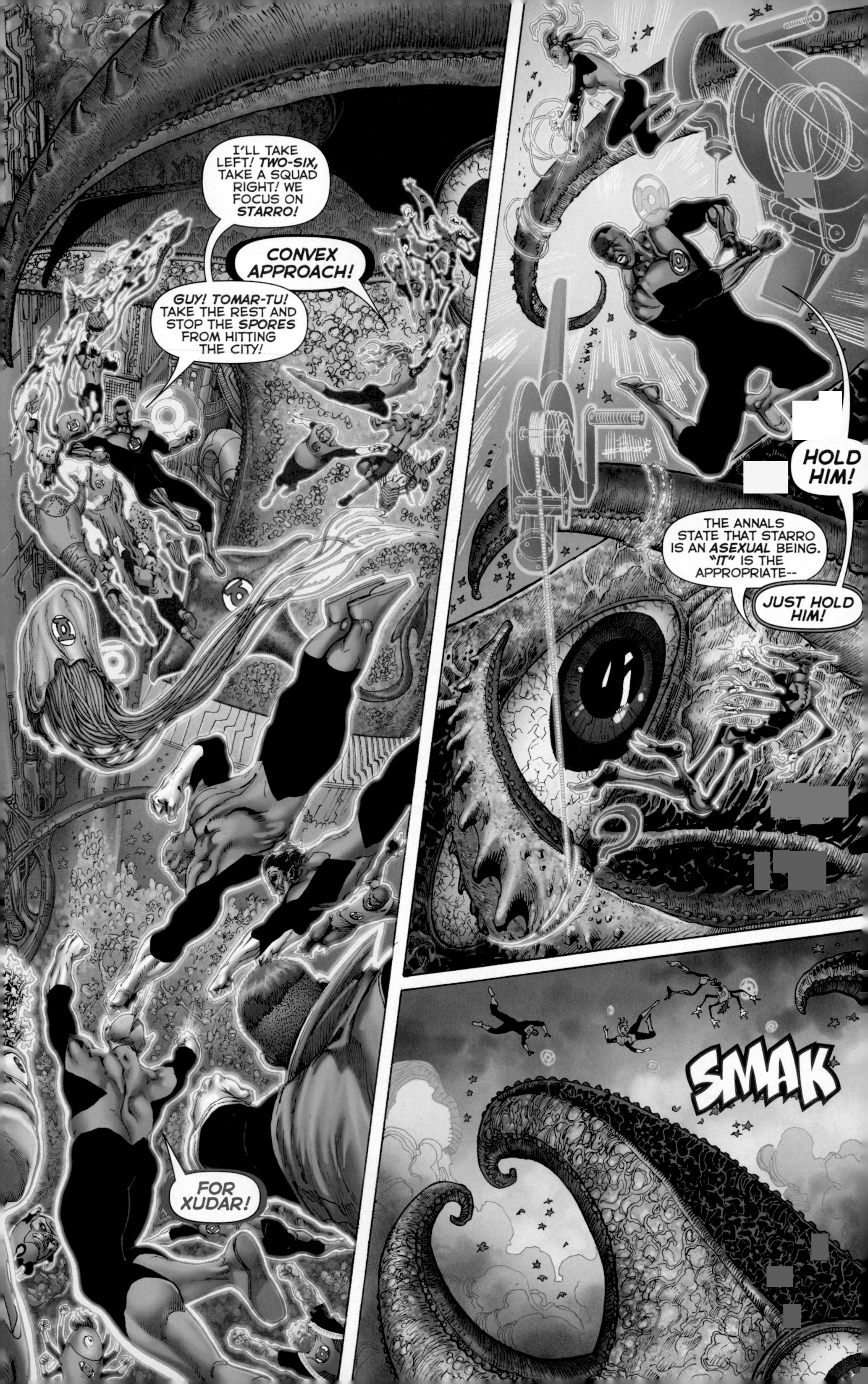
I'LL TAKE LEFT! TWO-SIX, TAKE A SQUAD RIGHT! WE FOCUS ON STARRO!
CONVEX APPROACH!
GUY! TOMAR-TU! TAKE THE REST AND STOP THE SPORES FROM HITTING THE CITY!
FOR XUDAR!
HOLD HIM!
THE ANNALS STATE THAT STARRO IS AN ASEXUAL BEING. "IT" IS THE APPROPRIATE--
JUST HOLD HIM!
SMAK

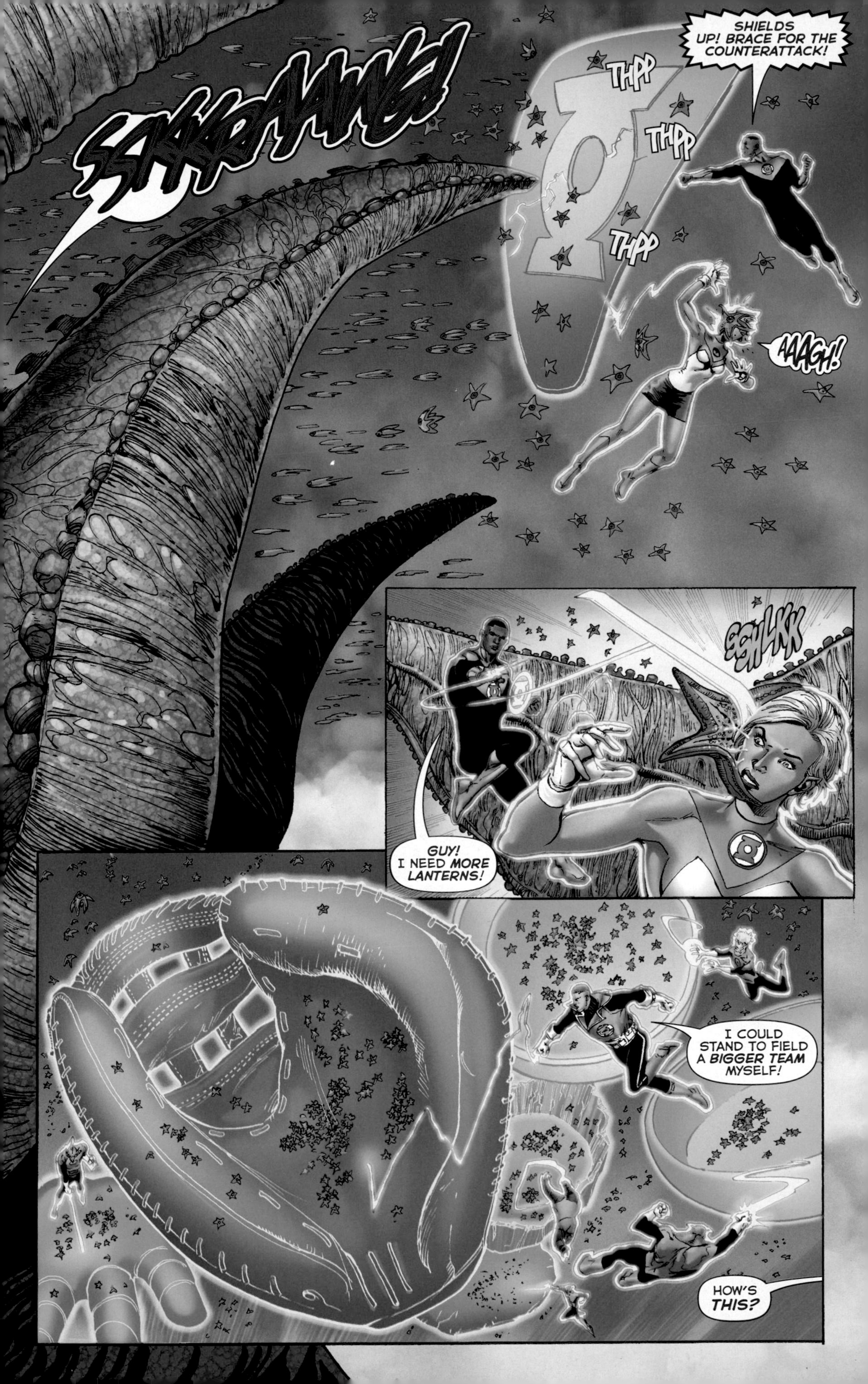
SSKRAAAWG!
SHIELDS UP! BRACE FOR THE COUNTERATTACK!
THPP
THPP
THPP
AAAGH!
SSCHLKK
GUY! I NEED MORE LANTERNS!
I COULD STAND TO FIELD A BIGGER TEAM MYSELF!
HOW'S THIS?

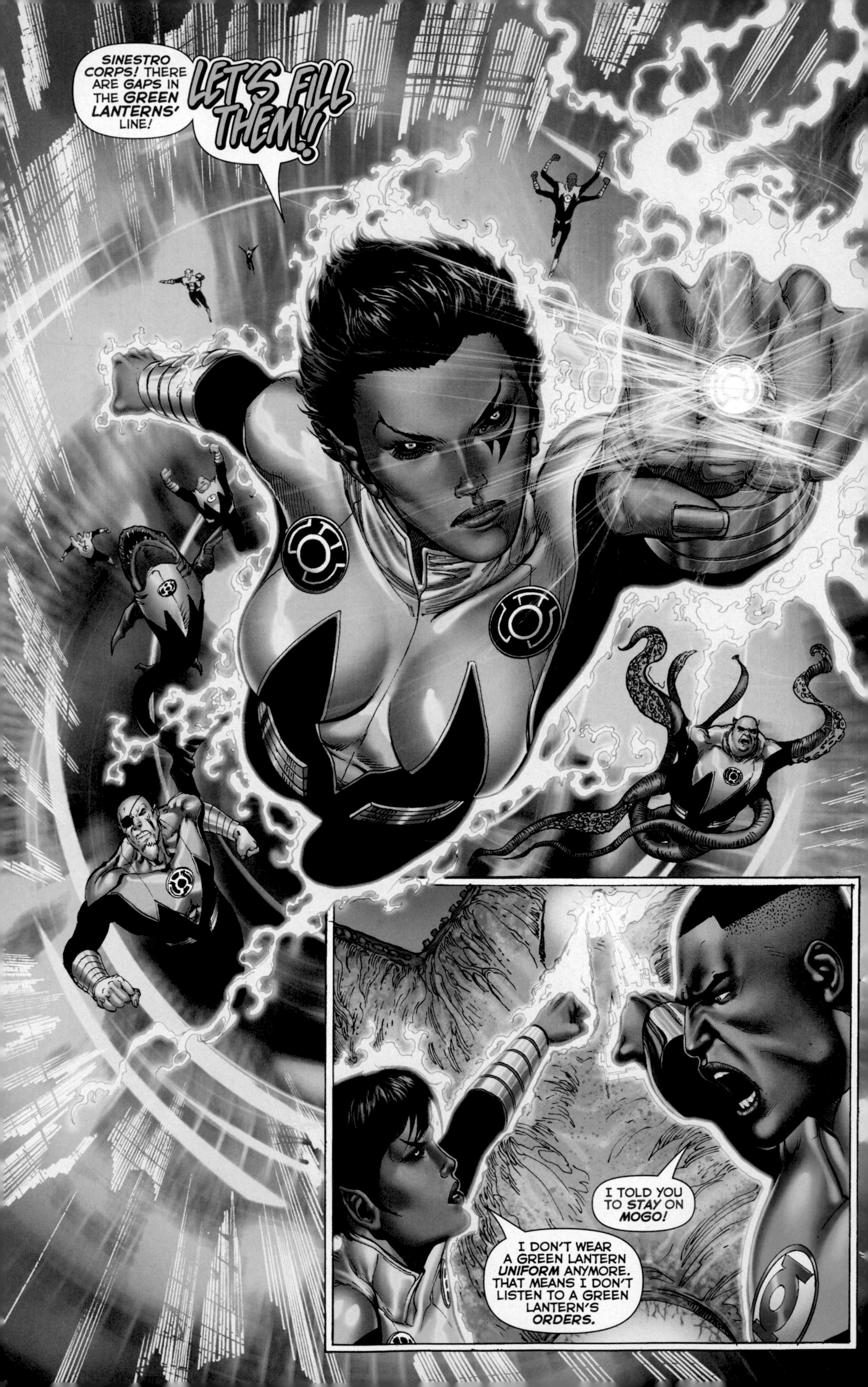
SINESTRO CORPS! THERE ARE GAPS IN THE GREEN LANTERNS' LINE!
LET'S FILL THEM!!
I TOLD YOU TO STAY ON MOGO!
I DON'T WEAR A GREEN LANTERN UNIFORM ANYMORE. THAT MEANS I DON'T LISTEN TO A GREEN LANTERN'S ORDERS.

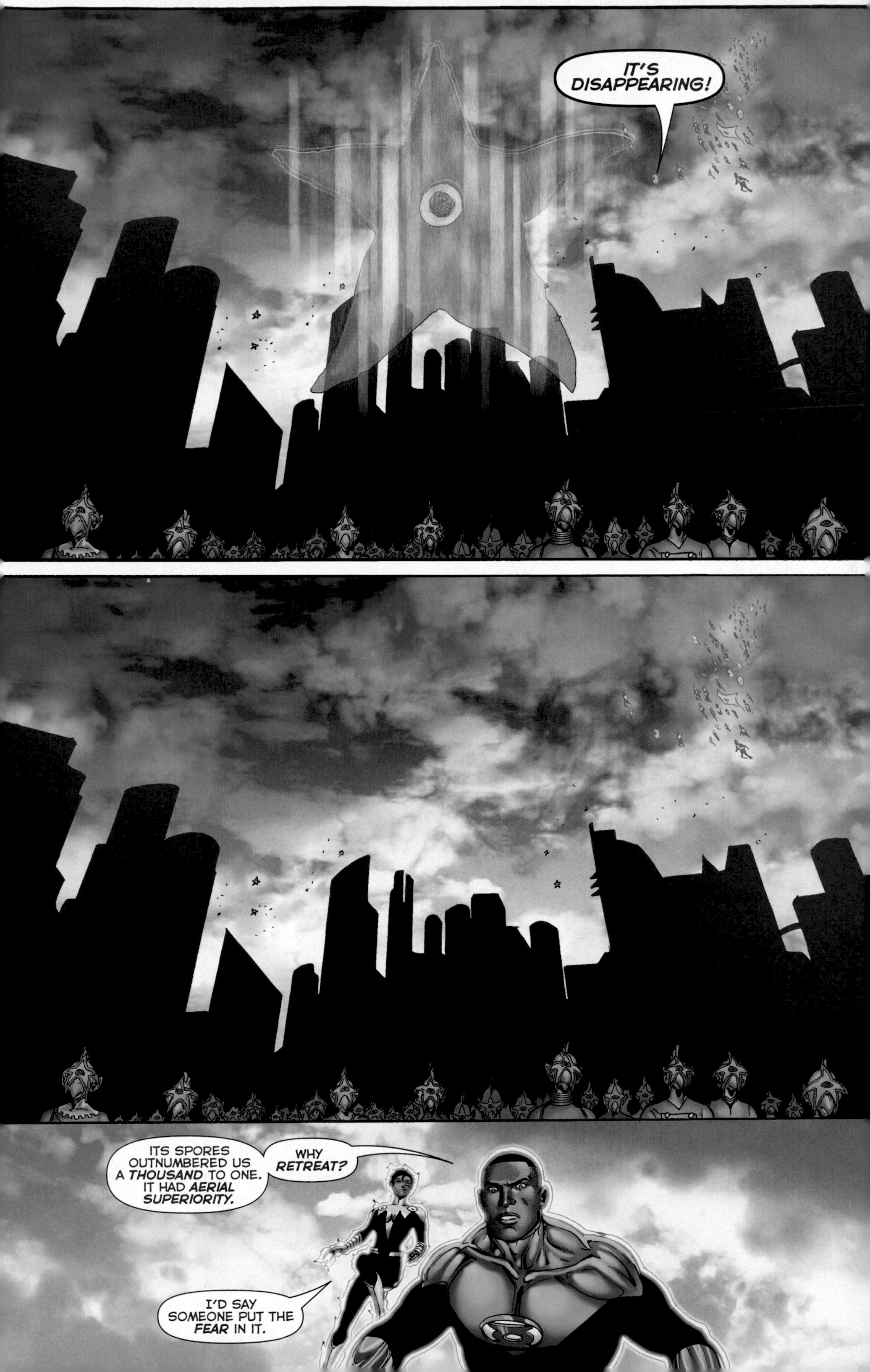
IT'S DISAPPEARING!
ITS SPORES OUTNUMBERED US A *THOUSAND* TO ONE. IT HAD *AERIAL SUPERIORITY.*
WHY *RETREAT?*
I'D SAY SOMEONE PUT THE *FEAR* IN IT.

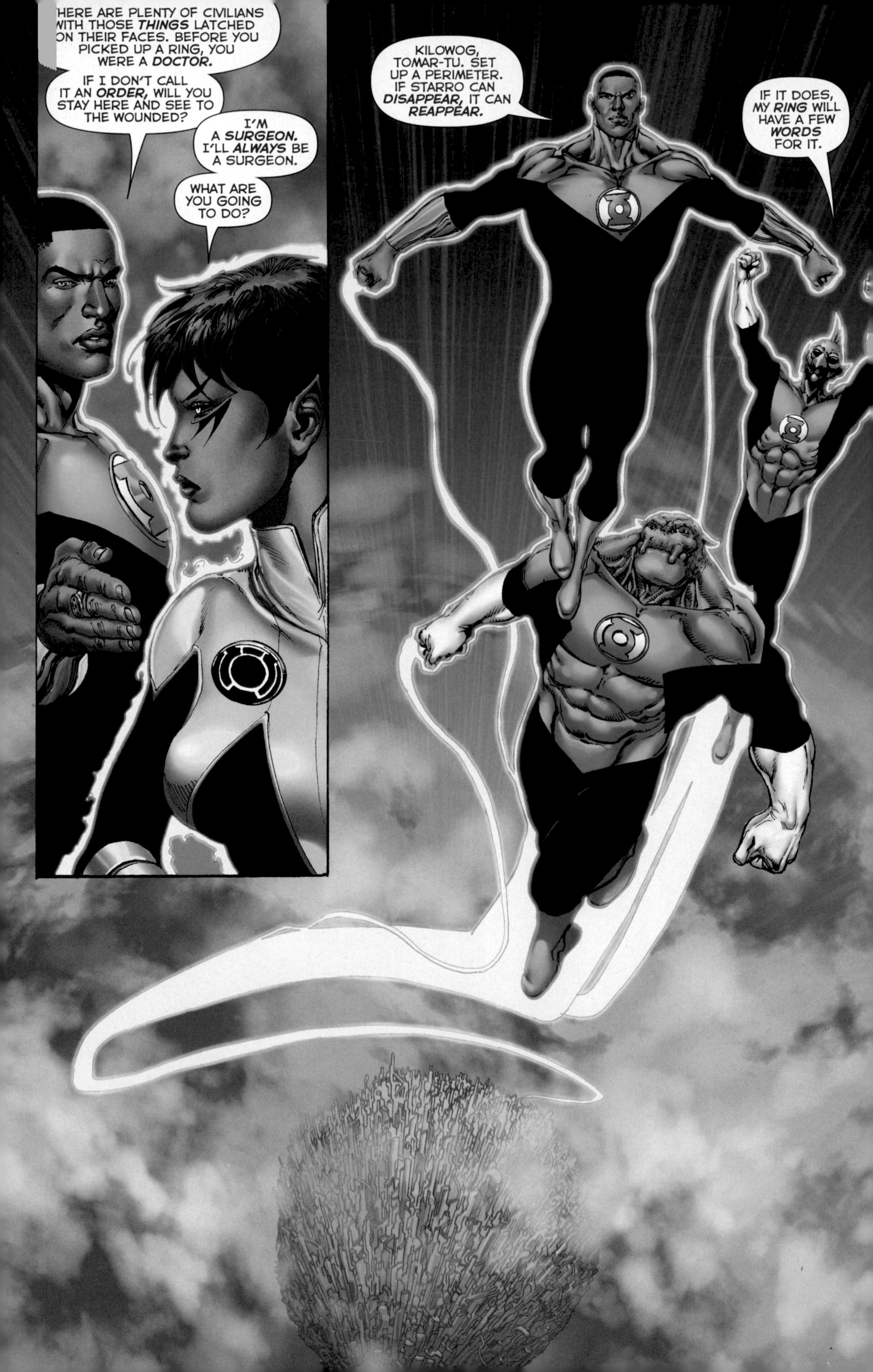
THERE ARE PLENTY OF CIVILIANS WITH THOSE THINGS LATCHED ON THEIR FACES. BEFORE YOU PICKED UP A RING, YOU WERE A DOCTOR.
IF I DON'T CALL IT AN ORDER, WILL YOU STAY HERE AND SEE TO THE WOUNDED?
I'M A SURGEON. I'LL ALWAYS BE A SURGEON.
WHAT ARE YOU GOING TO DO?
KILOWOG, TOMAR-TU. SET UP A PERIMETER. IF STARRO CAN DISAPPEAR, IT CAN REAPPEAR.
IF IT DOES, MY RING WILL HAVE A FEW WORDS FOR IT.

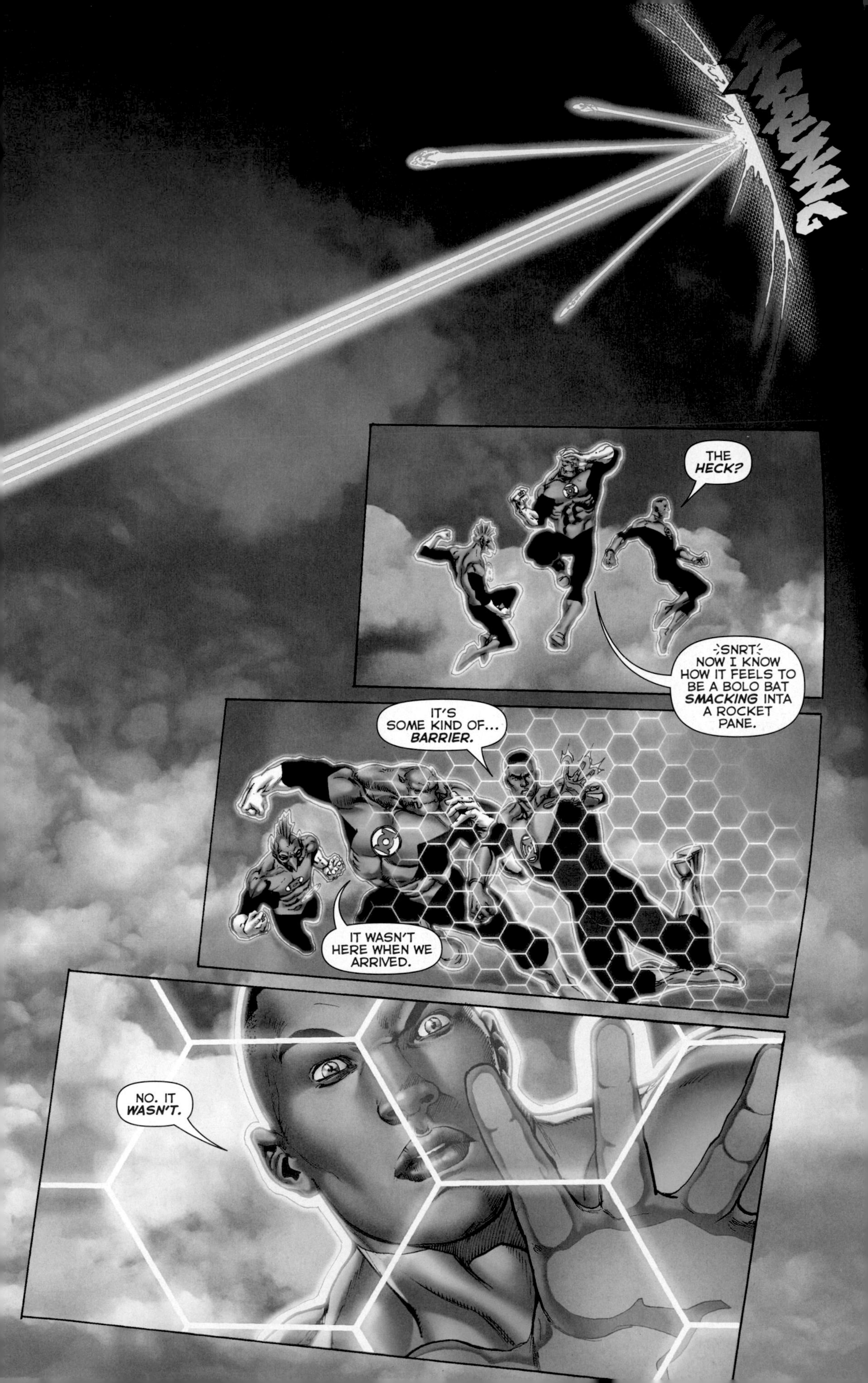
KRANNNG
THE HECK?
SNRT NOW I KNOW HOW IT FEELS TO BE A BOLO BAT SMACKING INTA A ROCKET PANE.
IT'S SOME KIND OF... BARRIER.
IT WASN'T HERE WHEN WE ARRIVED.
NO. IT WASN'T.

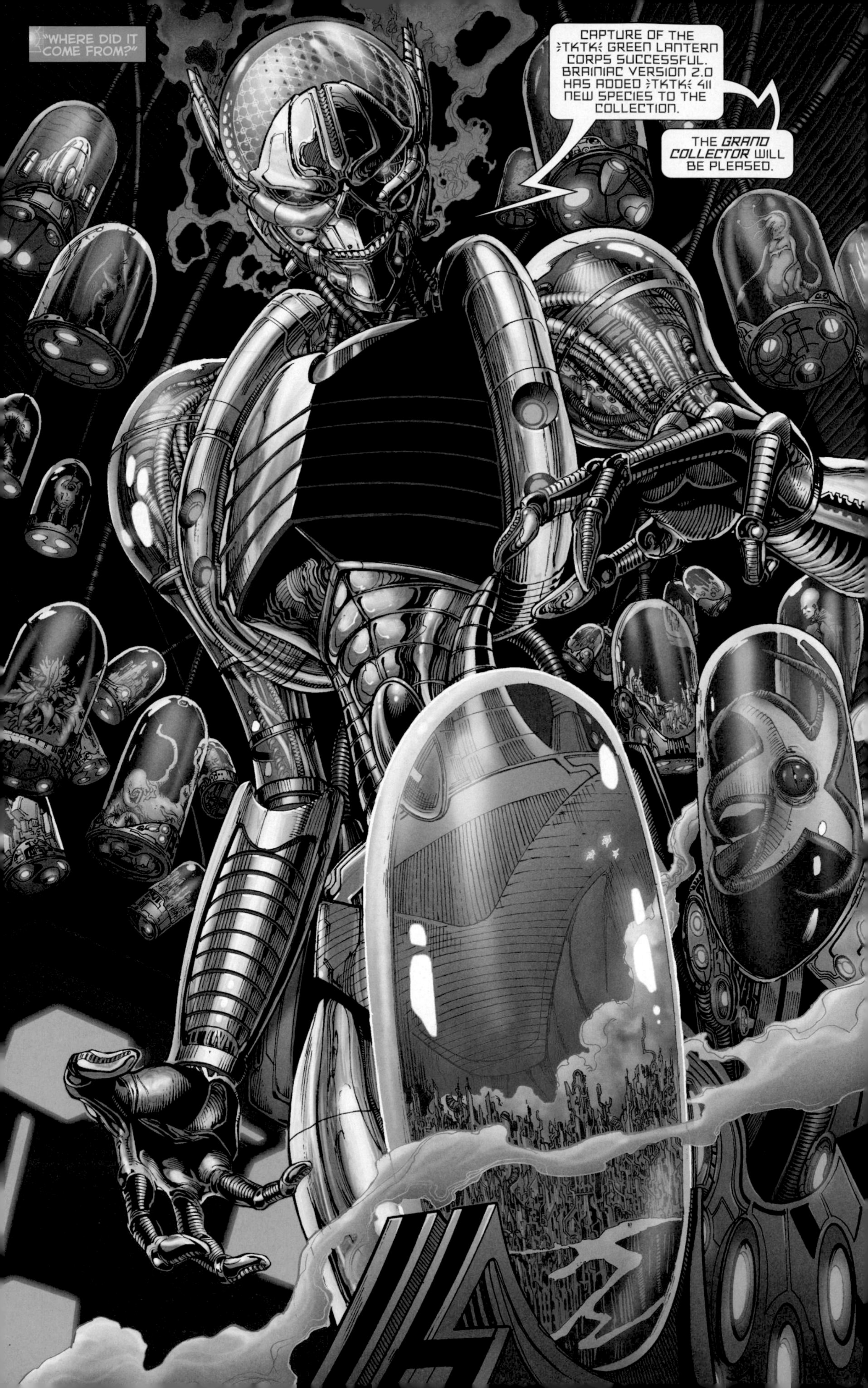
"WHERE DID IT COME FROM?"
CAPTURE OF THE ›TKTK‹ GREEN LANTERN CORPS SUCCESSFUL. BRAINIAC VERSION 2.0 HAS ADDED ›TKTK‹ 411 NEW SPECIES TO THE COLLECTION.
THE *GRAND COLLECTOR* WILL BE PLEASED.

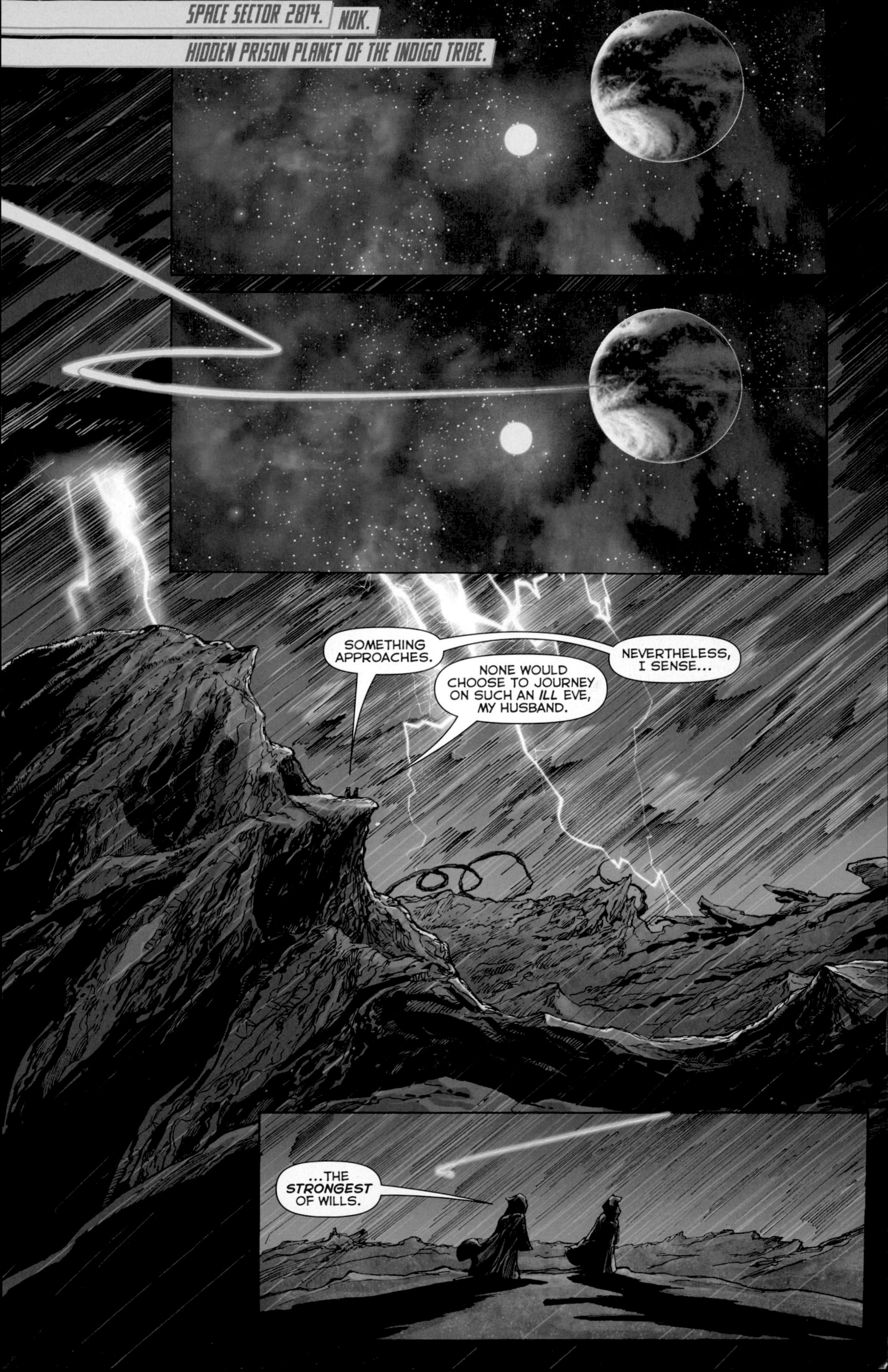
SPACE SECTOR 2814.
NOK.
HIDDEN PRISON PLANET OF THE INDIGO TRIBE.
SOMETHING APPROACHES.
NEVERTHELESS, I SENSE...
NONE WOULD CHOOSE TO JOURNEY ON SUCH AN *ILL* EVE, MY HUSBAND.
...THE *STRONGEST* OF WILLS.

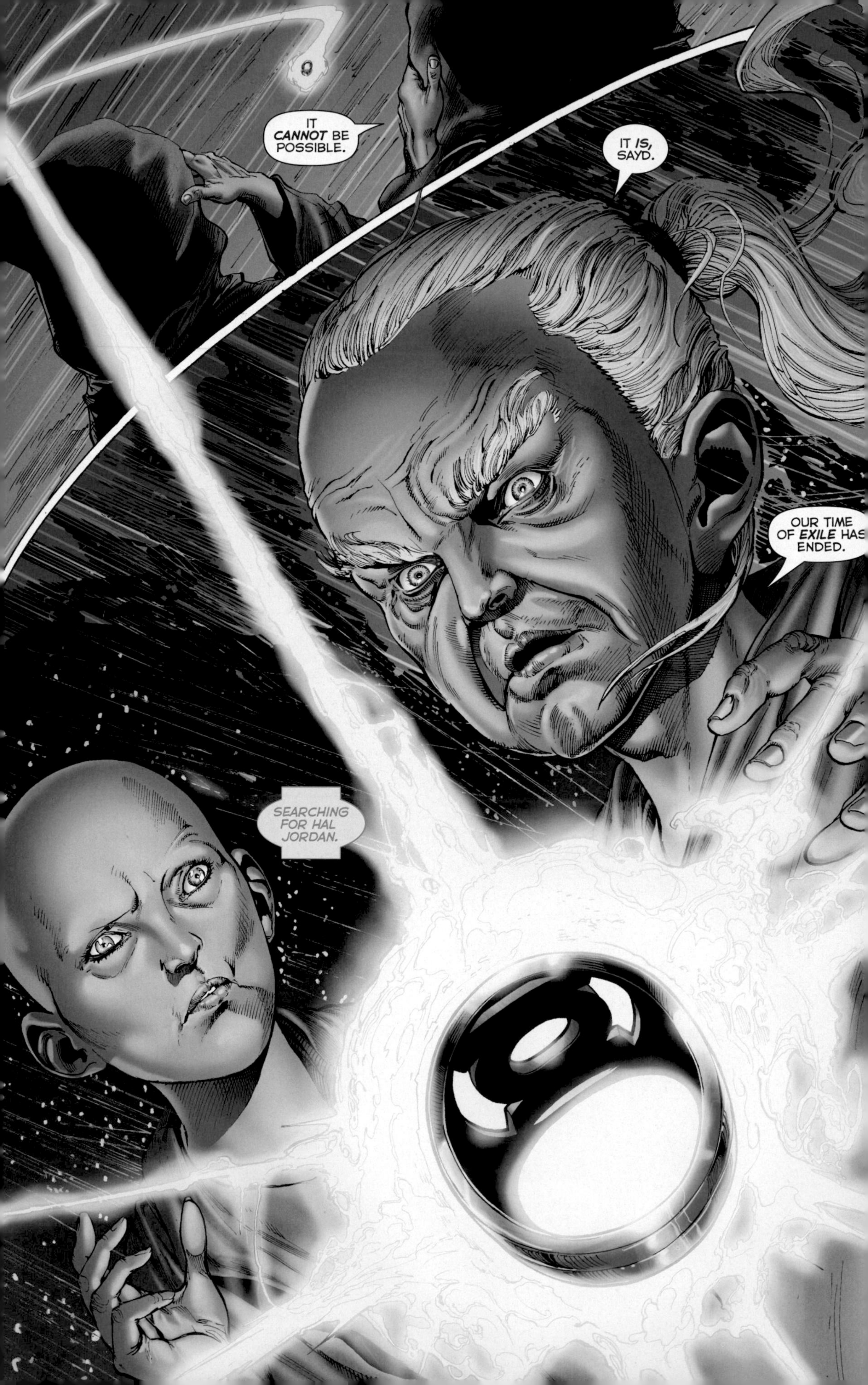
IT *CANNOT* BE POSSIBLE.
IT *IS*, SAYD.
OUR TIME OF *EXILE* HAS ENDED.
SEARCHING FOR HAL JORDAN.

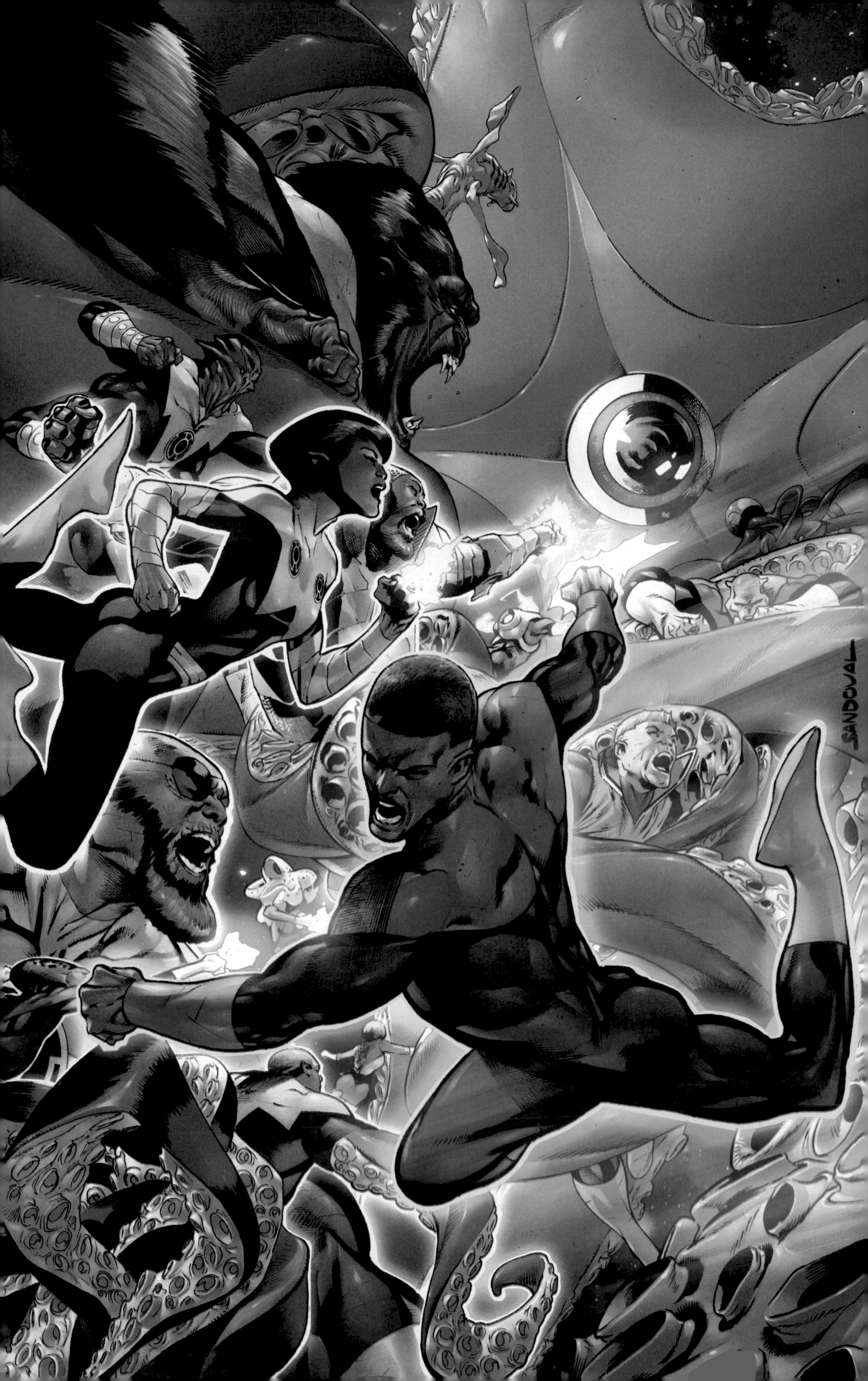
SANDOVAL

"BOTTLED LIGHT PART 2: BRAINIAC"

RAFA SANDOVAL penciller * JORDI TARRAGONA inker * TOMEU MOREY colorist

RAFA SANDOVAL, JORDI TARRAGONA and TOMEU MOREY cover artists

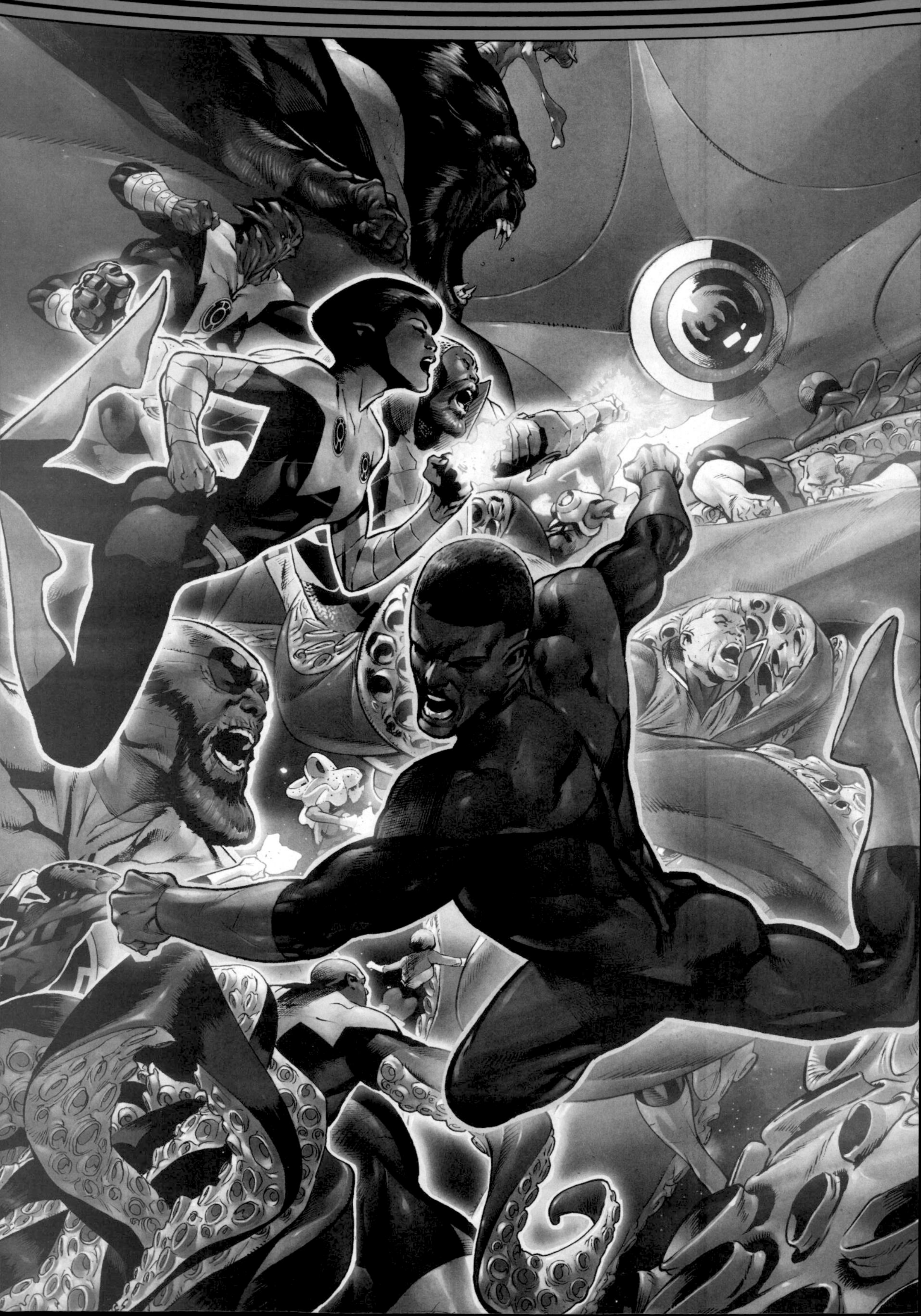

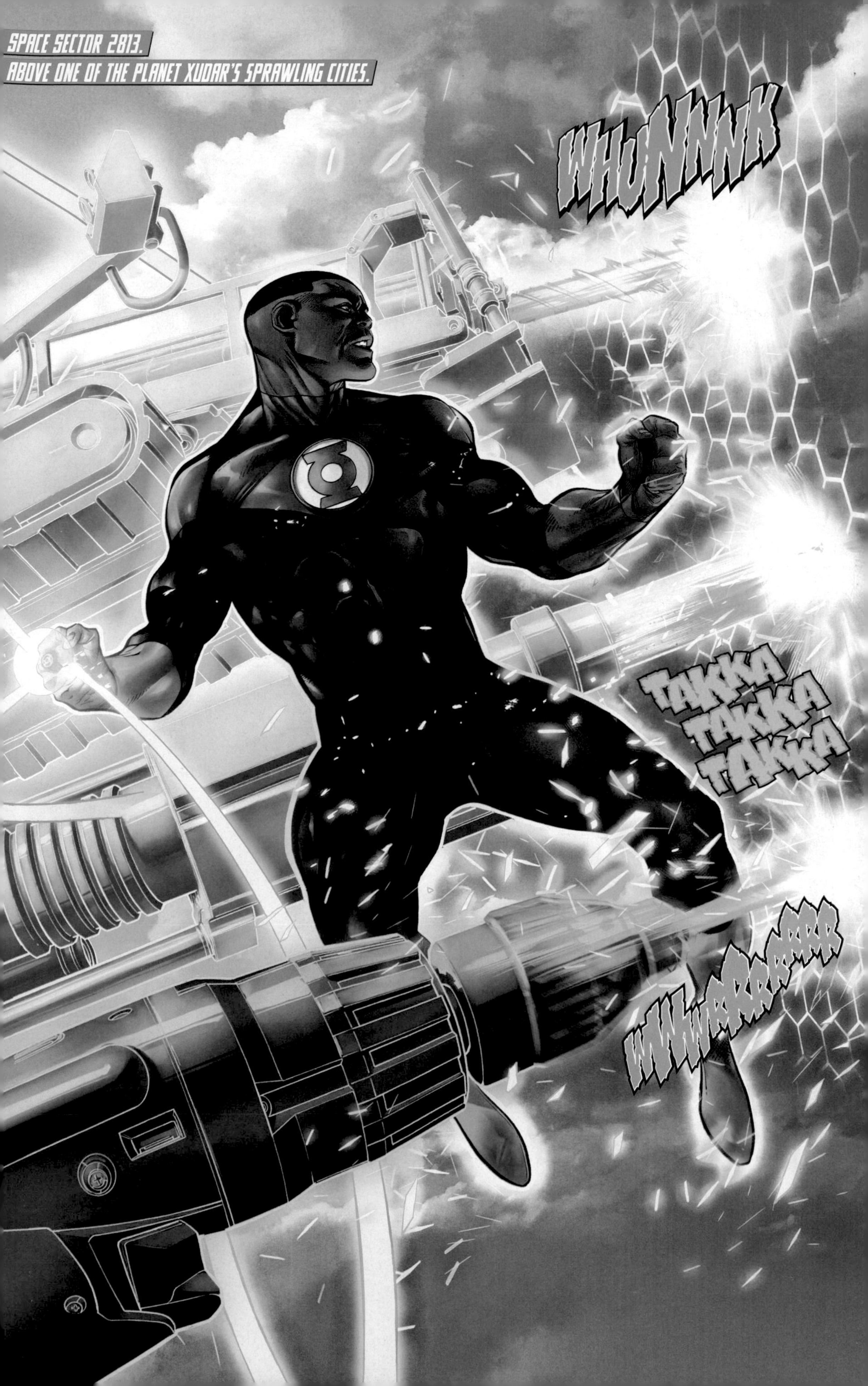
SPACE SECTOR 2813.
ABOVE ONE OF THE PLANET XUDAR'S SPRAWLING CITIES.
WHUNNNNK
TAKKA TAKKA TAKKA
WWWARRRRR

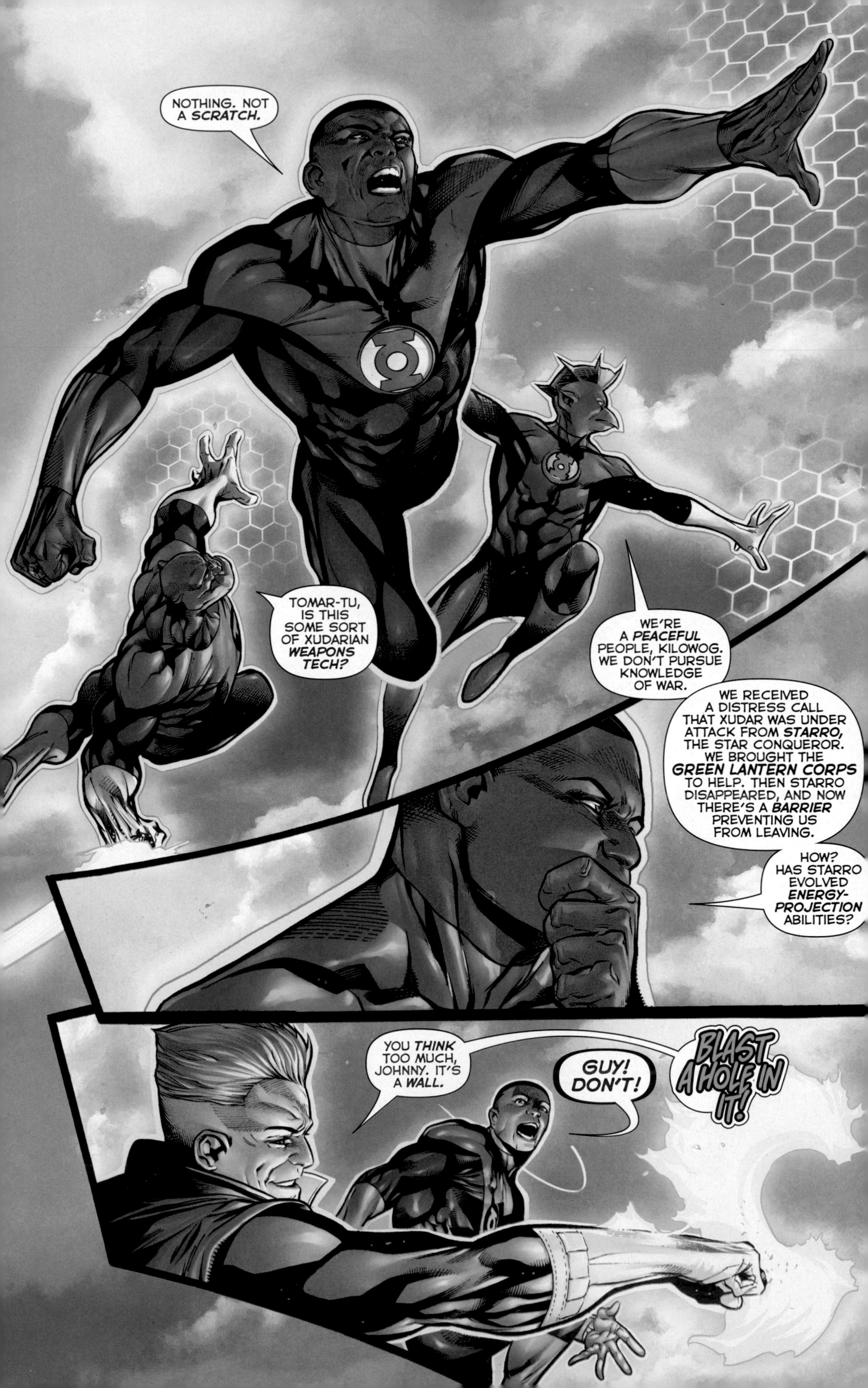
NOTHING. NOT A SCRATCH.
TOMAR-TU, IS THIS SOME SORT OF XUDARIAN WEAPONS TECH?
WE'RE A PEACEFUL PEOPLE, KILOWOG. WE DON'T PURSUE KNOWLEDGE OF WAR.
WE RECEIVED A DISTRESS CALL THAT XUDAR WAS UNDER ATTACK FROM STARRO, THE STAR CONQUEROR. WE BROUGHT THE GREEN LANTERN CORPS TO HELP. THEN STARRO DISAPPEARED, AND NOW THERE'S A BARRIER PREVENTING US FROM LEAVING.
HOW? HAS STARRO EVOLVED ENERGY-PROJECTION ABILITIES?
YOU THINK TOO MUCH, JOHNNY. IT'S A WALL.
BLAST A HOLE IN IT!
GUY! DON'T!

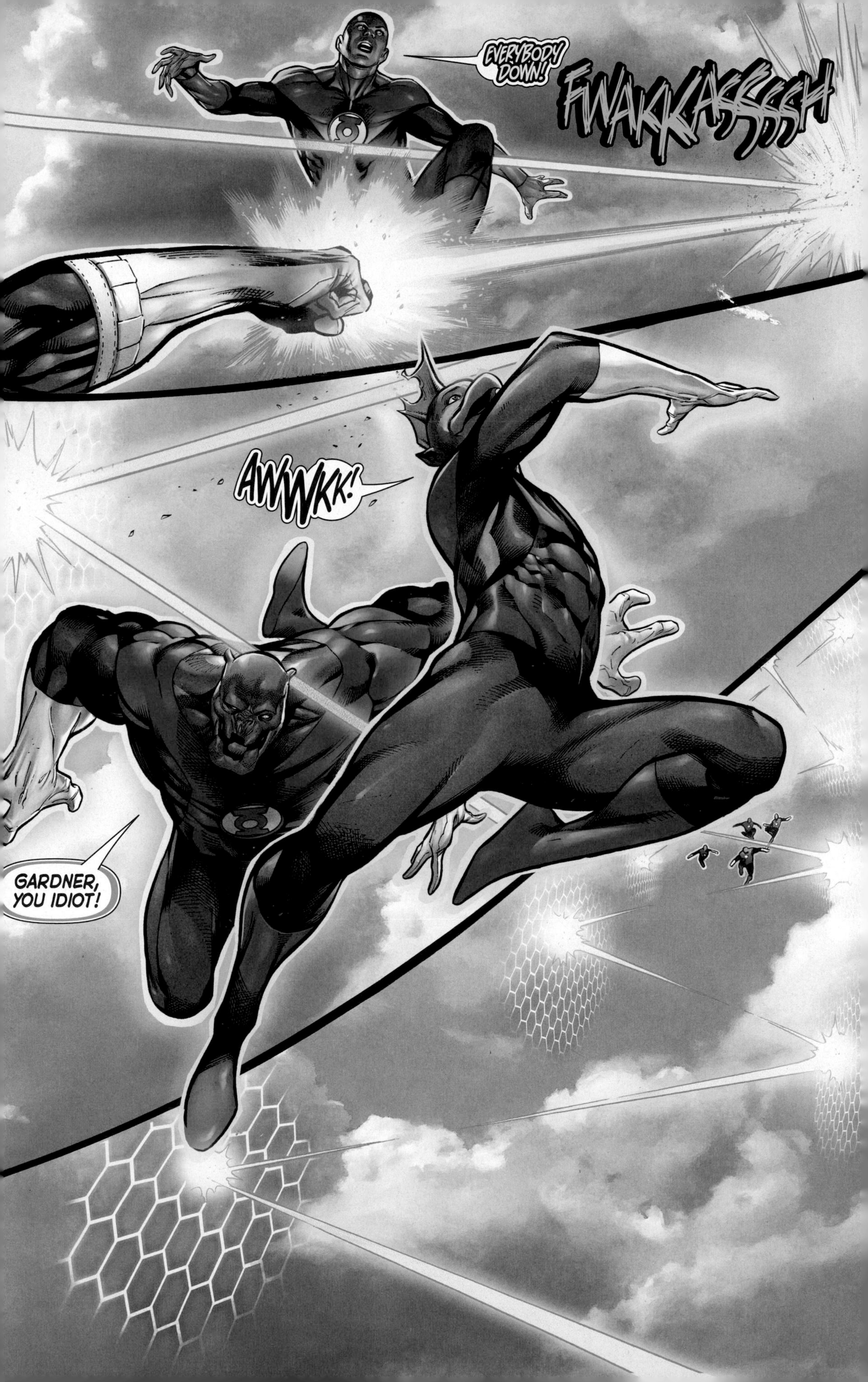
EVERYBODY DOWN!
FWAKKASSSSH
AWWKK!
GARDNER, YOU IDIOT!

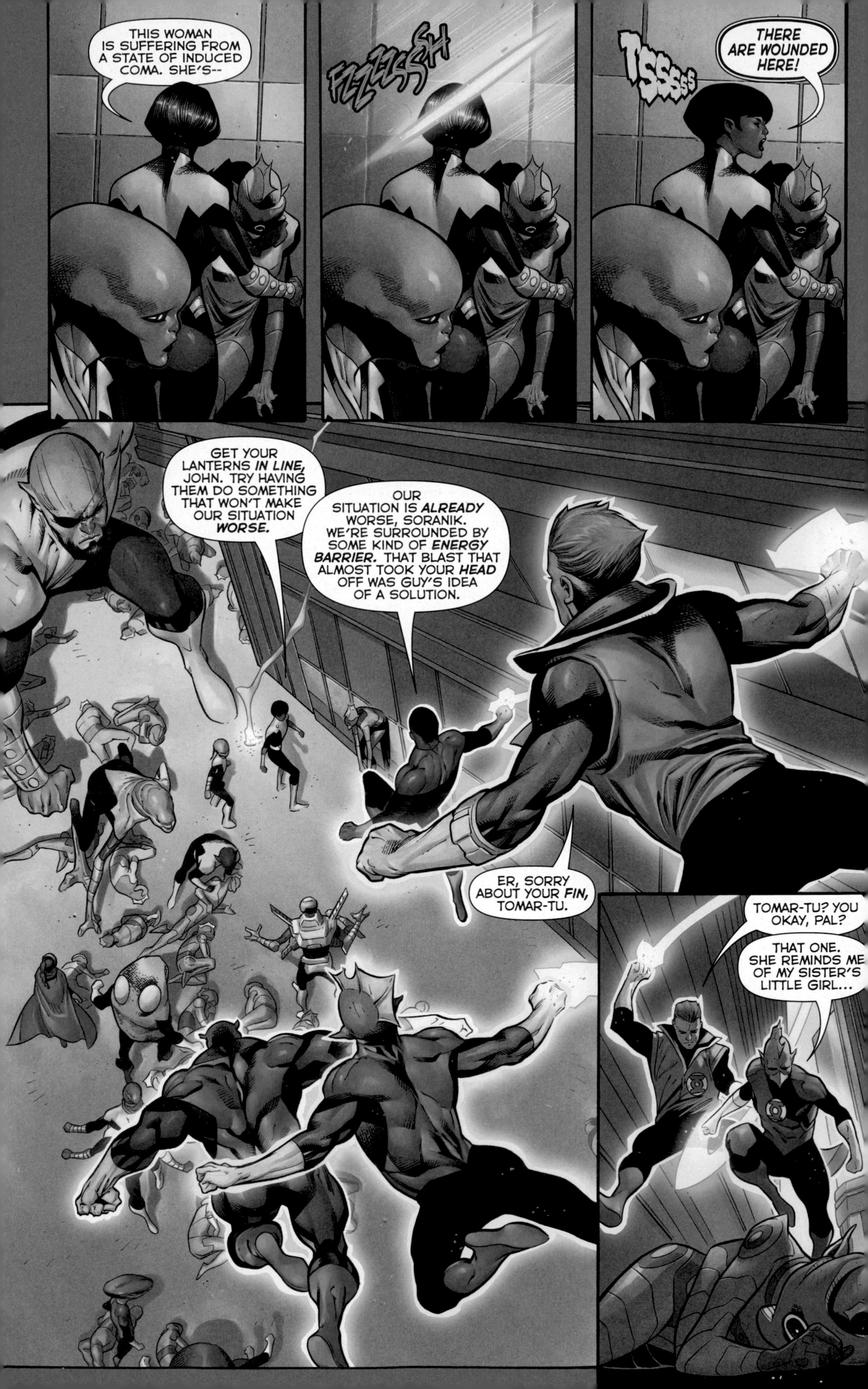
THIS WOMAN IS SUFFERING FROM A STATE OF INDUCED COMA. SHE'S--
FZZZZSSSH
TSSSSS
THERE ARE WOUNDED HERE!
GET YOUR LANTERNS IN LINE, JOHN. TRY HAVING THEM DO SOMETHING THAT WON'T MAKE OUR SITUATION WORSE.
OUR SITUATION IS ALREADY WORSE, SORANIK. WE'RE SURROUNDED BY SOME KIND OF ENERGY BARRIER. THAT BLAST THAT ALMOST TOOK YOUR HEAD OFF WAS GUY'S IDEA OF A SOLUTION.
ER, SORRY ABOUT YOUR FIN, TOMAR-TU.
TOMAR-TU? YOU OKAY, PAL?
THAT ONE. SHE REMINDS ME OF MY SISTER'S LITTLE GIRL...

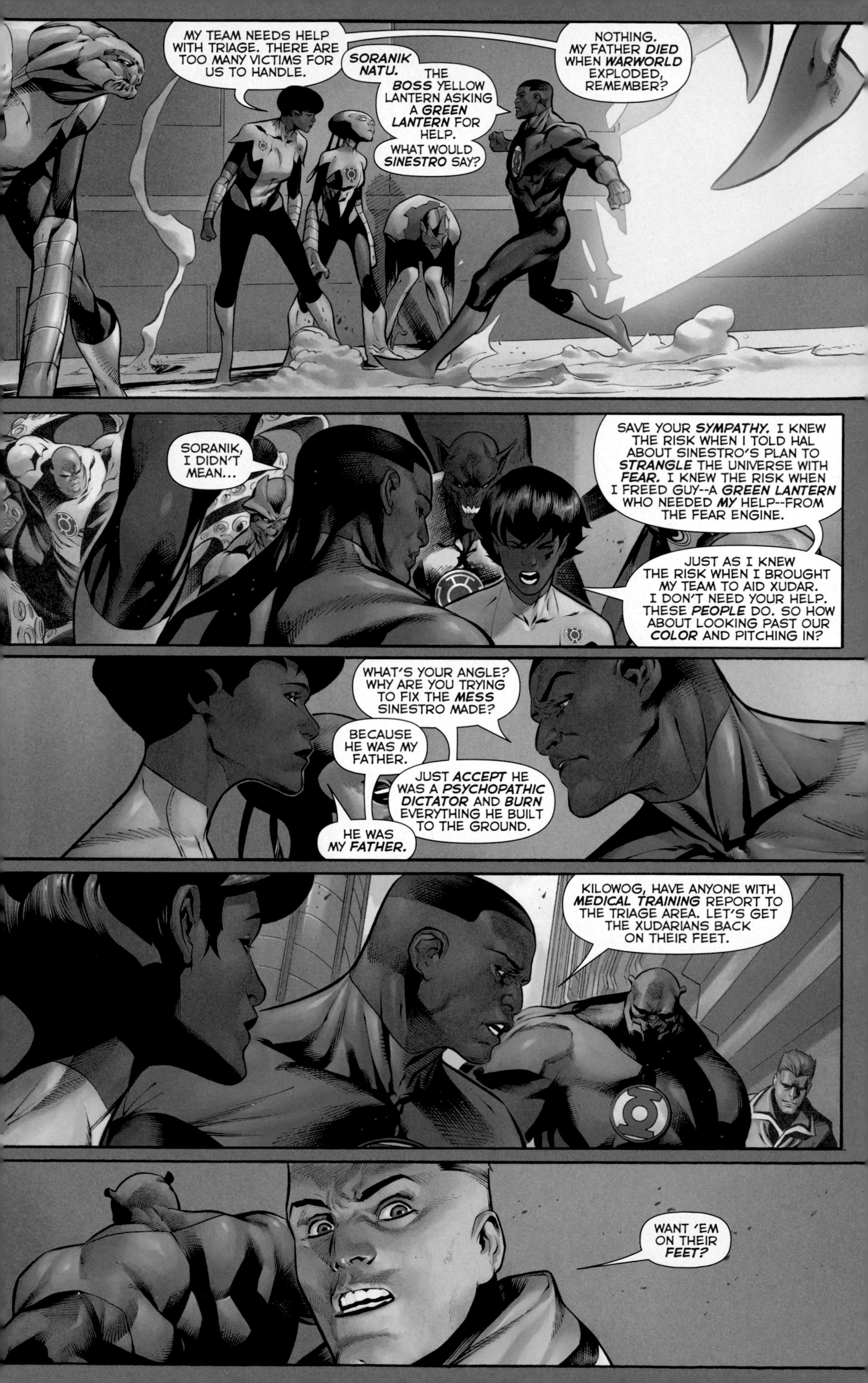
MY TEAM NEEDS HELP WITH TRIAGE. THERE ARE TOO MANY VICTIMS FOR US TO HANDLE.
SORANIK NATU.
THE BOSS YELLOW LANTERN ASKING A GREEN LANTERN FOR HELP. WHAT WOULD SINESTRO SAY?
NOTHING. MY FATHER DIED WHEN WARWORLD EXPLODED, REMEMBER?
SORANIK, I DIDN'T MEAN...
SAVE YOUR SYMPATHY. I KNEW THE RISK WHEN I TOLD HAL ABOUT SINESTRO'S PLAN TO STRANGLE THE UNIVERSE WITH FEAR. I KNEW THE RISK WHEN I FREED GUY--A GREEN LANTERN WHO NEEDED MY HELP--FROM THE FEAR ENGINE.
JUST AS I KNEW THE RISK WHEN I BROUGHT MY TEAM TO AID XUDAR. I DON'T NEED YOUR HELP. THESE PEOPLE DO. SO HOW ABOUT LOOKING PAST OUR COLOR AND PITCHING IN?
WHAT'S YOUR ANGLE? WHY ARE YOU TRYING TO FIX THE MESS SINESTRO MADE?
BECAUSE HE WAS MY FATHER.
JUST ACCEPT HE WAS A PSYCHOPATHIC DICTATOR AND BURN EVERYTHING HE BUILT TO THE GROUND.
HE WAS MY FATHER.
KILOWOG, HAVE ANYONE WITH MEDICAL TRAINING REPORT TO THE TRIAGE AREA. LET'S GET THE XUDARIANS BACK ON THEIR FEET.
WANT 'EM ON THEIR FEET?

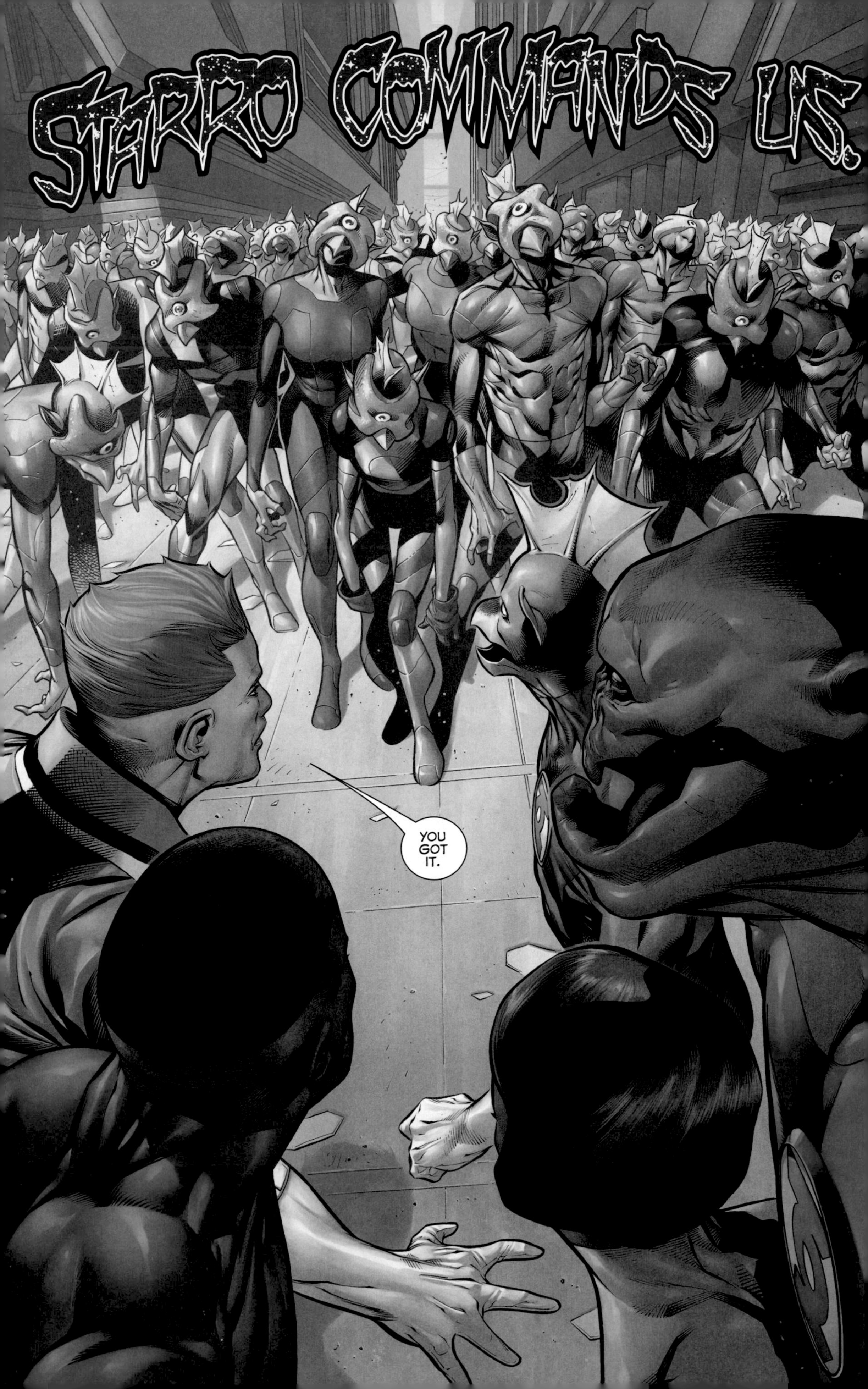
STARRO COMMANDS US.
YOU GOT IT.

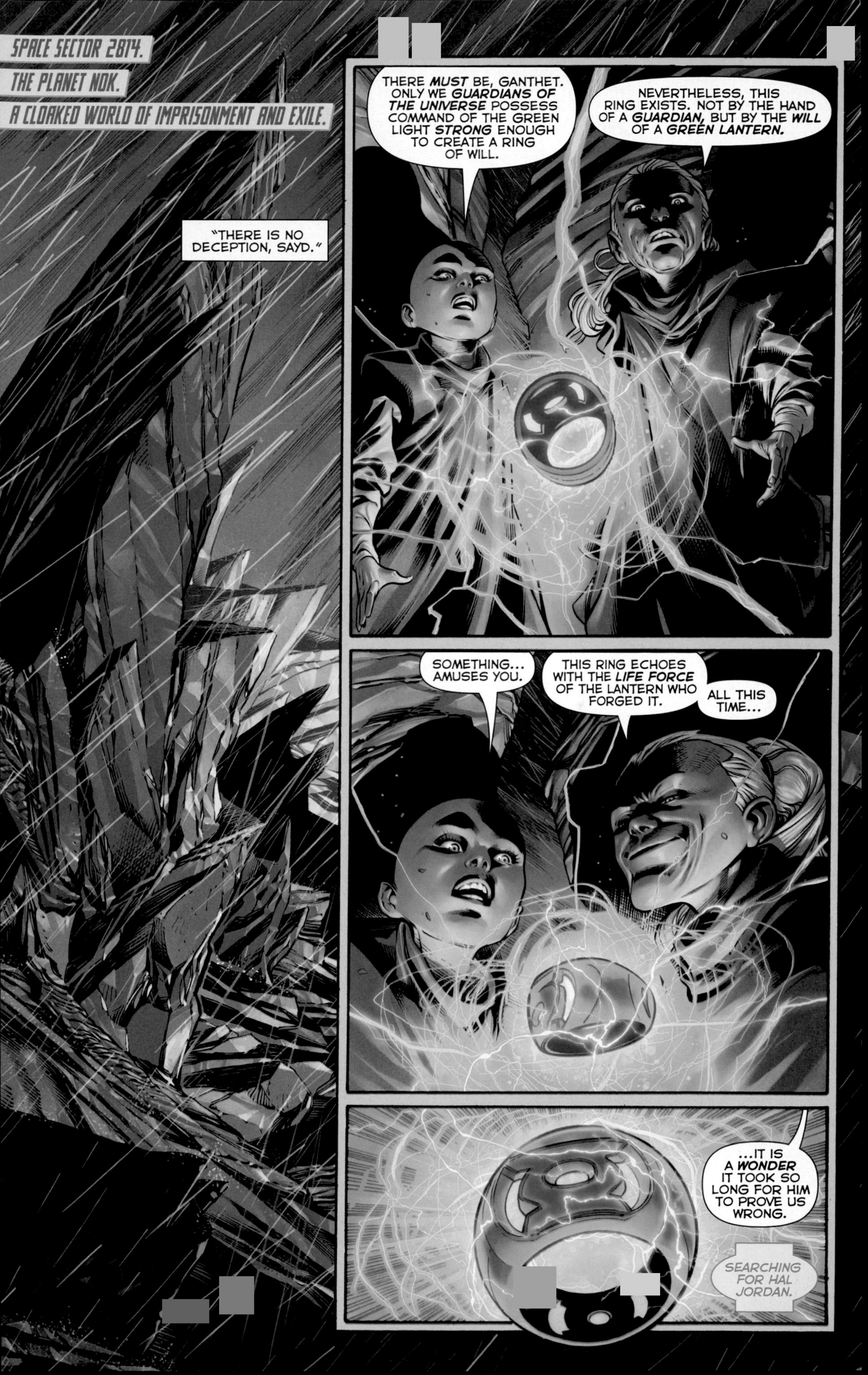
SPACE SECTOR 2814.
THE PLANET NOK.
A CLOAKED WORLD OF IMPRISONMENT AND EXILE.
"THERE IS NO DECEPTION, SAYD."
THERE *MUST* BE, GANTHET. ONLY WE ***GUARDIANS OF THE UNIVERSE*** POSSESS COMMAND OF THE GREEN LIGHT ***STRONG*** ENOUGH TO CREATE A RING OF WILL.
NEVERTHELESS, THIS RING EXISTS. NOT BY THE HAND OF A ***GUARDIAN,*** BUT BY THE ***WILL*** OF A ***GREEN LANTERN.***
SOMETHING... AMUSES YOU.
THIS RING ECHOES WITH THE ***LIFE FORCE*** OF THE LANTERN WHO FORGED IT.
ALL THIS TIME...
...IT IS A ***WONDER*** IT TOOK SO LONG FOR HIM TO PROVE US WRONG.
SEARCHING FOR HAL JORDAN.

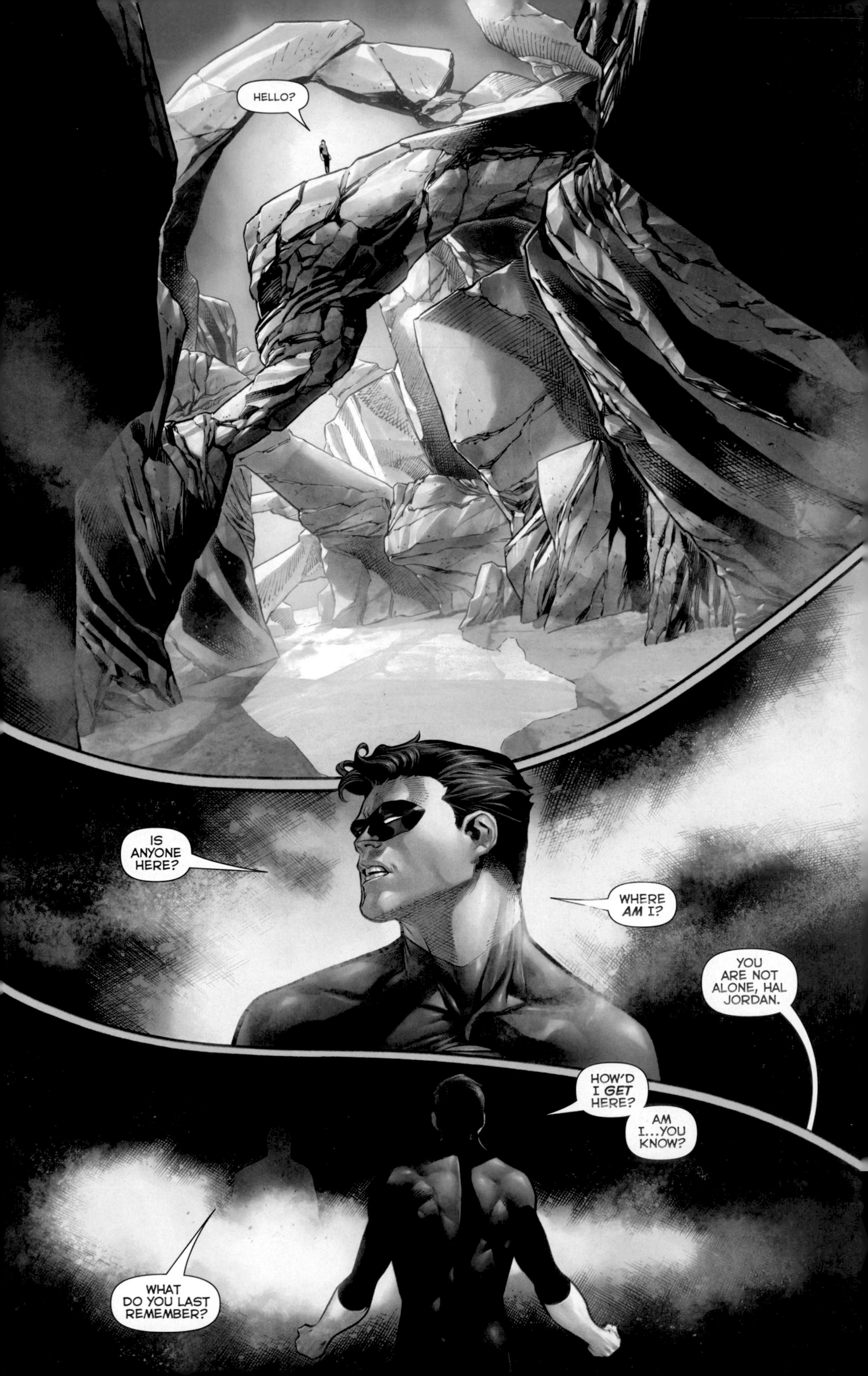
HELLO?
IS ANYONE HERE?
WHERE AM I?
YOU ARE NOT ALONE, HAL JORDAN.
HOW'D I GET HERE?
AM I...YOU KNOW?
WHAT DO YOU LAST REMEMBER?

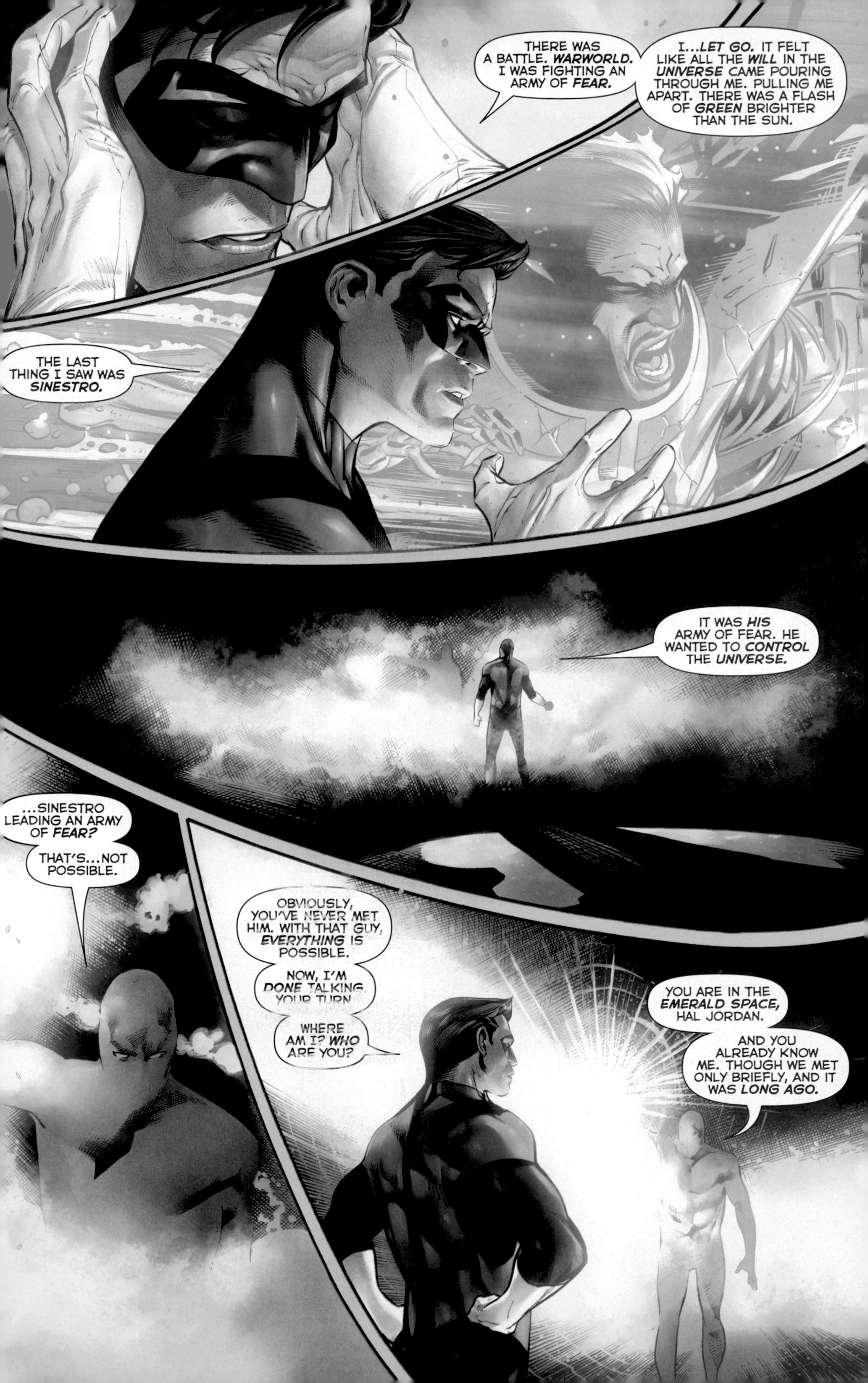
THERE WAS A BATTLE. WARWORLD. I WAS FIGHTING AN ARMY OF FEAR.
I...LET GO. IT FELT LIKE ALL THE WILL IN THE UNIVERSE CAME POURING THROUGH ME. PULLING ME APART. THERE WAS A FLASH OF GREEN BRIGHTER THAN THE SUN.
THE LAST THING I SAW WAS SINESTRO.
IT WAS HIS ARMY OF FEAR. HE WANTED TO CONTROL THE UNIVERSE.
...SINESTRO LEADING AN ARMY OF FEAR?
THAT'S...NOT POSSIBLE.
OBVIOUSLY, YOU'VE NEVER MET HIM. WITH THAT GUY, EVERYTHING IS POSSIBLE.
NOW, I'M DONE TALKING. YOUR TURN.
WHERE AM I? WHO ARE YOU?
YOU ARE IN THE EMERALD SPACE, HAL JORDAN.
AND YOU ALREADY KNOW ME. THOUGH WE MET ONLY BRIEFLY, AND IT WAS LONG AGO.

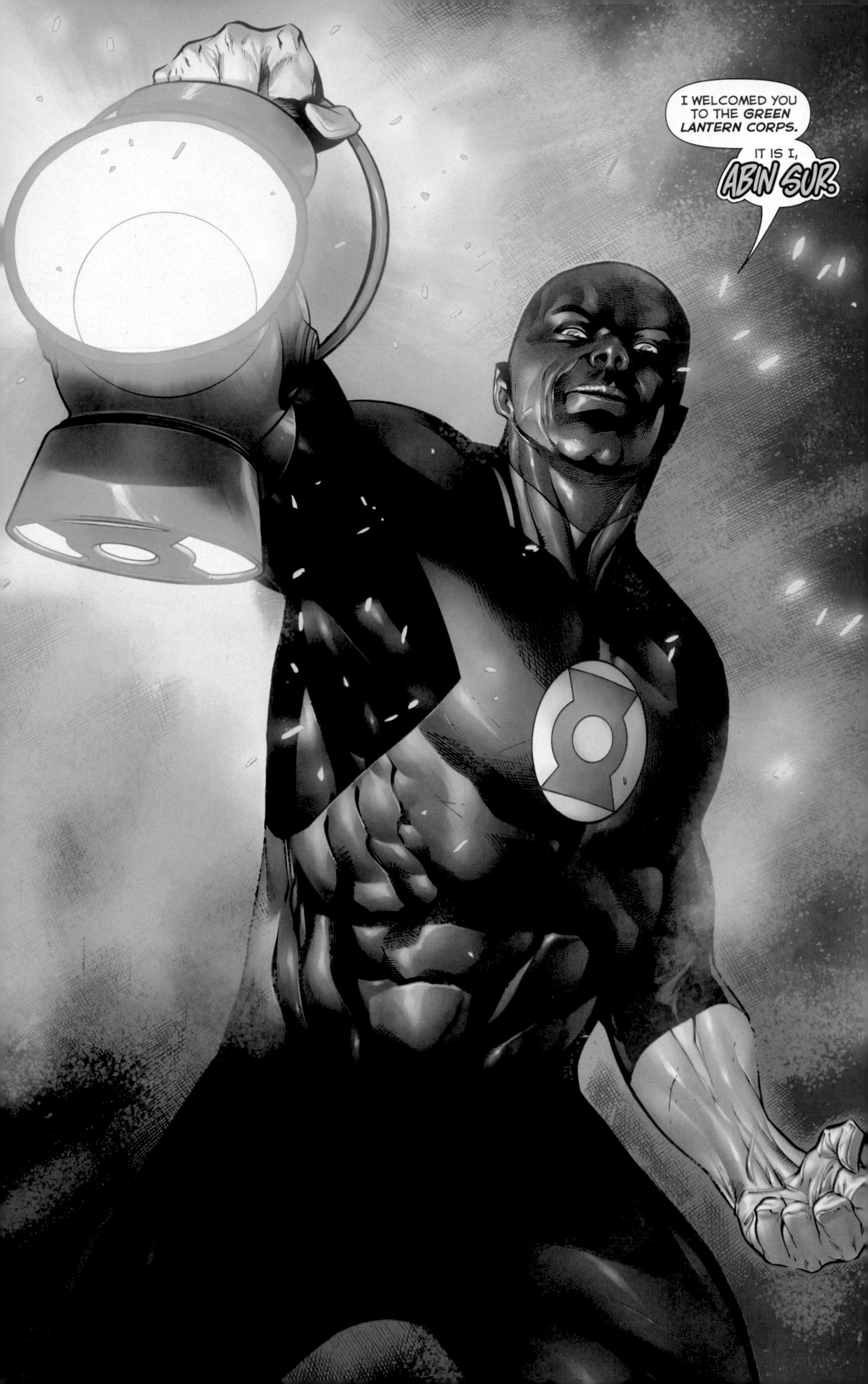
I WELCOMED YOU TO THE GREEN LANTERN CORPS.
IT IS I, ABIN SUR.

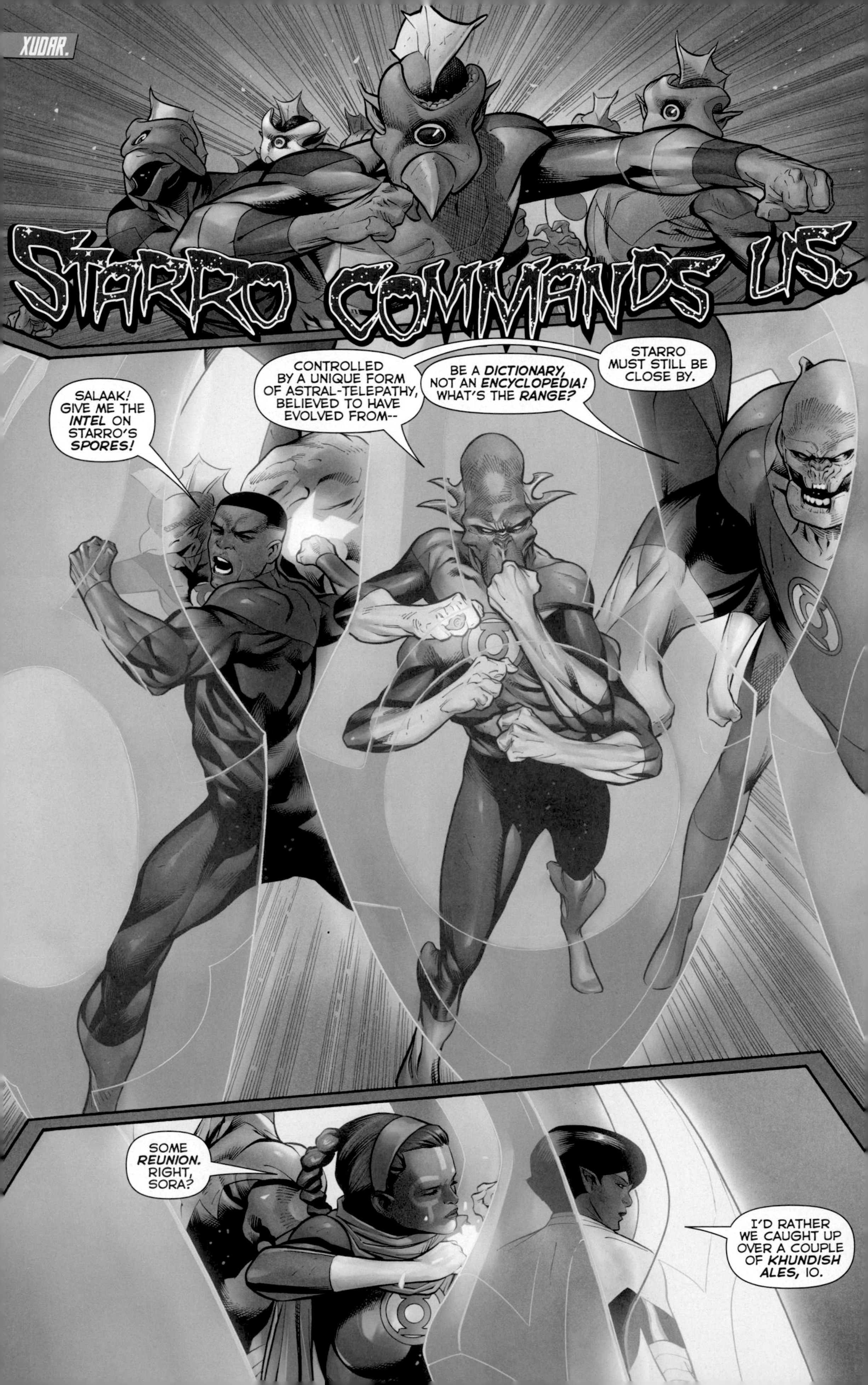
XUDAR.
STARRO COMMANDS US.
SALAAK! GIVE ME THE INTEL ON STARRO'S SPORES!
CONTROLLED BY A UNIQUE FORM OF ASTRAL-TELEPATHY, BELIEVED TO HAVE EVOLVED FROM--
BE A DICTIONARY, NOT AN ENCYCLOPEDIA! WHAT'S THE RANGE?
STARRO MUST STILL BE CLOSE BY.
SOME REUNION. RIGHT, SORA?
I'D RATHER WE CAUGHT UP OVER A COUPLE OF KHUNDISH ALES, IO.

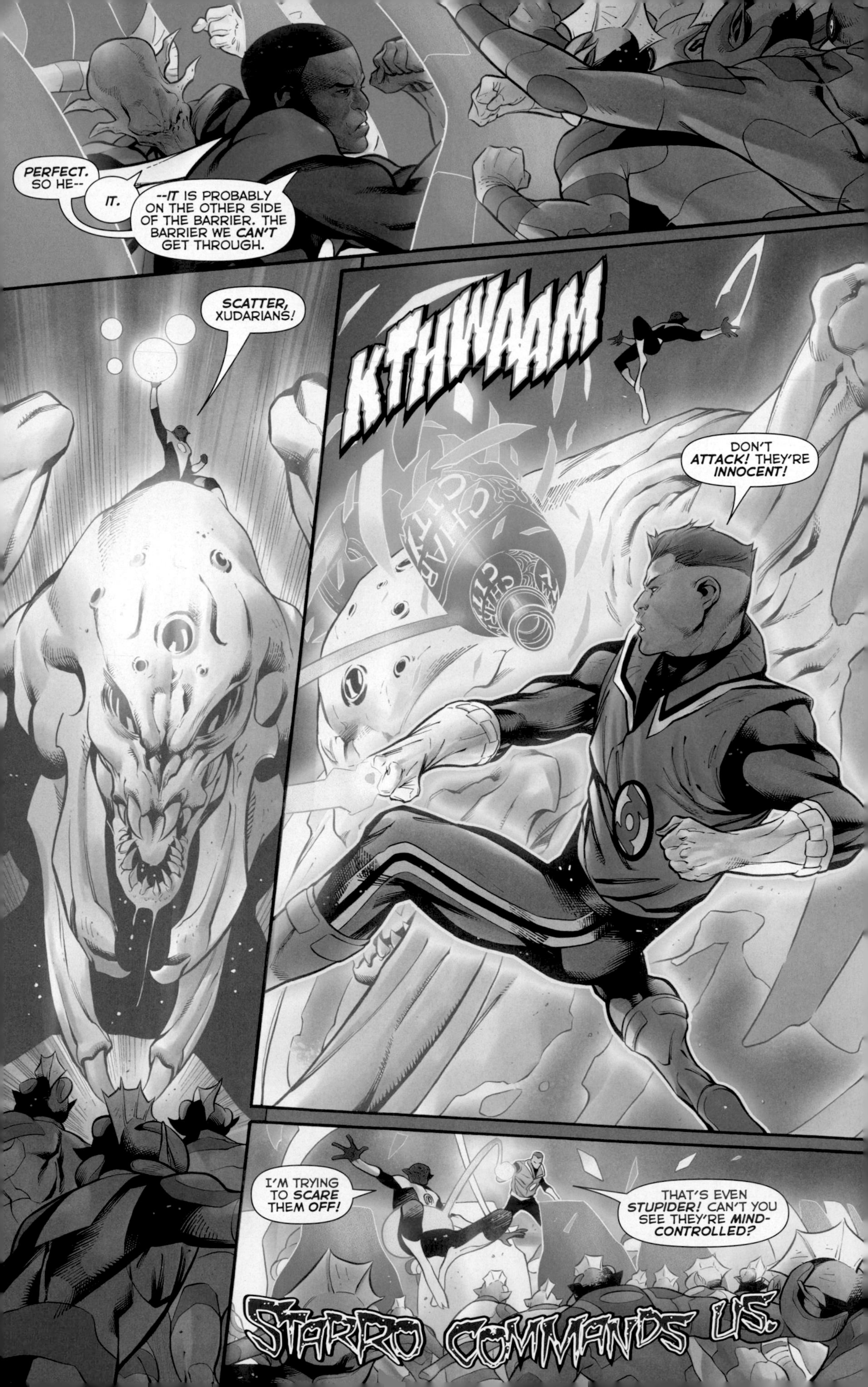
PERFECT. SO HE--
IT.
--IT IS PROBABLY ON THE OTHER SIDE OF THE BARRIER. THE BARRIER WE CAN'T GET THROUGH.
SCATTER, XUDARIANS!
KTHWAAM
DON'T ATTACK! THEY'RE INNOCENT!
I'M TRYING TO SCARE THEM OFF!
THAT'S EVEN STUPIDER! CAN'T YOU SEE THEY'RE MIND-CONTROLLED?
STARRO COMMANDS US.

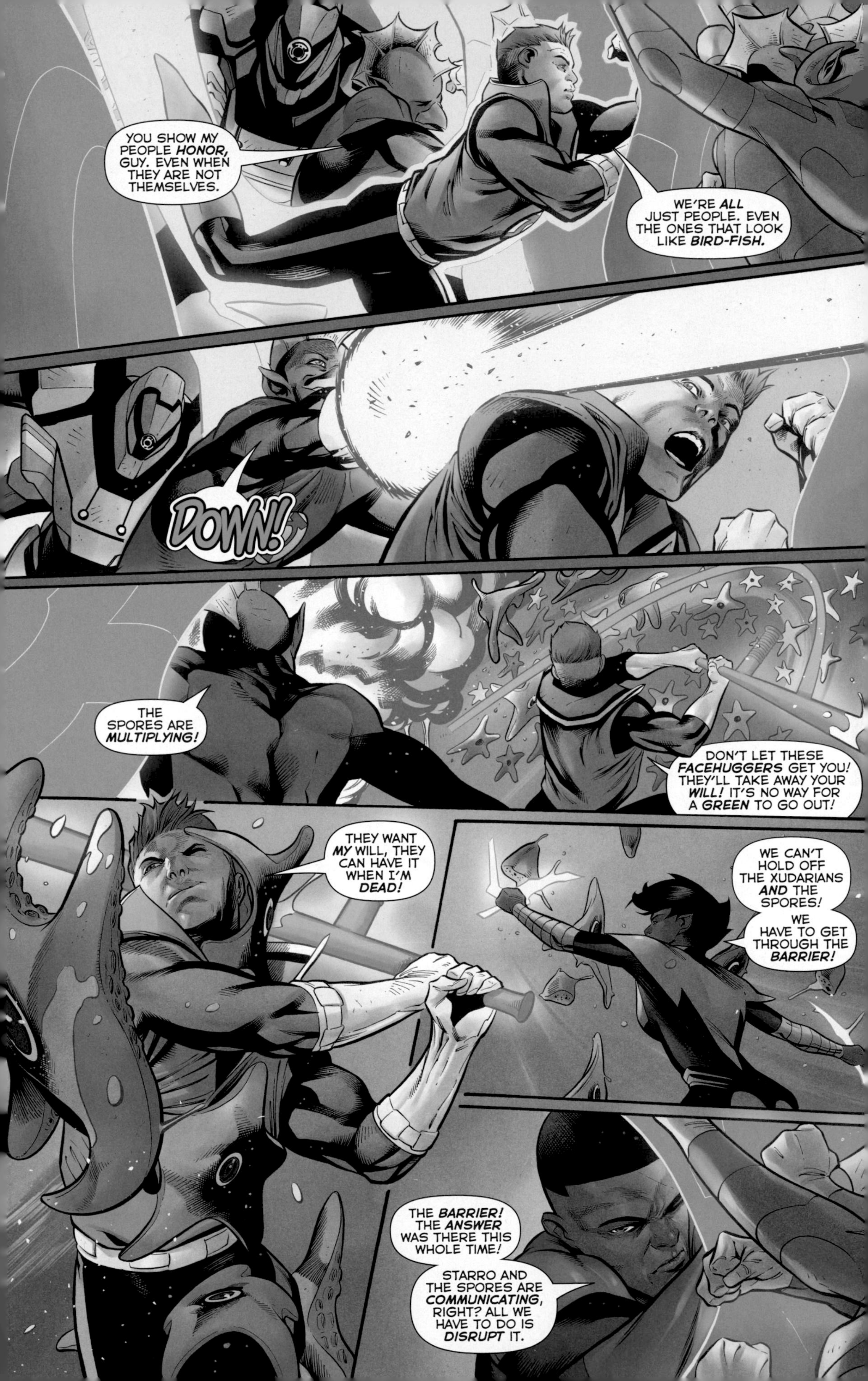
YOU SHOW MY PEOPLE HONOR, GUY. EVEN WHEN THEY ARE NOT THEMSELVES.
WE'RE ALL JUST PEOPLE. EVEN THE ONES THAT LOOK LIKE BIRD-FISH.
DOWN!
THE SPORES ARE MULTIPLYING!
DON'T LET THESE FACEHUGGERS GET YOU! THEY'LL TAKE AWAY YOUR WILL! IT'S NO WAY FOR A GREEN TO GO OUT!
THEY WANT MY WILL, THEY CAN HAVE IT WHEN I'M DEAD!
WE CAN'T HOLD OFF THE XUDARIANS AND THE SPORES!
WE HAVE TO GET THROUGH THE BARRIER!
THE BARRIER! THE ANSWER WAS THERE THIS WHOLE TIME!
STARRO AND THE SPORES ARE COMMUNICATING, RIGHT? ALL WE HAVE TO DO IS DISRUPT IT.

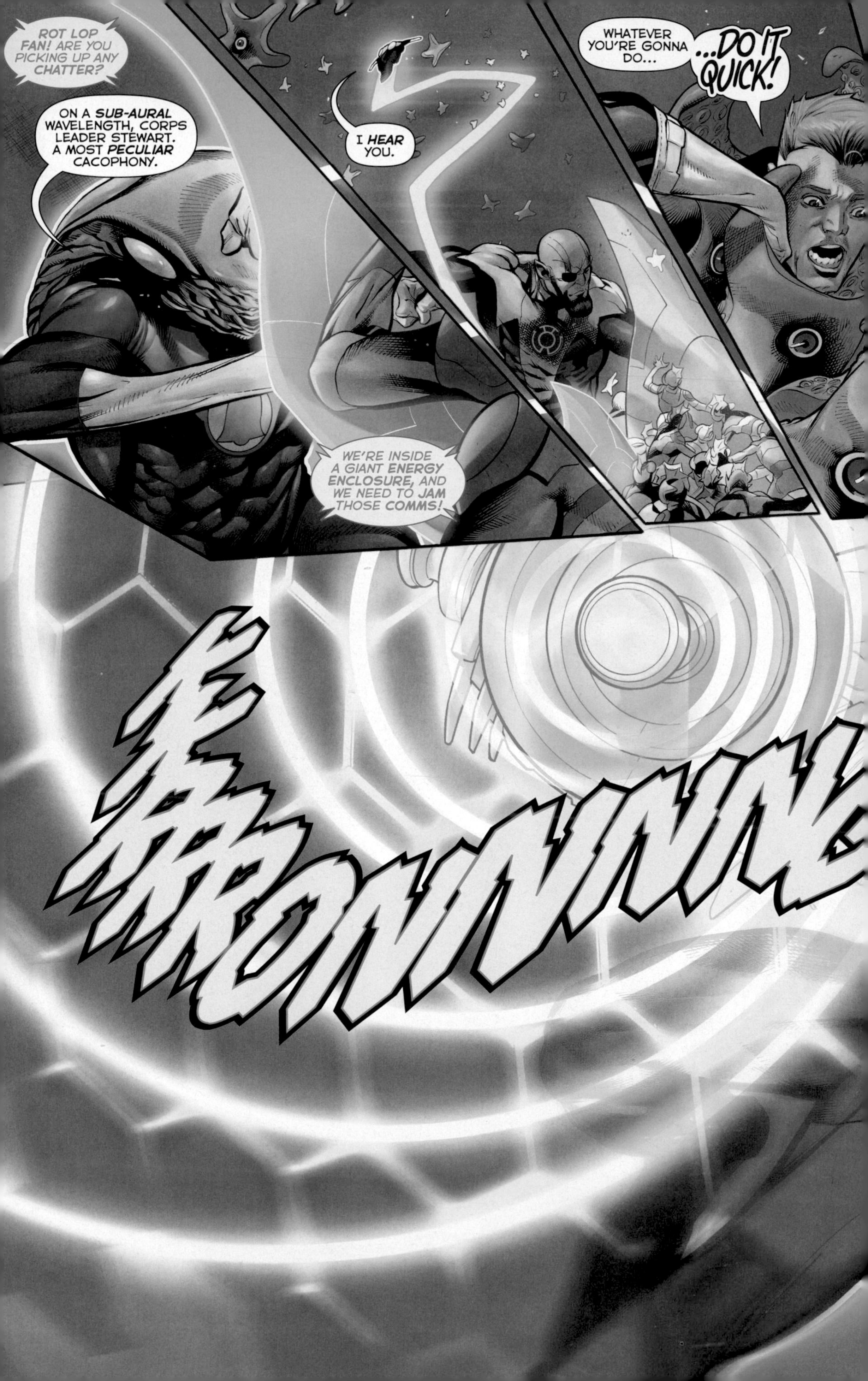
ROT LOP FAN! ARE YOU PICKING UP ANY CHATTER?
ON A SUB-AURAL WAVELENGTH, CORPS LEADER STEWART. A MOST PECULIAR CACOPHONY.
I HEAR YOU.
WE'RE INSIDE A GIANT ENERGY ENCLOSURE, AND WE NEED TO JAM THOSE COMMS!
WHATEVER YOU'RE GONNA DO...
...DO IT QUICK!
KRONNNN

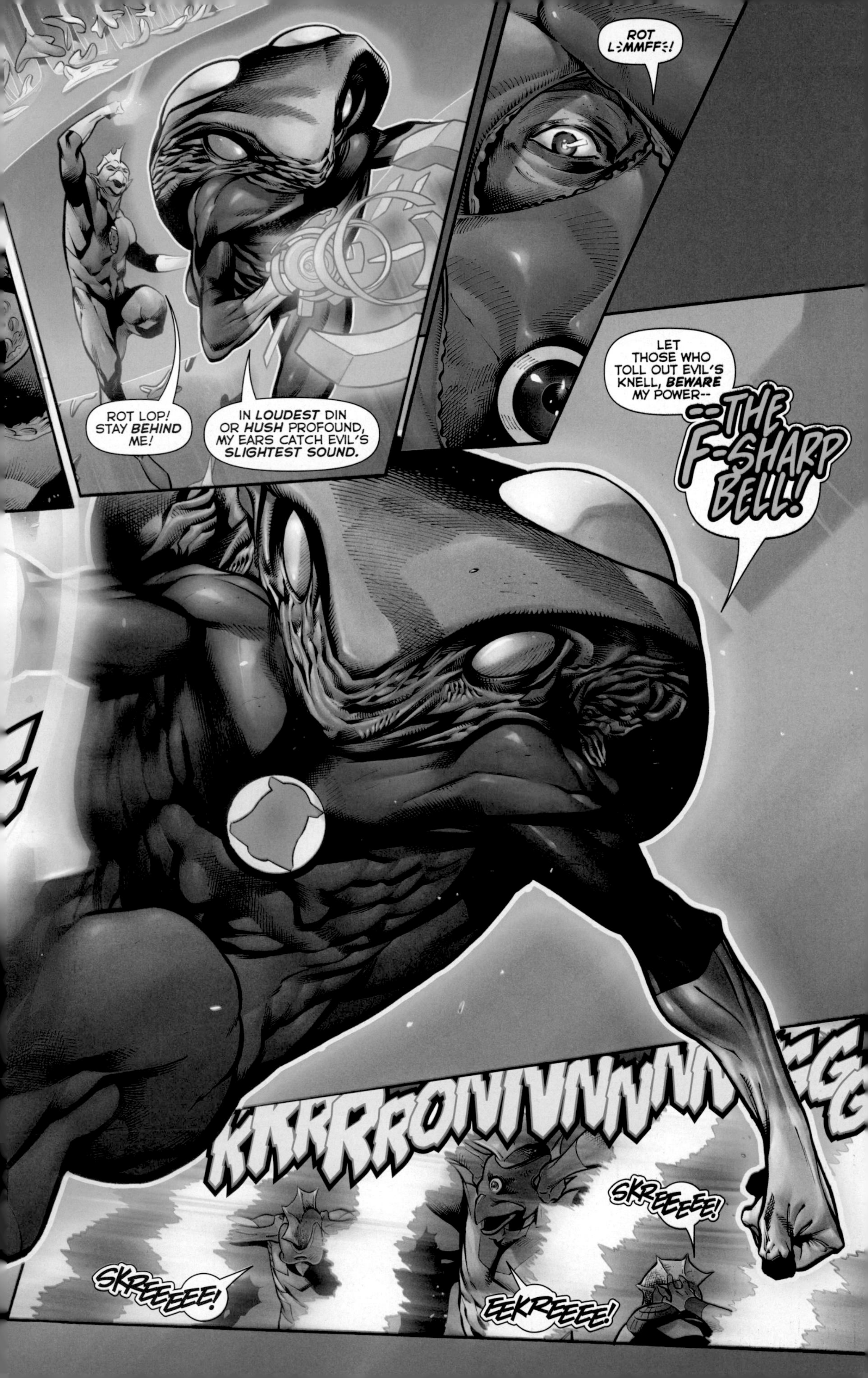

ROT LOP! STAY BEHIND ME!
IN LOUDEST DIN OR HUSH PROFOUND, MY EARS CATCH EVIL'S SLIGHTEST SOUND.
ROT L>MMFF<!
LET THOSE WHO TOLL OUT EVIL'S KNELL, BEWARE MY POWER--
--THE F-SHARP BELL!
KRRRRONNNNNNNGG
SKREEEEEE!
SKREEEEEE!
EEKREEEE!

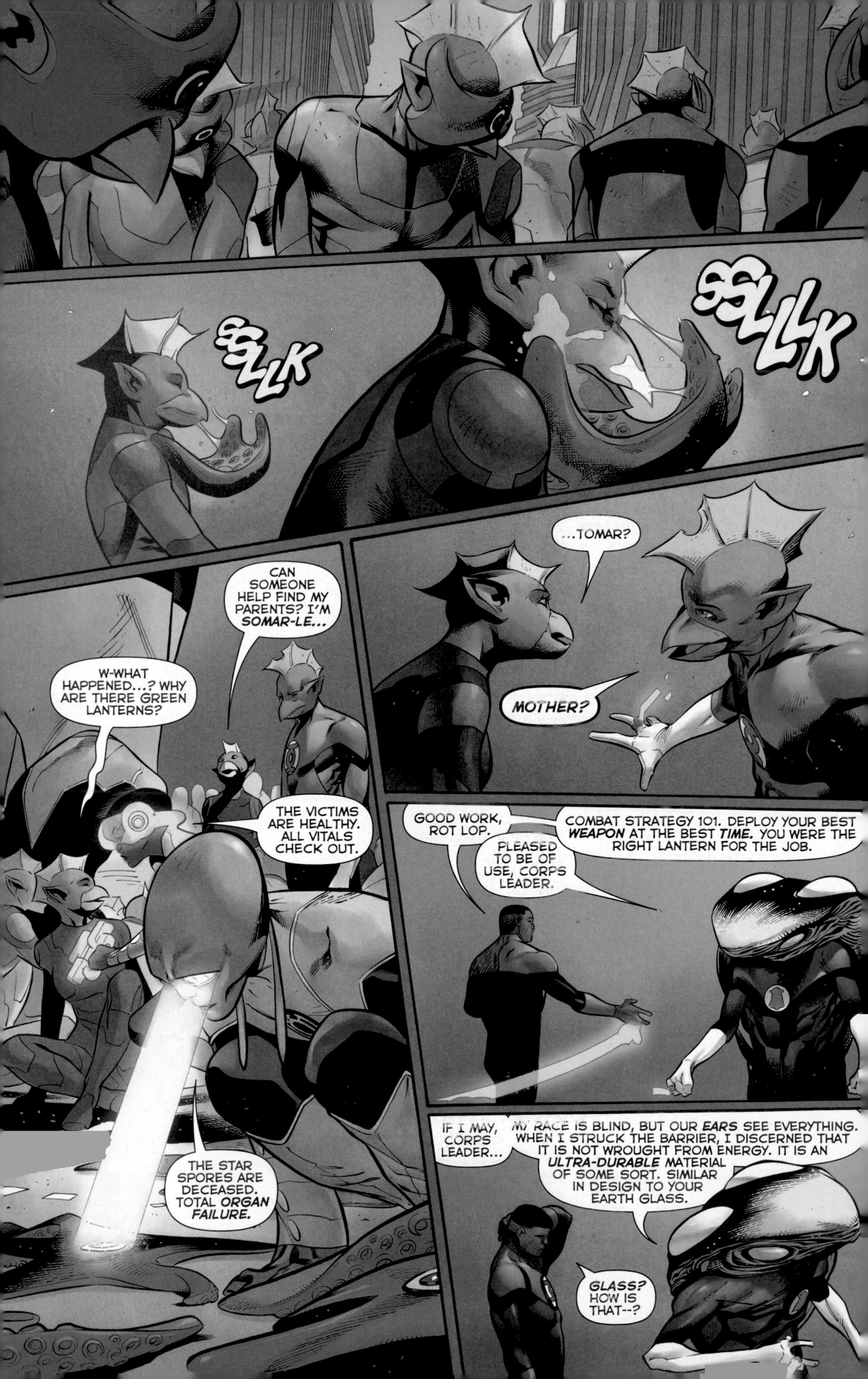
SSLLK
SSLLLK
...TOMAR?
MOTHER?
W-WHAT HAPPENED...? WHY ARE THERE GREEN LANTERNS?
CAN SOMEONE HELP FIND MY PARENTS? I'M SOMAR-LE...
THE VICTIMS ARE HEALTHY. ALL VITALS CHECK OUT.
THE STAR SPORES ARE DECEASED. TOTAL ORGAN FAILURE.
GOOD WORK, ROT LOP.
COMBAT STRATEGY 101. DEPLOY YOUR BEST WEAPON AT THE BEST TIME. YOU WERE THE RIGHT LANTERN FOR THE JOB.
PLEASED TO BE OF USE, CORPS LEADER.
IF I MAY, CORPS LEADER...
MY RACE IS BLIND, BUT OUR EARS SEE EVERYTHING. WHEN I STRUCK THE BARRIER, I DISCERNED THAT IT IS NOT WROUGHT FROM ENERGY. IT IS AN ULTRA-DURABLE MATERIAL OF SOME SORT. SIMILAR IN DESIGN TO YOUR EARTH GLASS.
GLASS? HOW IS THAT--?

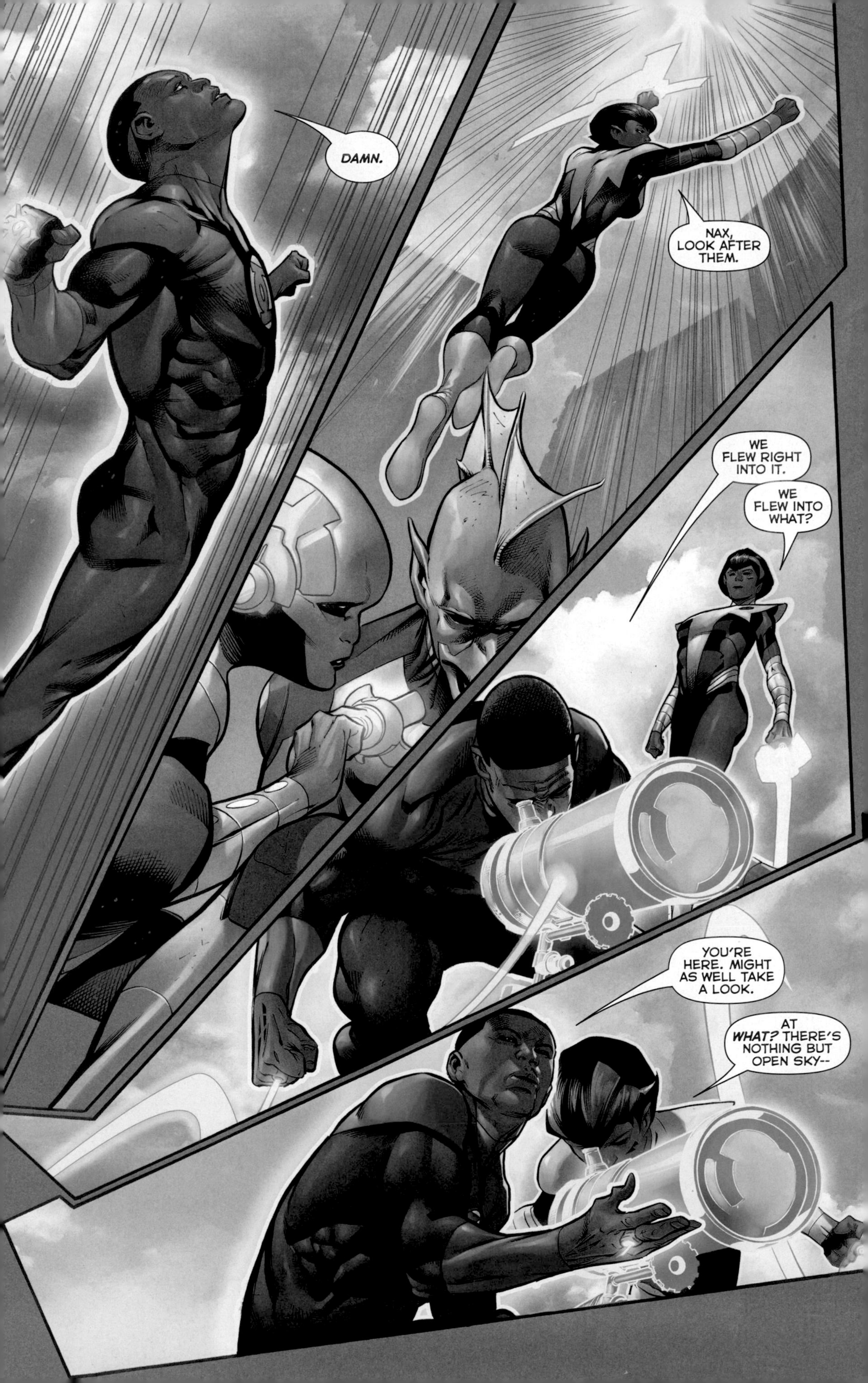
DAMN.
NAX, LOOK AFTER THEM.
WE FLEW RIGHT INTO IT.
WE FLEW INTO WHAT?
YOU'RE HERE. MIGHT AS WELL TAKE A LOOK.
AT *WHAT?* THERE'S NOTHING BUT OPEN SKY--

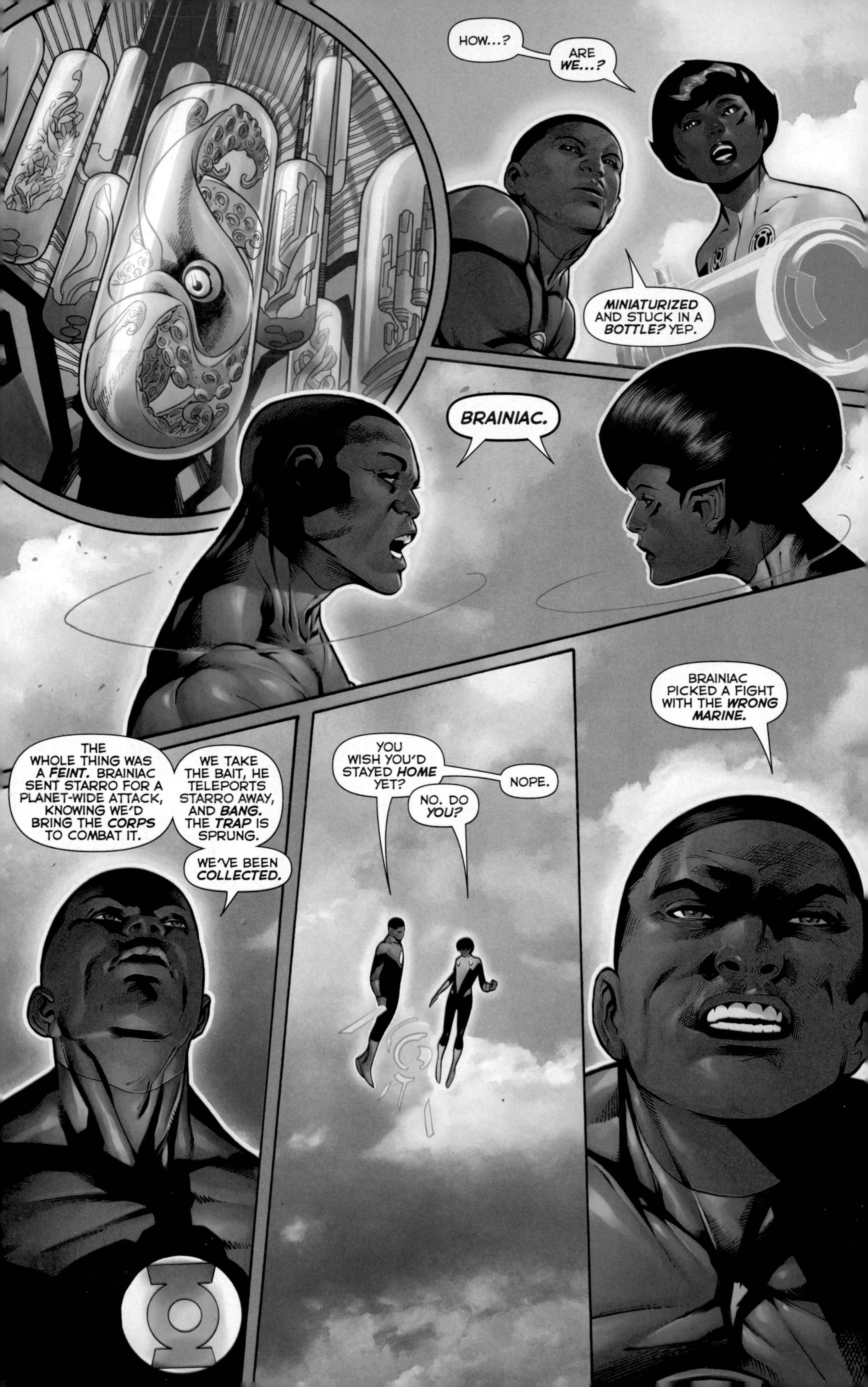
HOW...?
ARE WE...?
MINIATURIZED AND STUCK IN A BOTTLE? YEP.
BRAINIAC.
BRAINIAC PICKED A FIGHT WITH THE WRONG MARINE.
THE WHOLE THING WAS A FEINT. BRAINIAC SENT STARRO FOR A PLANET-WIDE ATTACK, KNOWING WE'D BRING THE CORPS TO COMBAT IT.
WE TAKE THE BAIT, HE TELEPORTS STARRO AWAY, AND BANG. THE TRAP IS SPRUNG.
WE'VE BEEN COLLECTED.
YOU WISH YOU'D STAYED HOME YET?
NOPE.
NO. DO YOU?

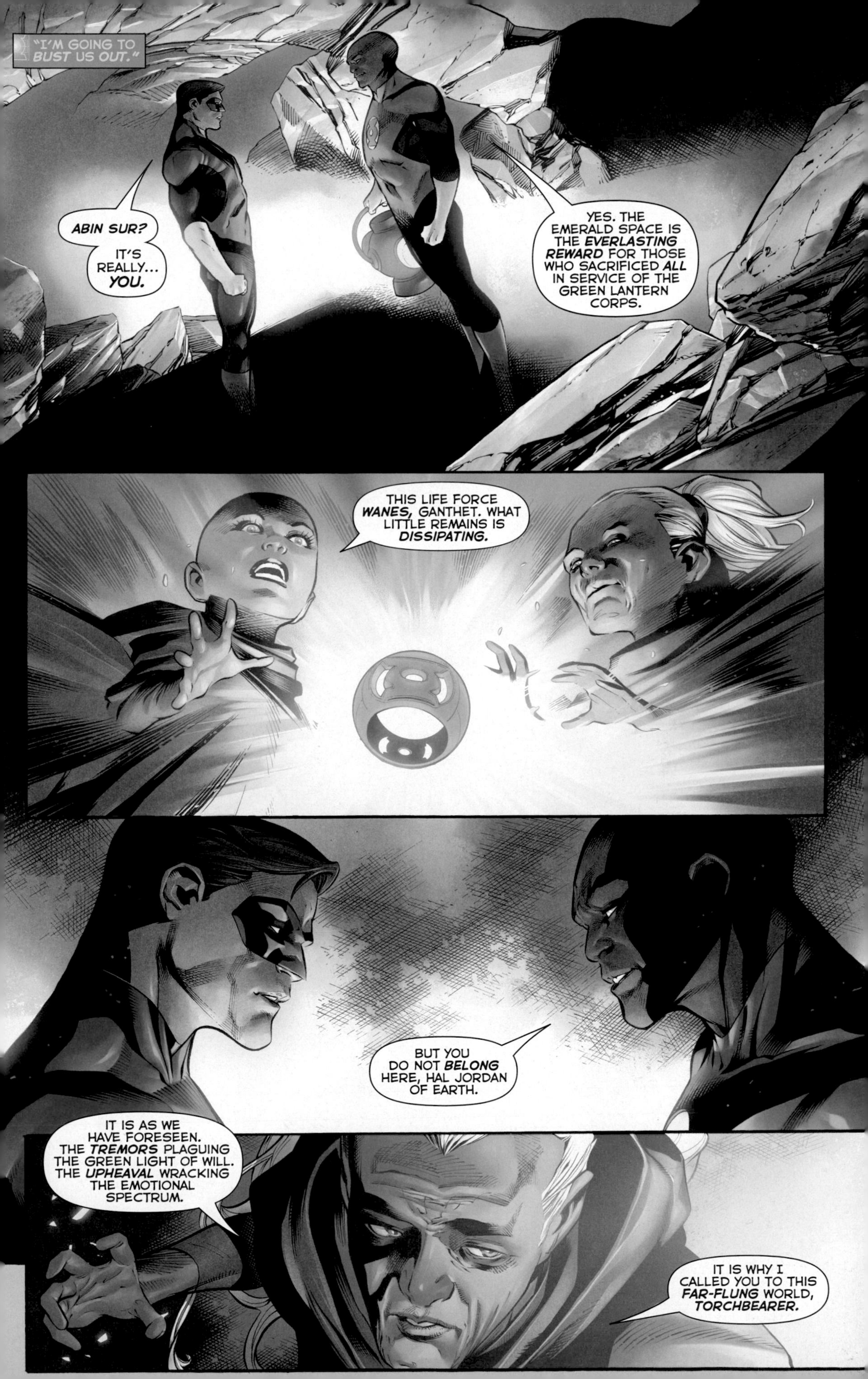
"I'M GOING TO BUST US OUT."
ABIN SUR? IT'S REALLY... YOU.
YES. THE EMERALD SPACE IS THE EVERLASTING REWARD FOR THOSE WHO SACRIFICED ALL IN SERVICE OF THE GREEN LANTERN CORPS.
THIS LIFE FORCE WANES, GANTHET. WHAT LITTLE REMAINS IS DISSIPATING.
BUT YOU DO NOT BELONG HERE, HAL JORDAN OF EARTH.
IT IS AS WE HAVE FORESEEN. THE TREMORS PLAGUING THE GREEN LIGHT OF WILL. THE UPHEAVAL WRACKING THE EMOTIONAL SPECTRUM.
IT IS WHY I CALLED YOU TO THIS FAR-FLUNG WORLD, TORCHBEARER.

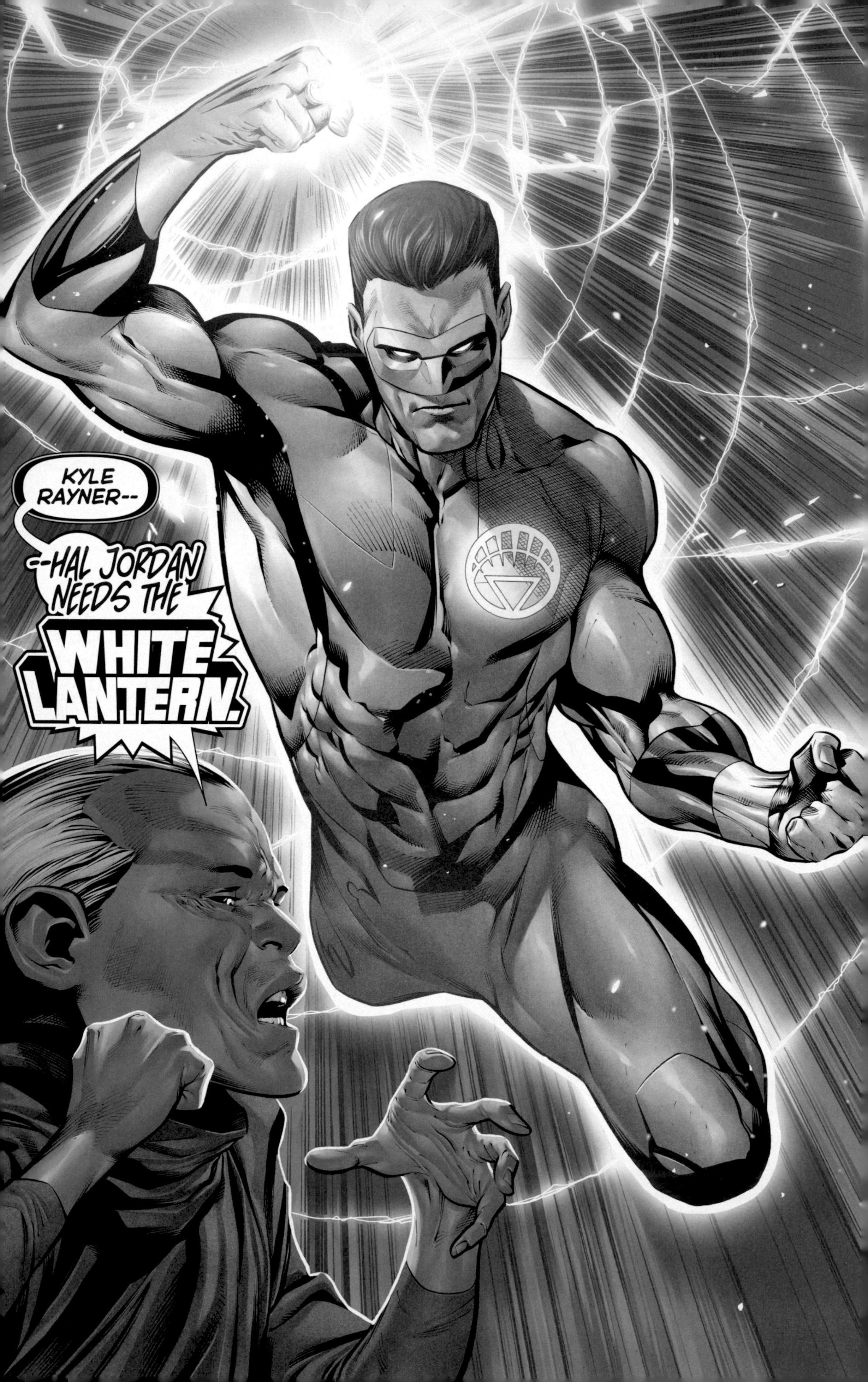

KYLE RAYNER--
--HAL JORDAN NEEDS THE
WHITE LANTERN.

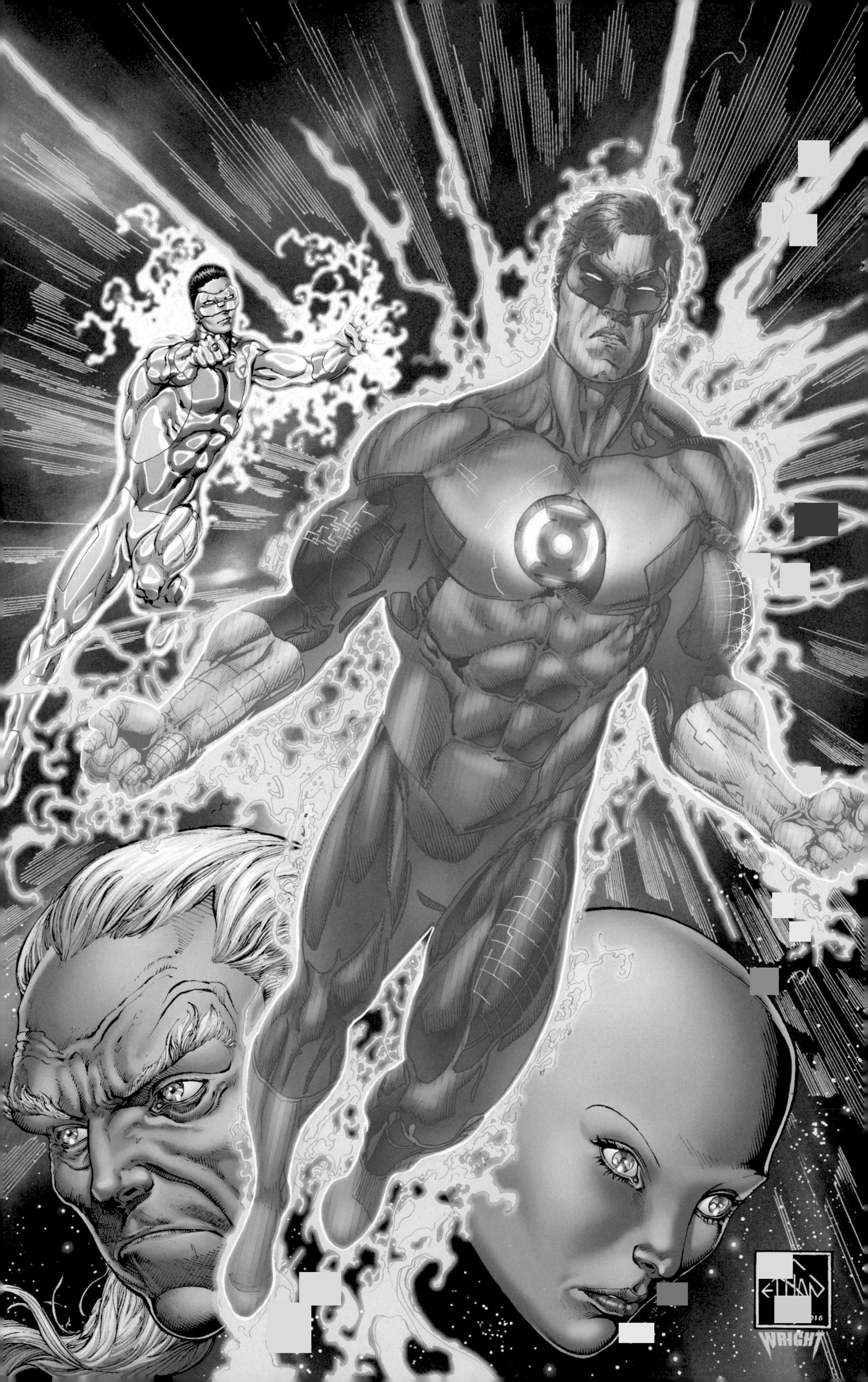

"BOTTLED LIGHT PART 3: BY LANTERN'S LIGHT"

ED BENES artist ∗ **JASON WRIGHT** colorist

ETHAN VAN SCIVER and **JASON WRIGHT** cover artists

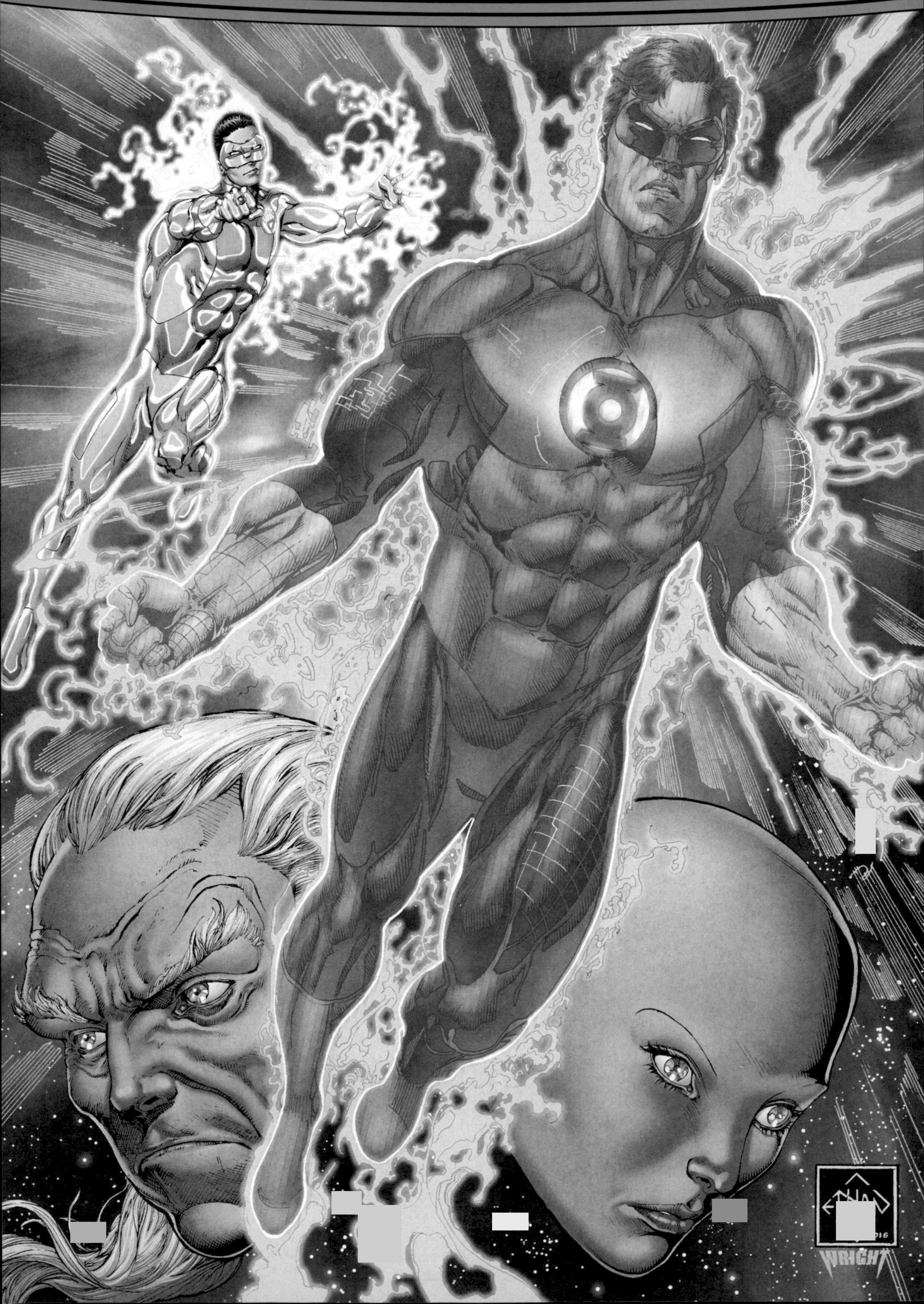

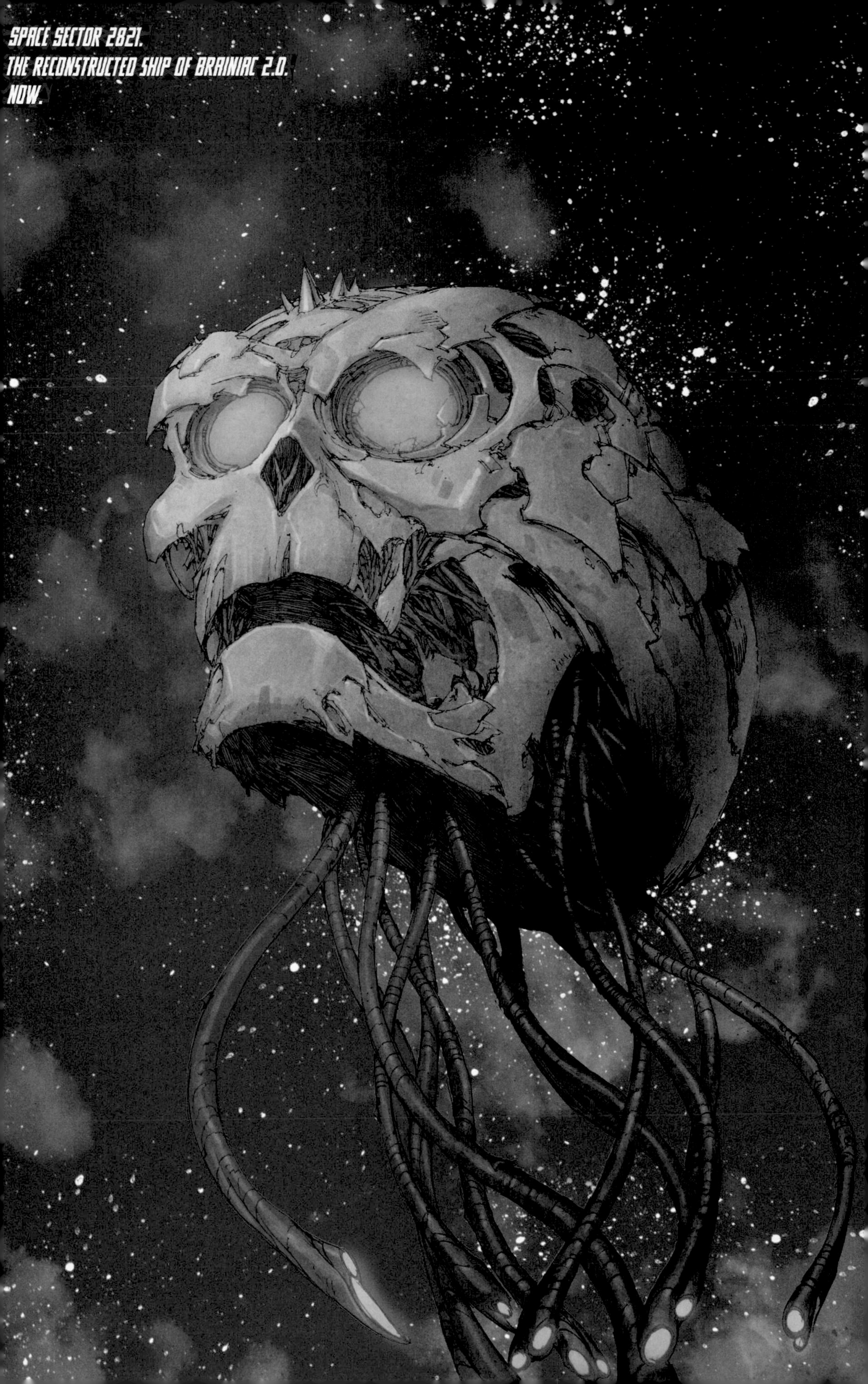
SPACE SECTOR 2821.
THE RECONSTRUCTED SHIP OF BRAINIAC 2.0.
NOW.

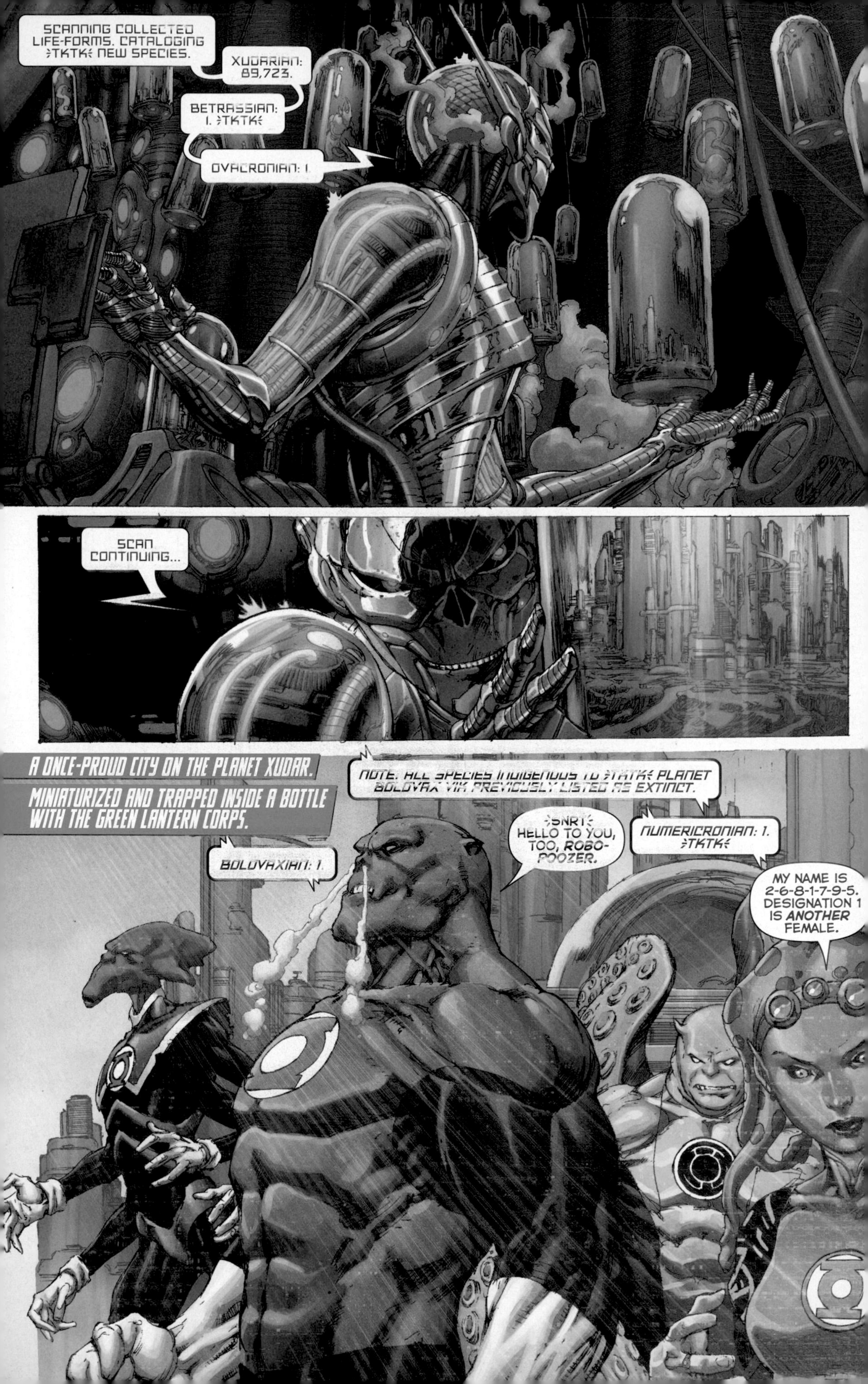
SCANNING COLLECTED LIFE-FORMS. CATALOGING ⋟TKTK⋞ NEW SPECIES.
XUDARIAN: 89,723.
BETRASSIAN: 1. ⋟TKTK⋞
OVACRONIAN: 1.
SCAN CONTINUING...
A ONCE-PROUD CITY ON THE PLANET XUDAR.
MINIATURIZED AND TRAPPED INSIDE A BOTTLE WITH THE GREEN LANTERN CORPS.
NOTE: ALL SPECIES INDIGENOUS TO ⋟TKTK⋞ PLANET BOLOVAX VIK PREVIOUSLY LISTED AS EXTINCT.
BOLOVAXIAN: 1.
⋟SNRT⋞ HELLO TO YOU, TOO, ROBO-POOZER.
NUMERICRONIAN: 1. ⋟TKTK⋞
MY NAME IS 2-6-8-1-7-9-5. DESIGNATION 1 IS ANOTHER FEMALE.

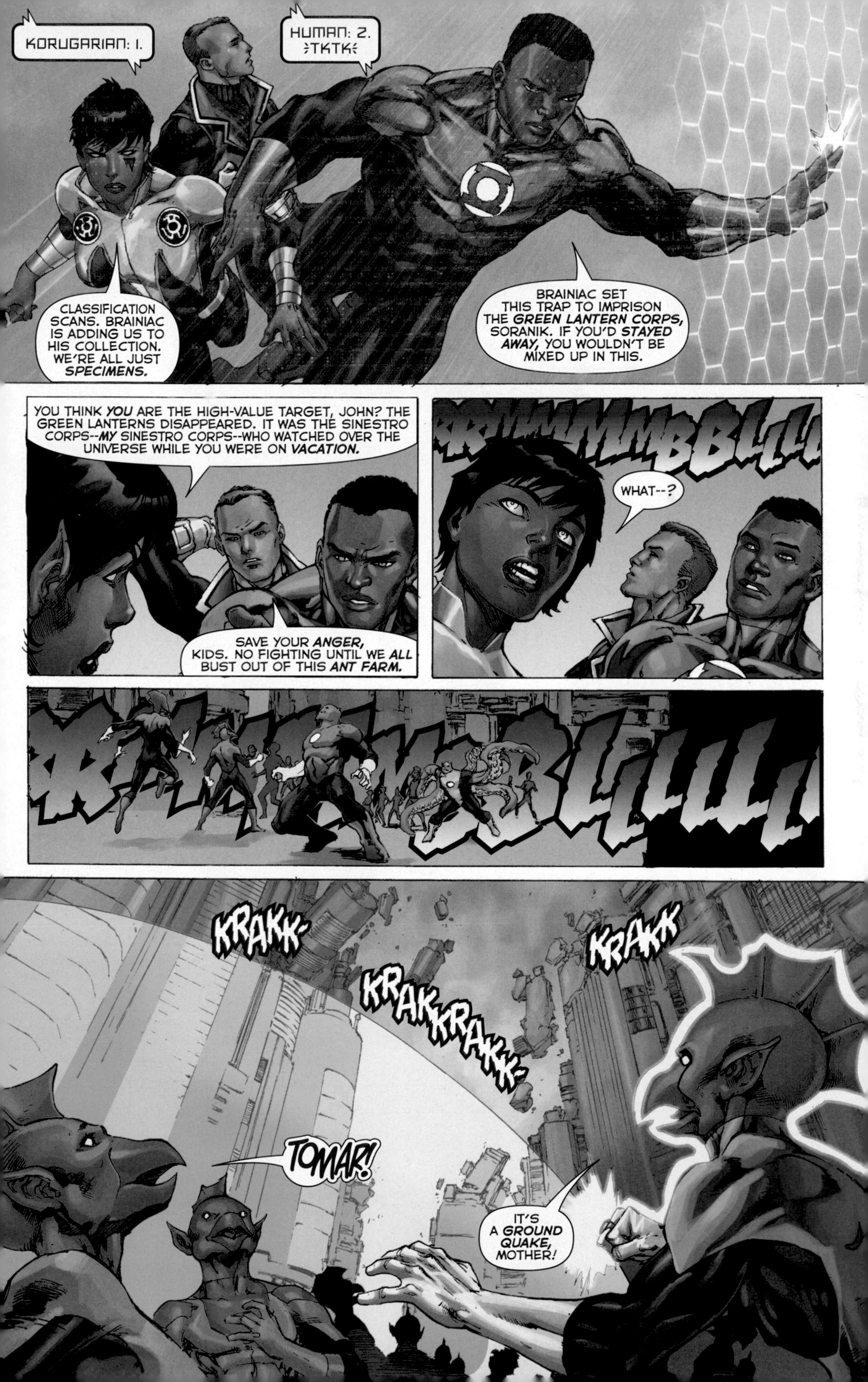
KORUGARIAN: 1.
HUMAN: 2.
TKTK
CLASSIFICATION SCANS. BRAINIAC IS ADDING US TO HIS COLLECTION. WE'RE ALL JUST SPECIMENS.
BRAINIAC SET THIS TRAP TO IMPRISON THE GREEN LANTERN CORPS, SORANIK. IF YOU'D STAYED AWAY, YOU WOULDN'T BE MIXED UP IN THIS.
YOU THINK YOU ARE THE HIGH-VALUE TARGET, JOHN? THE GREEN LANTERNS DISAPPEARED. IT WAS THE SINESTRO CORPS--MY SINESTRO CORPS--WHO WATCHED OVER THE UNIVERSE WHILE YOU WERE ON VACATION.
SAVE YOUR ANGER, KIDS. NO FIGHTING UNTIL WE ALL BUST OUT OF THIS ANT FARM.
RRMMMMMMBBLLLL
WHAT--?
KRAKK-
KRAKKRAKK-
KRAKK
TOMAR!
IT'S A GROUND QUAKE, MOTHER!

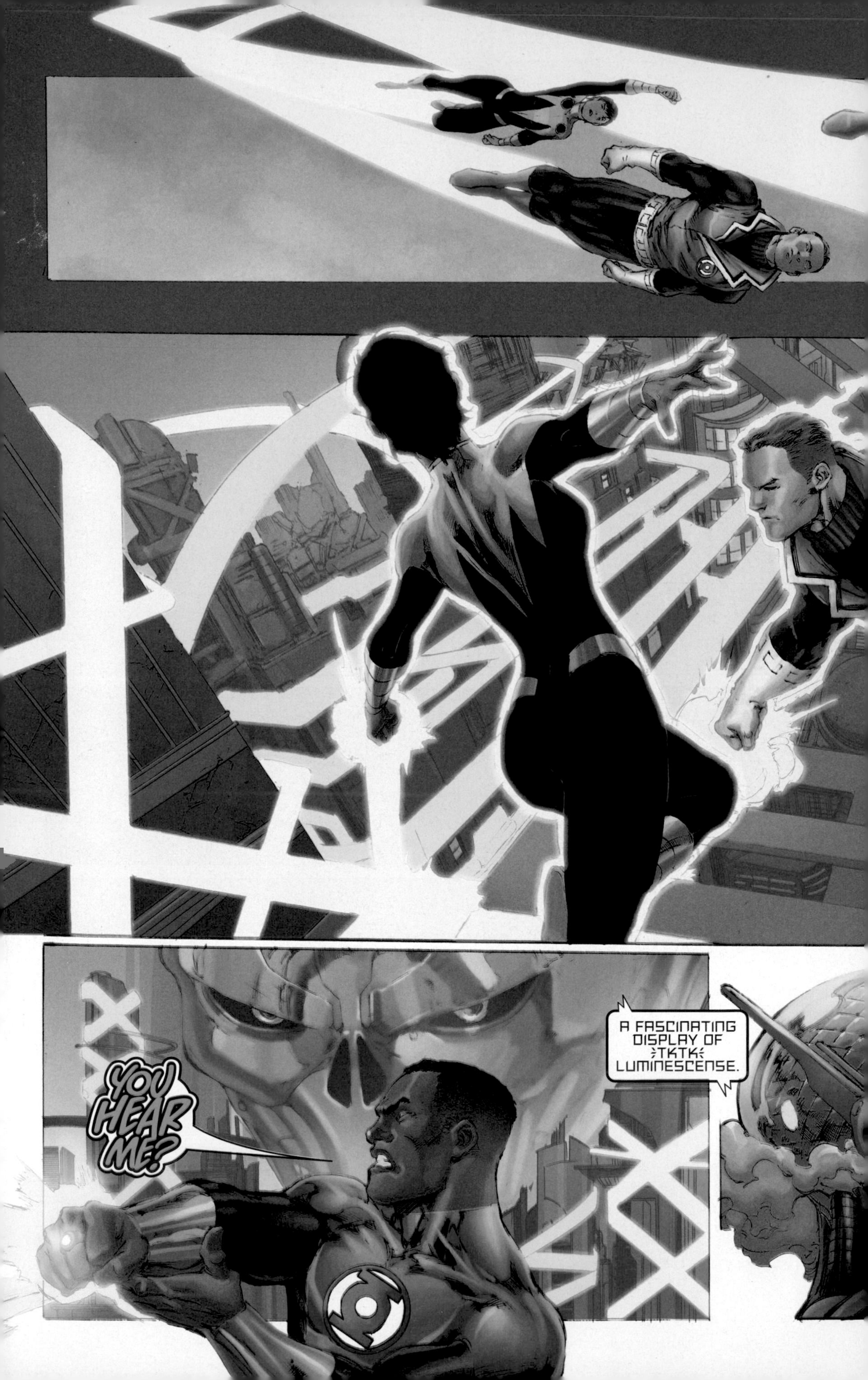
A FASCINATING DISPLAY OF TKTK LUMINESCENSE.
YOU HEAR ME?

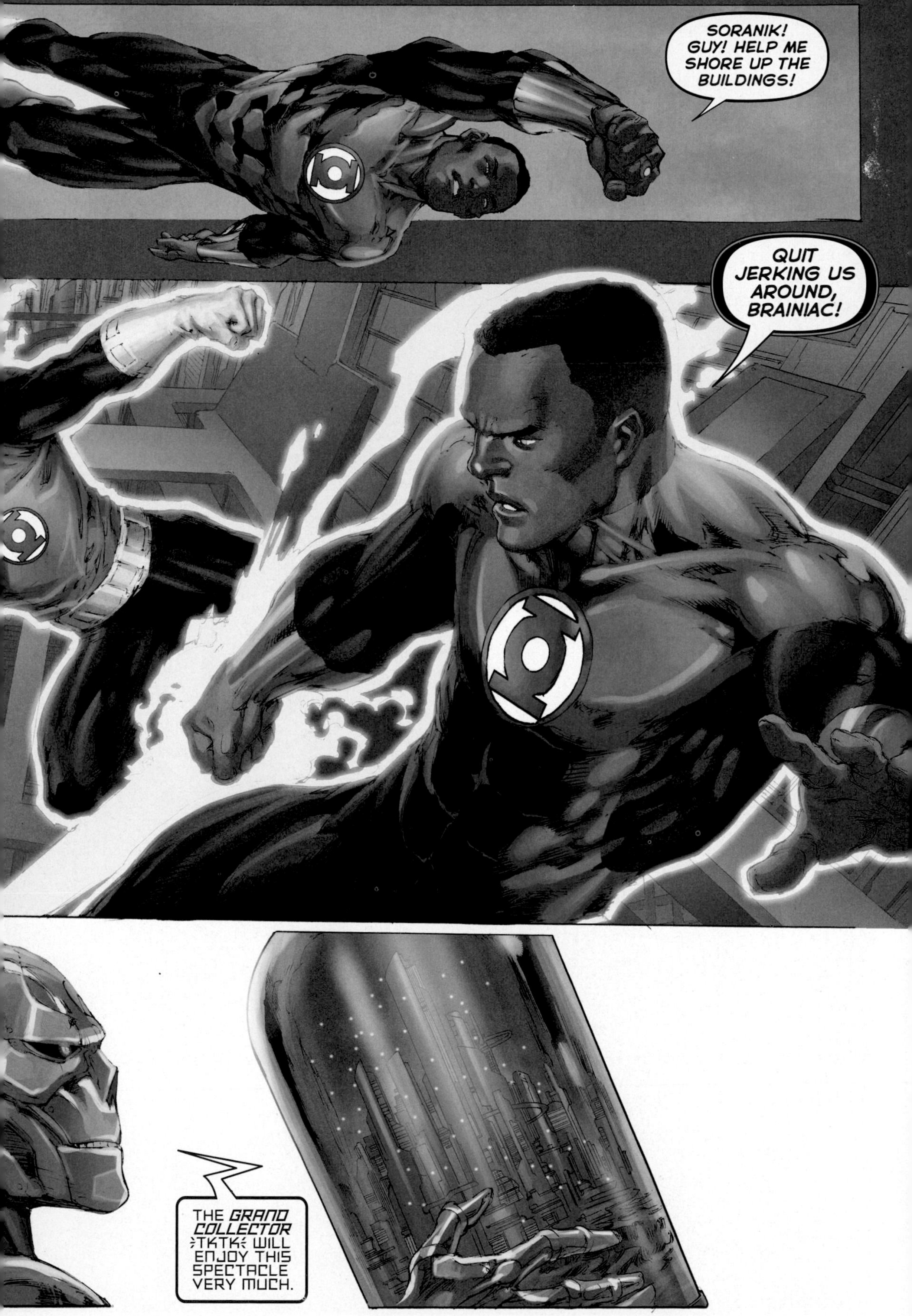
SORANIK! GUY! HELP ME SHORE UP THE BUILDINGS!
QUIT JERKING US AROUND, BRAINIAC!
THE GRAND COLLECTOR ›TKTK‹ WILL ENJOY THIS SPECTACLE VERY MUCH.

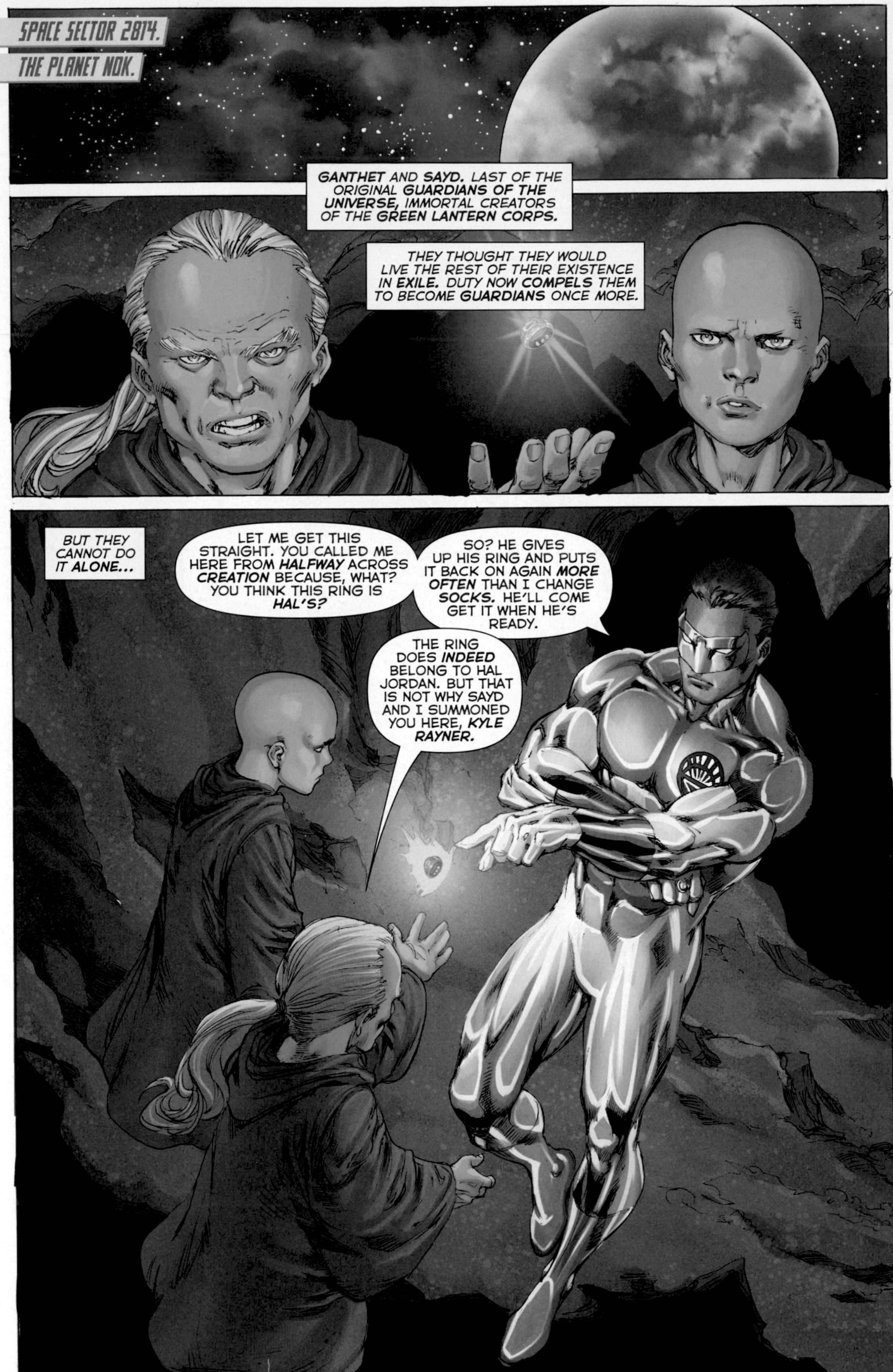
SPACE SECTOR 2814.
THE PLANET NOK.
GANTHET AND SAYD. LAST OF THE ORIGINAL GUARDIANS OF THE UNIVERSE, IMMORTAL CREATORS OF THE GREEN LANTERN CORPS.
THEY THOUGHT THEY WOULD LIVE THE REST OF THEIR EXISTENCE IN EXILE. DUTY NOW COMPELS THEM TO BECOME GUARDIANS ONCE MORE.
BUT THEY CANNOT DO IT ALONE...
LET ME GET THIS STRAIGHT. YOU CALLED ME HERE FROM HALFWAY ACROSS CREATION BECAUSE, WHAT? YOU THINK THIS RING IS HAL'S?
SO? HE GIVES UP HIS RING AND PUTS IT BACK ON AGAIN MORE OFTEN THAN I CHANGE SOCKS. HE'LL COME GET IT WHEN HE'S READY.
THE RING DOES INDEED BELONG TO HAL JORDAN. BUT THAT IS NOT WHY SAYD AND I SUMMONED YOU HERE, KYLE RAYNER.

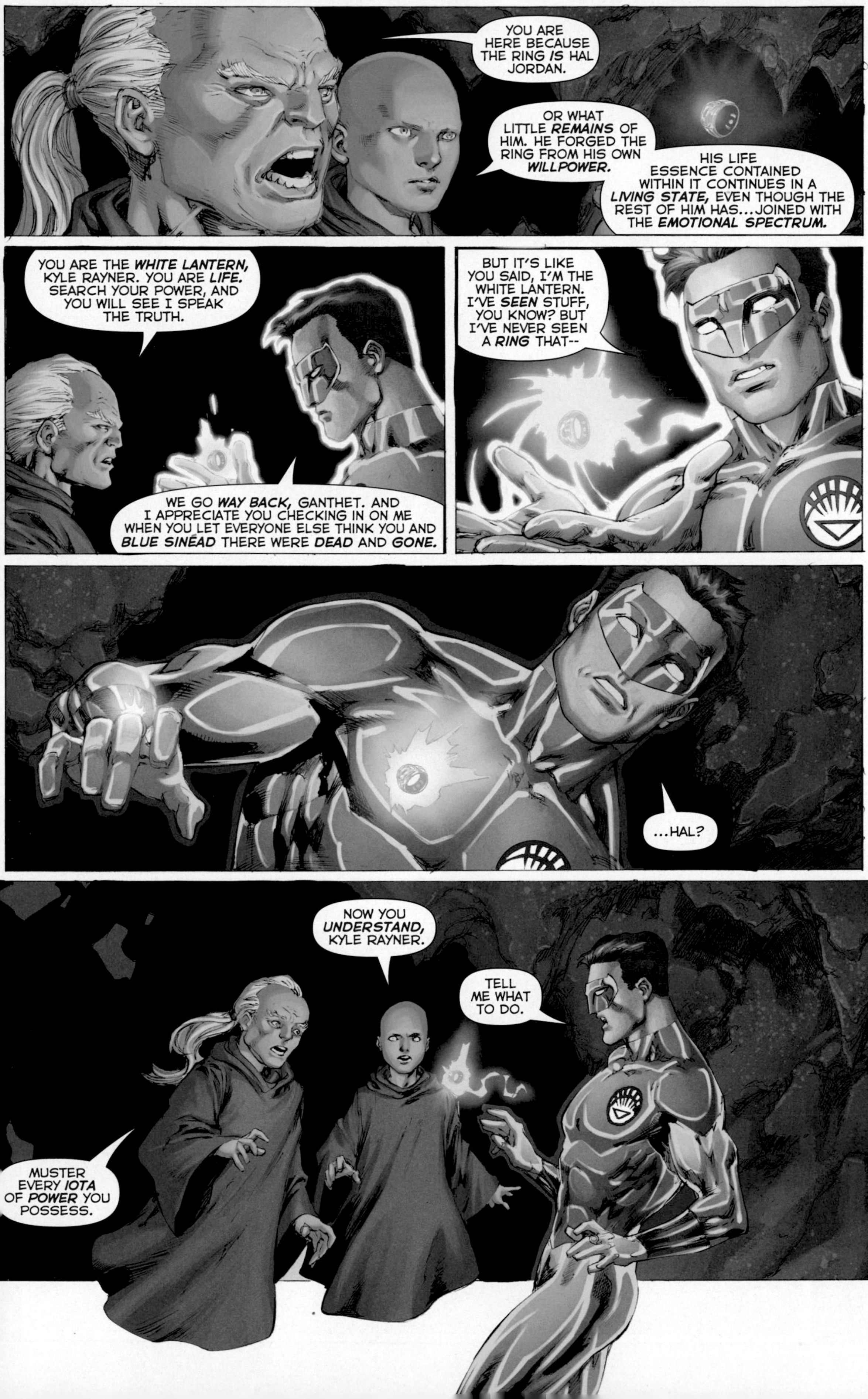
YOU ARE HERE BECAUSE THE RING *IS* HAL JORDAN.
OR WHAT LITTLE ***REMAINS*** OF HIM. HE FORGED THE RING FROM HIS OWN ***WILLPOWER.***
HIS LIFE ESSENCE CONTAINED WITHIN IT CONTINUES IN A ***LIVING STATE,*** EVEN THOUGH THE REST OF HIM HAS...JOINED WITH THE ***EMOTIONAL SPECTRUM.***
YOU ARE THE ***WHITE LANTERN,*** KYLE RAYNER. YOU ARE ***LIFE.*** SEARCH YOUR POWER, AND YOU WILL SEE I SPEAK THE TRUTH.
WE GO ***WAY BACK,*** GANTHET. AND I APPRECIATE YOU CHECKING IN ON ME WHEN YOU LET EVERYONE ELSE THINK YOU AND ***BLUE SINEAD*** THERE WERE ***DEAD*** AND ***GONE.***
BUT IT'S LIKE YOU SAID, I'M THE WHITE LANTERN. I'VE ***SEEN*** STUFF, YOU KNOW? BUT I'VE NEVER SEEN A ***RING*** THAT--
...HAL?
NOW YOU ***UNDERSTAND,*** KYLE RAYNER.
TELL ME WHAT TO DO.
MUSTER EVERY ***IOTA*** OF ***POWER*** YOU POSSESS.

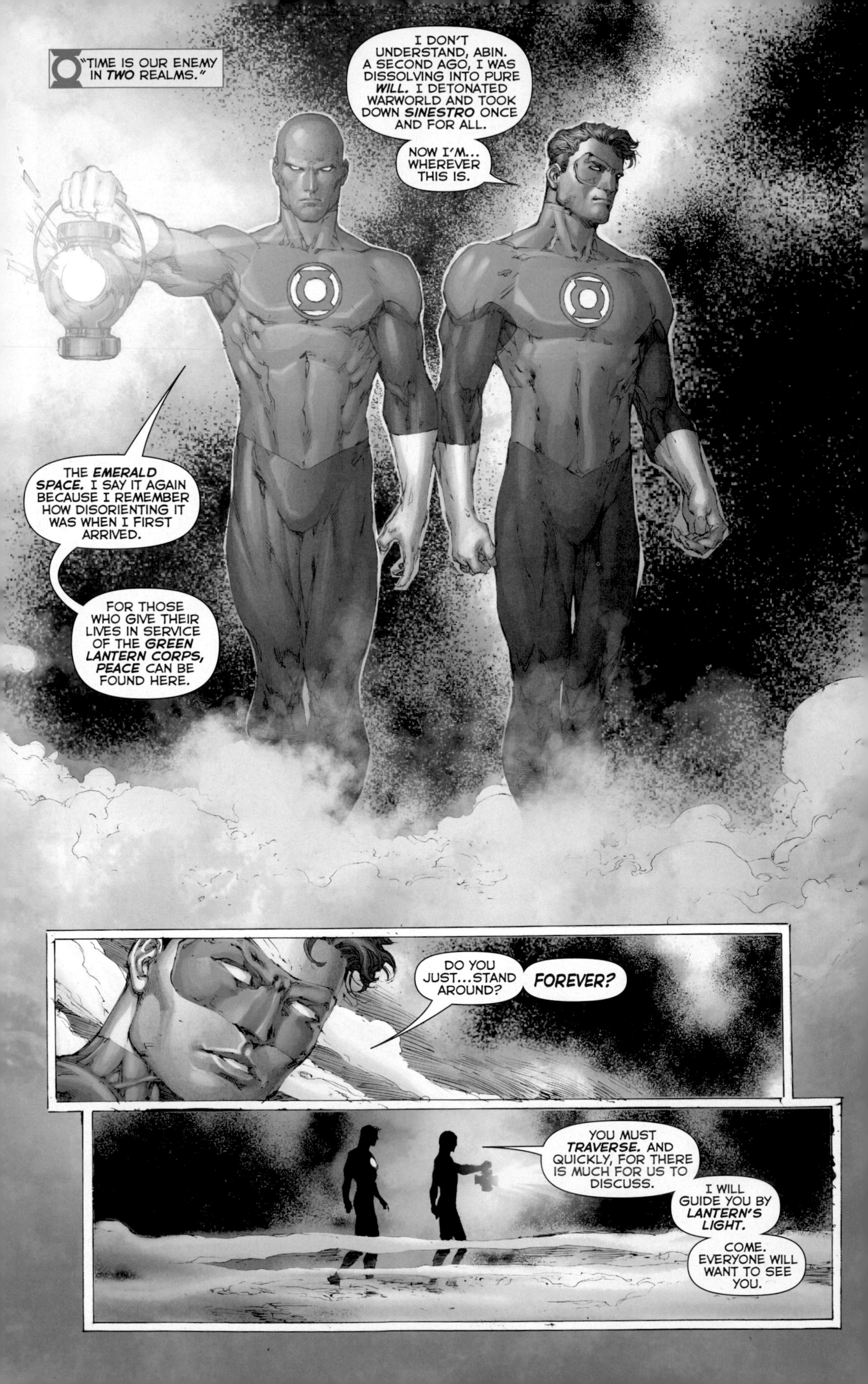
"TIME IS OUR ENEMY IN *TWO* REALMS."
I DON'T UNDERSTAND, ABIN. A SECOND AGO, I WAS DISSOLVING INTO PURE *WILL.* I DETONATED WARWORLD AND TOOK DOWN *SINESTRO* ONCE AND FOR ALL.
NOW I'M... WHEREVER THIS IS.
THE *EMERALD SPACE.* I SAY IT AGAIN BECAUSE I REMEMBER HOW DISORIENTING IT WAS WHEN I FIRST ARRIVED.
FOR THOSE WHO GIVE THEIR LIVES IN SERVICE OF THE *GREEN LANTERN CORPS, PEACE* CAN BE FOUND HERE.
DO YOU JUST...STAND AROUND?
FOREVER?
YOU MUST *TRAVERSE.* AND QUICKLY, FOR THERE IS MUCH FOR US TO DISCUSS.
I WILL GUIDE YOU BY *LANTERN'S LIGHT.*
COME. EVERYONE WILL WANT TO SEE YOU.

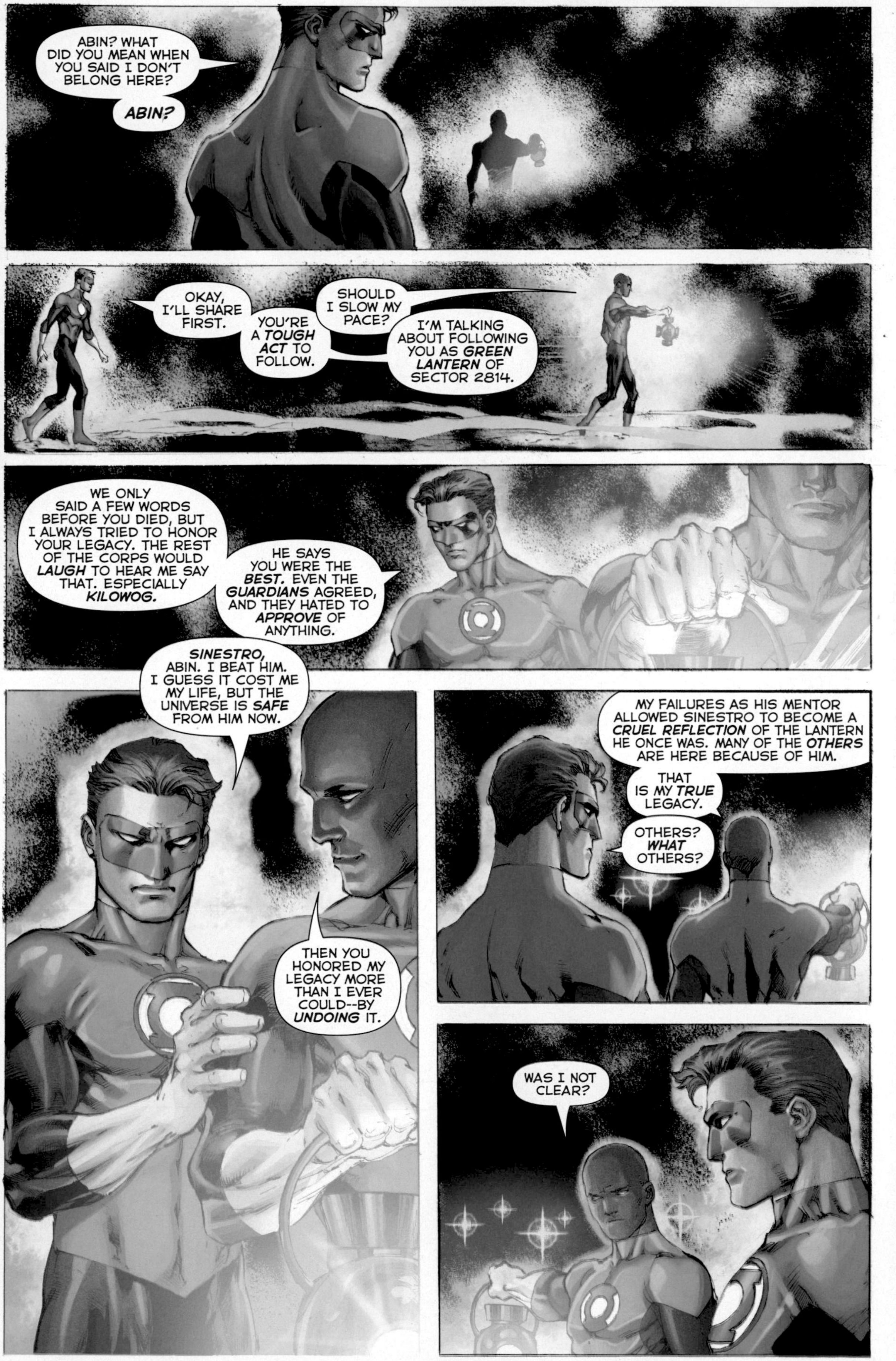
ABIN? WHAT DID YOU MEAN WHEN YOU SAID I DON'T BELONG HERE?
ABIN?
OKAY, I'LL SHARE FIRST.
YOU'RE A TOUGH ACT TO FOLLOW.
SHOULD I SLOW MY PACE?
I'M TALKING ABOUT FOLLOWING YOU AS GREEN LANTERN OF SECTOR 2814.
WE ONLY SAID A FEW WORDS BEFORE YOU DIED, BUT I ALWAYS TRIED TO HONOR YOUR LEGACY. THE REST OF THE CORPS WOULD LAUGH TO HEAR ME SAY THAT. ESPECIALLY KILOWOG.
HE SAYS YOU WERE THE BEST. EVEN THE GUARDIANS AGREED, AND THEY HATED TO APPROVE OF ANYTHING.
SINESTRO, ABIN. I BEAT HIM. I GUESS IT COST ME MY LIFE, BUT THE UNIVERSE IS SAFE FROM HIM NOW.
THEN YOU HONORED MY LEGACY MORE THAN I EVER COULD--BY UNDOING IT.
MY FAILURES AS HIS MENTOR ALLOWED SINESTRO TO BECOME A CRUEL REFLECTION OF THE LANTERN HE ONCE WAS. MANY OF THE OTHERS ARE HERE BECAUSE OF HIM.
THAT IS MY TRUE LEGACY.
OTHERS? WHAT OTHERS?
WAS I NOT CLEAR?

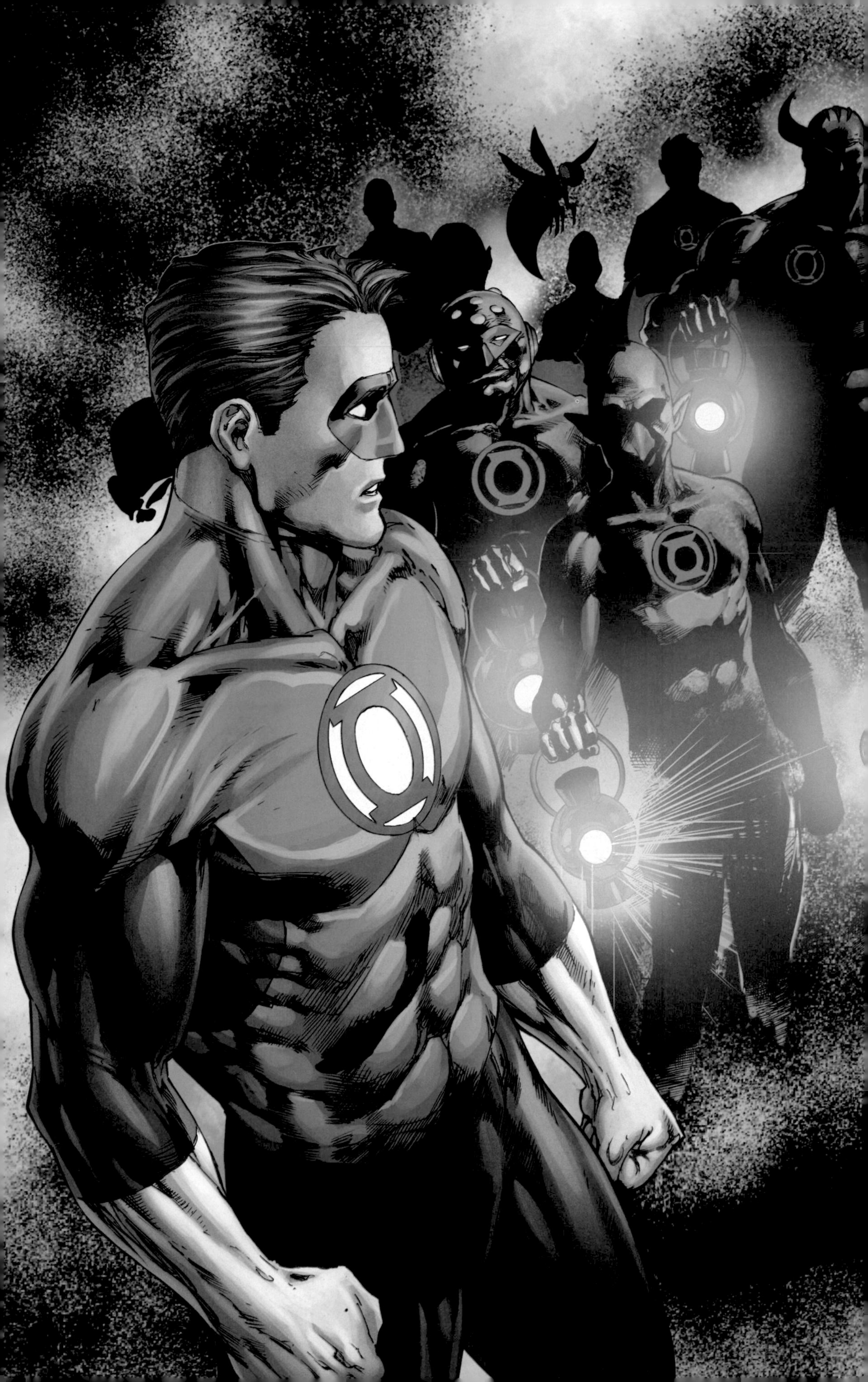

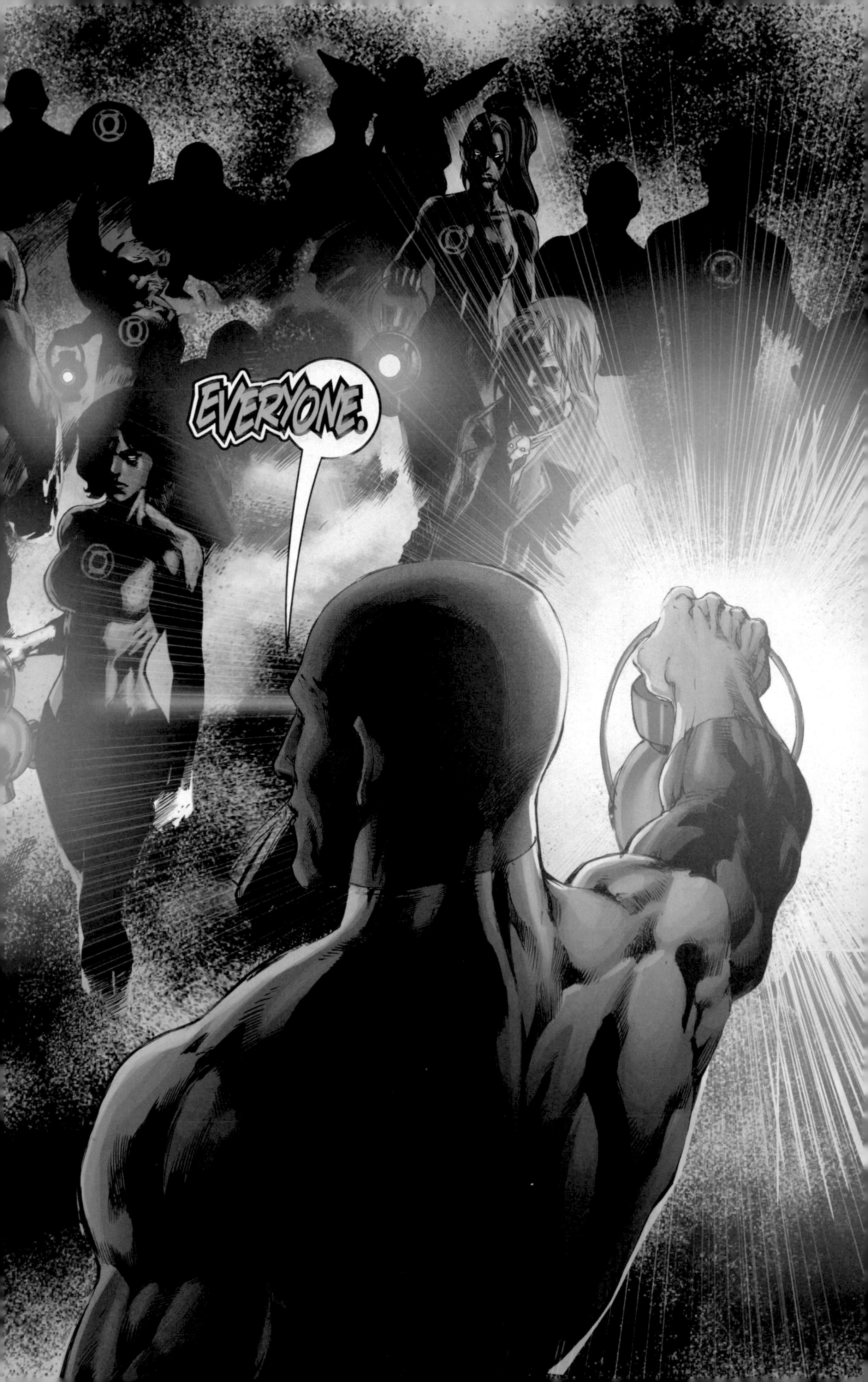
EVERYONE.

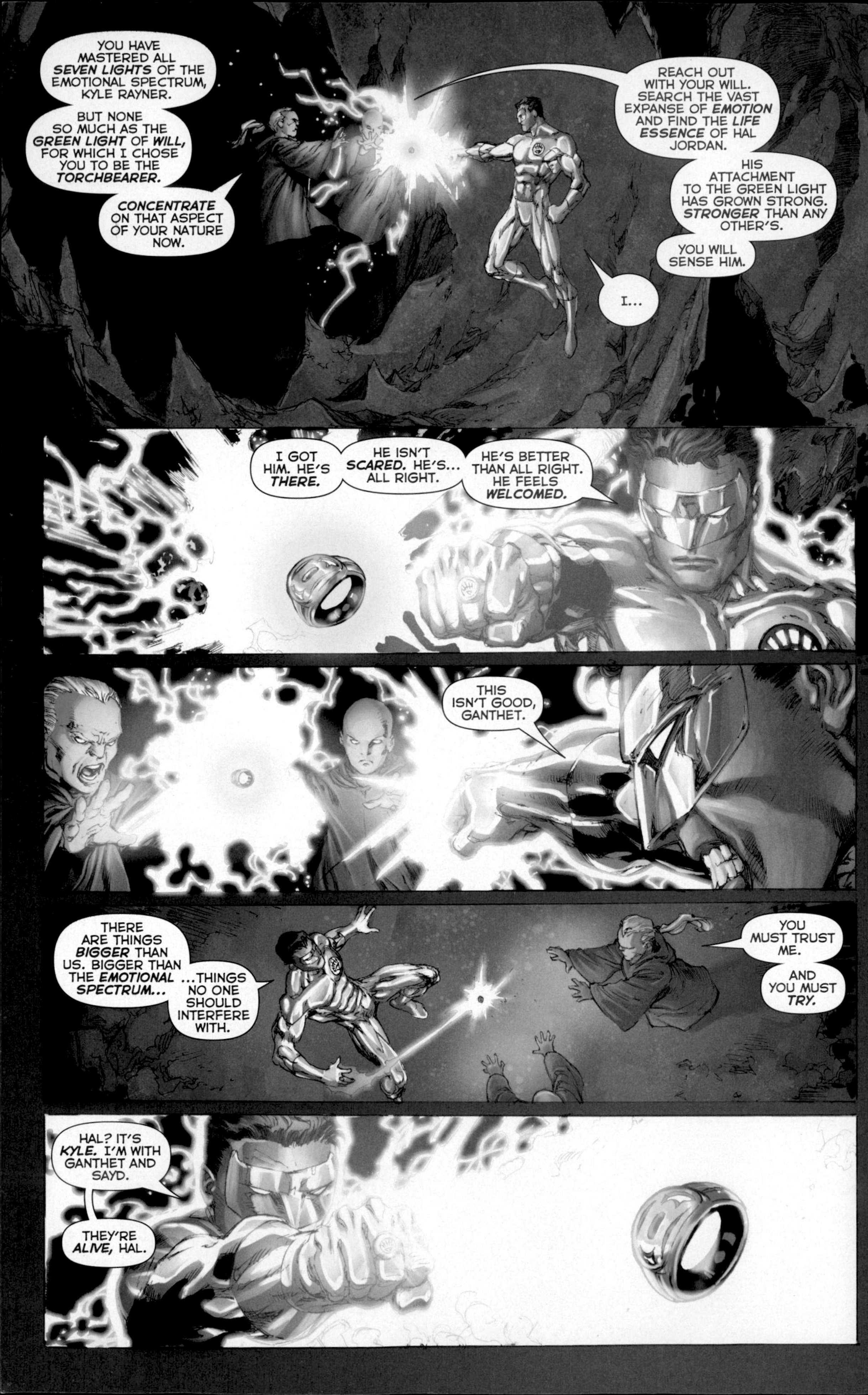
YOU HAVE MASTERED ALL SEVEN LIGHTS OF THE EMOTIONAL SPECTRUM, KYLE RAYNER.
BUT NONE SO MUCH AS THE GREEN LIGHT OF WILL, FOR WHICH I CHOSE YOU TO BE THE TORCHBEARER.
CONCENTRATE ON THAT ASPECT OF YOUR NATURE NOW.
REACH OUT WITH YOUR WILL. SEARCH THE VAST EXPANSE OF EMOTION AND FIND THE LIFE ESSENCE OF HAL JORDAN.
HIS ATTACHMENT TO THE GREEN LIGHT HAS GROWN STRONG. STRONGER THAN ANY OTHER'S.
YOU WILL SENSE HIM.
I...
I GOT HIM. HE'S THERE.
HE ISN'T SCARED. HE'S... ALL RIGHT.
HE'S BETTER THAN ALL RIGHT. HE FEELS WELCOMED.
THIS ISN'T GOOD, GANTHET.
THERE ARE THINGS BIGGER THAN US. BIGGER THAN THE EMOTIONAL SPECTRUM...
...THINGS NO ONE SHOULD INTERFERE WITH.
YOU MUST TRUST ME.
AND YOU MUST TRY.
HAL? IT'S KYLE. I'M WITH GANTHET AND SAYD.
THEY'RE ALIVE, HAL.

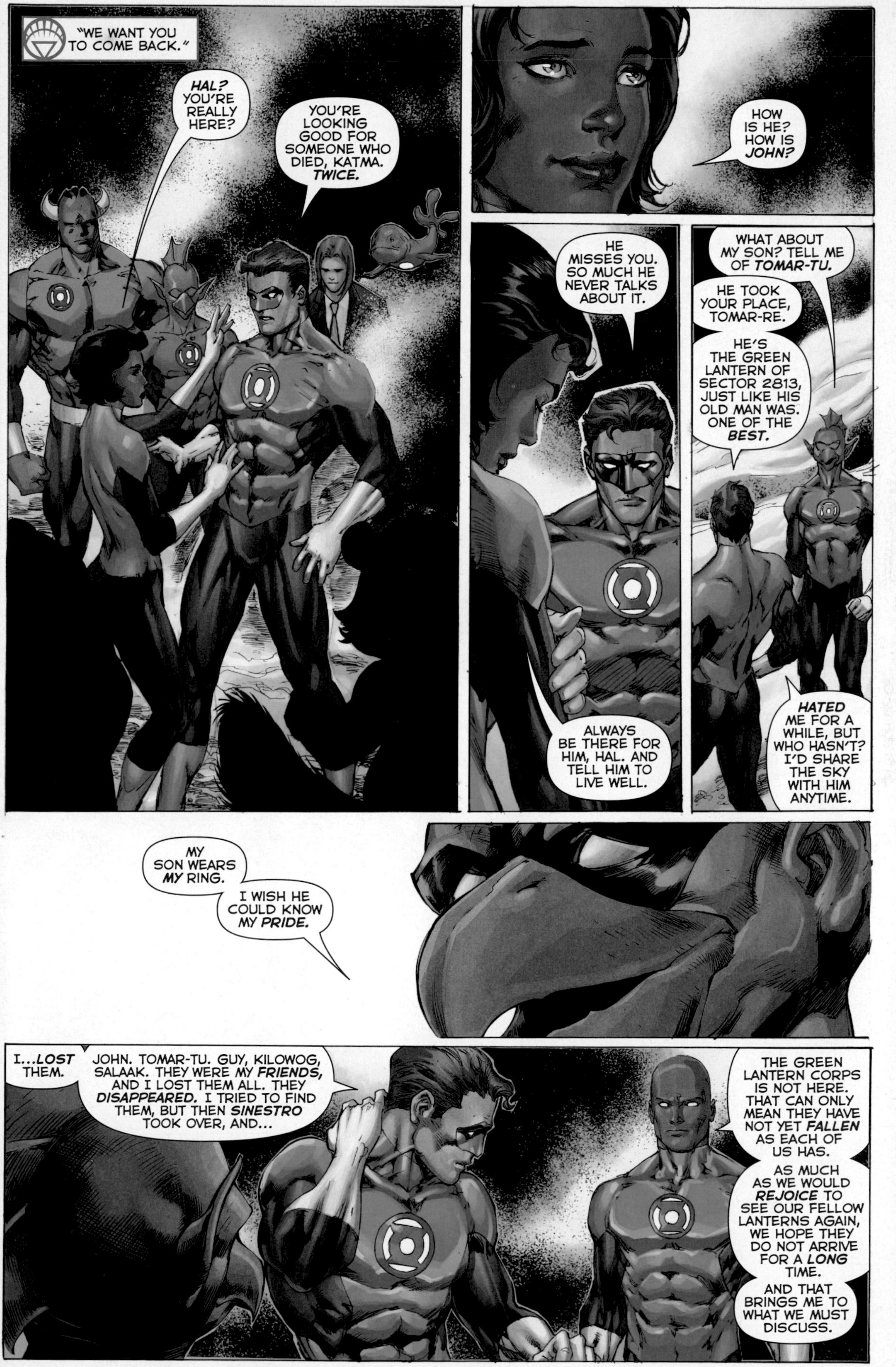
"WE WANT YOU TO COME BACK."
HAL? YOU'RE REALLY HERE?
YOU'RE LOOKING GOOD FOR SOMEONE WHO DIED, KATMA. TWICE.
HOW IS HE? HOW IS JOHN?
HE MISSES YOU. SO MUCH HE NEVER TALKS ABOUT IT.
ALWAYS BE THERE FOR HIM, HAL. AND TELL HIM TO LIVE WELL.
WHAT ABOUT MY SON? TELL ME OF TOMAR-TU.
HE TOOK YOUR PLACE, TOMAR-RE.
HE'S THE GREEN LANTERN OF SECTOR 2813, JUST LIKE HIS OLD MAN WAS. ONE OF THE BEST.
HATED ME FOR A WHILE, BUT WHO HASN'T? I'D SHARE THE SKY WITH HIM ANYTIME.
MY SON WEARS MY RING.
I WISH HE COULD KNOW MY PRIDE.
I...LOST THEM.
JOHN. TOMAR-TU. GUY, KILOWOG, SALAAK. THEY WERE MY FRIENDS, AND I LOST THEM ALL. THEY DISAPPEARED. I TRIED TO FIND THEM, BUT THEN SINESTRO TOOK OVER, AND...
THE GREEN LANTERN CORPS IS NOT HERE. THAT CAN ONLY MEAN THEY HAVE NOT YET FALLEN AS EACH OF US HAS.
AS MUCH AS WE WOULD REJOICE TO SEE OUR FELLOW LANTERNS AGAIN, WE HOPE THEY DO NOT ARRIVE FOR A LONG TIME.
AND THAT BRINGS ME TO WHAT WE MUST DISCUSS.

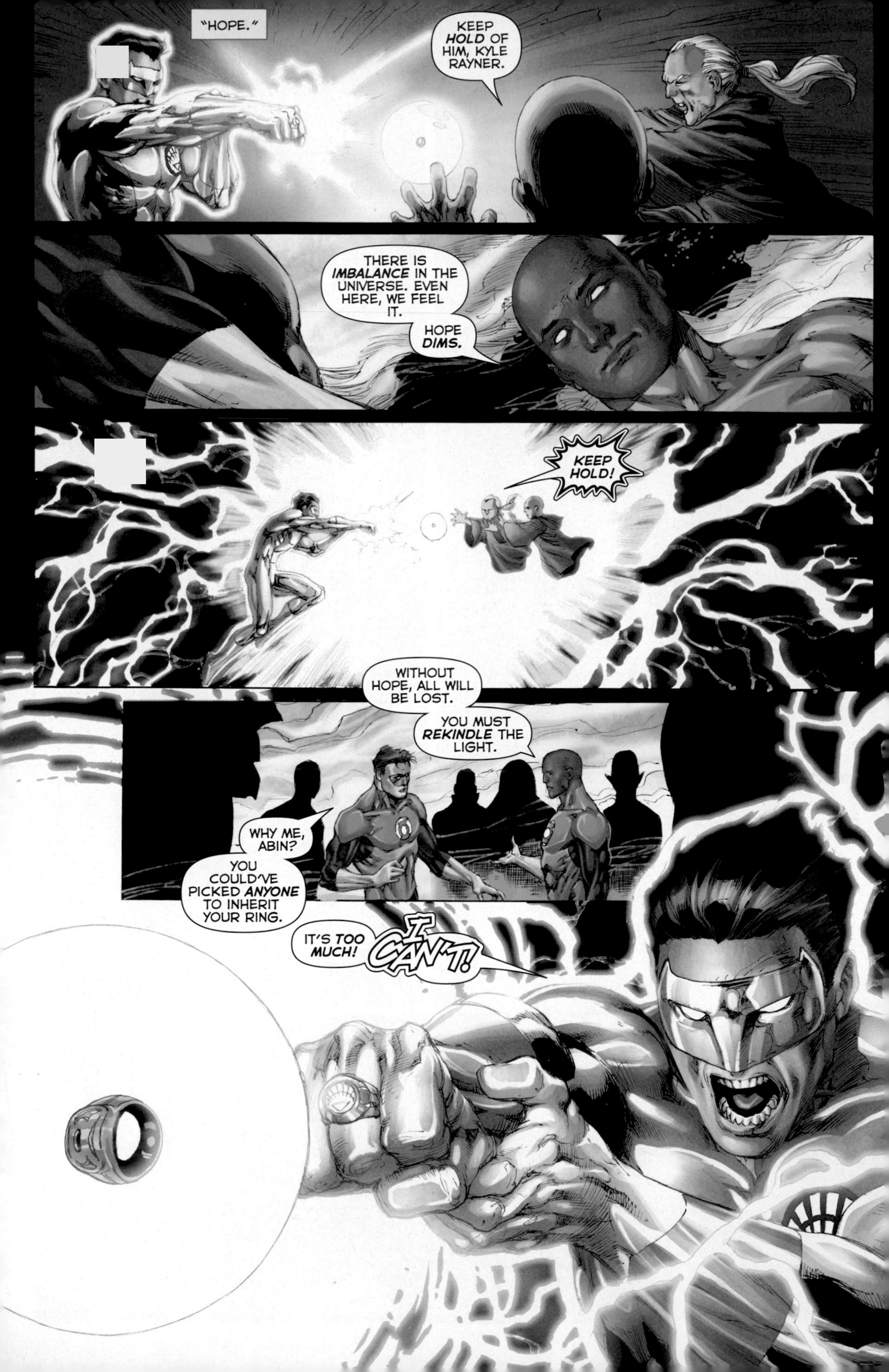
"HOPE."
KEEP HOLD OF HIM, KYLE RAYNER.
THERE IS IMBALANCE IN THE UNIVERSE. EVEN HERE, WE FEEL IT.
HOPE DIMS.
KEEP HOLD!
WITHOUT HOPE, ALL WILL BE LOST.
YOU MUST REKINDLE THE LIGHT.
WHY ME, ABIN?
YOU COULD'VE PICKED ANYONE TO INHERIT YOUR RING.
IT'S TOO MUCH!
I CAN'T!

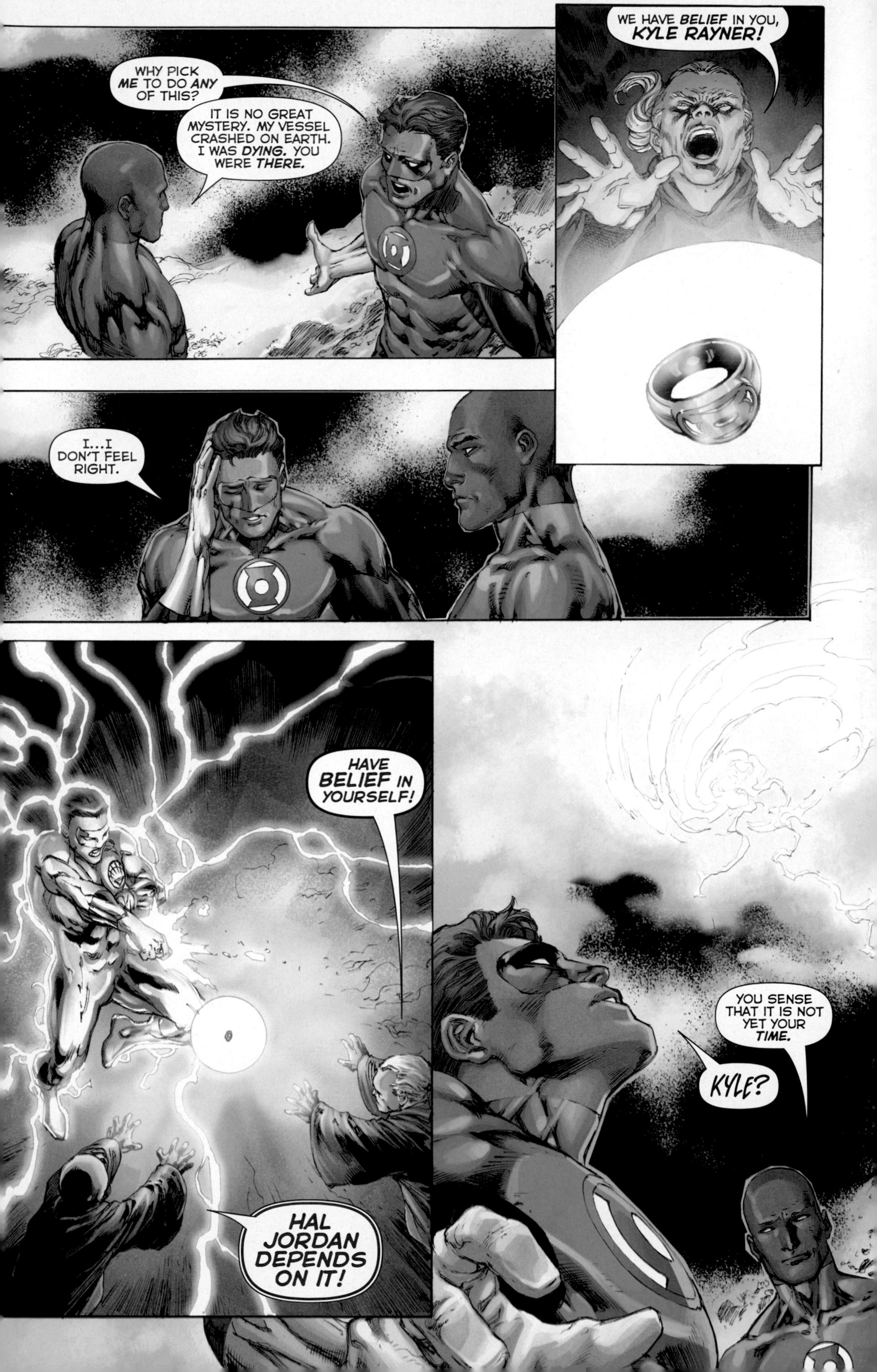
WHY PICK ME TO DO ANY OF THIS?
IT IS NO GREAT MYSTERY. MY VESSEL CRASHED ON EARTH. I WAS DYING. YOU WERE THERE.
WE HAVE BELIEF IN YOU, KYLE RAYNER!
I...I DON'T FEEL RIGHT.
HAVE BELIEF IN YOURSELF!
HAL JORDAN DEPENDS ON IT!
YOU SENSE THAT IT IS NOT YET YOUR TIME.
KYLE?

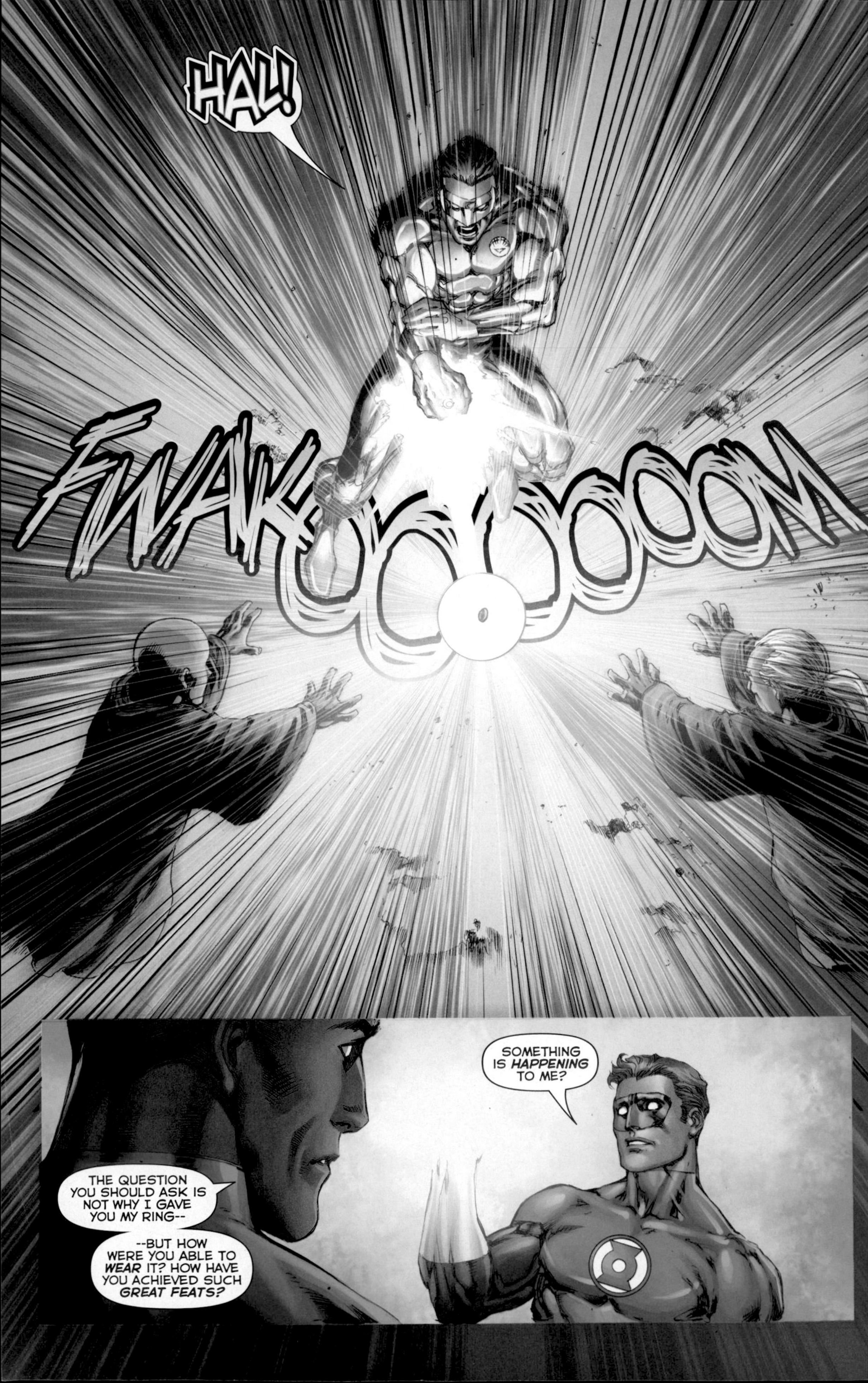
HAL!
FWAK!
OOOOOOOM
SOMETHING IS HAPPENING TO ME?
THE QUESTION YOU SHOULD ASK IS NOT WHY I GAVE YOU MY RING--
--BUT HOW WERE YOU ABLE TO WEAR IT? HOW HAVE YOU ACHIEVED SUCH GREAT FEATS?

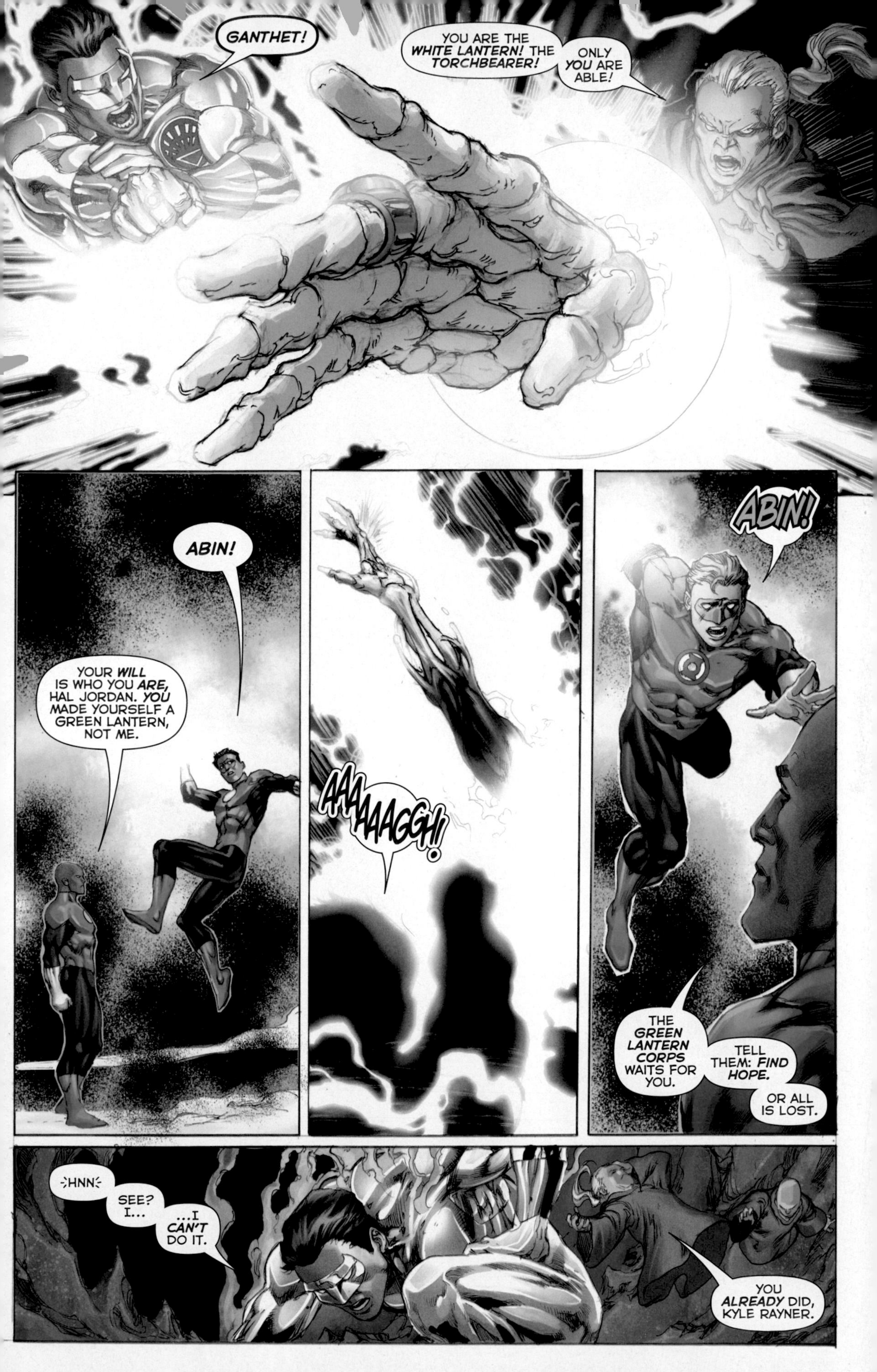

GANTHET!
YOU ARE THE WHITE LANTERN! THE TORCHBEARER!
ONLY YOU ARE ABLE!
ABIN!
YOUR WILL IS WHO YOU ARE, HAL JORDAN. YOU MADE YOURSELF A GREEN LANTERN, NOT ME.
AAAAAAAGGH!
ABIN!
THE GREEN LANTERN CORPS WAITS FOR YOU.
TELL THEM: FIND HOPE.
OR ALL IS LOST.
HNN
SEE? I...
...I CAN'T DO IT.
YOU ALREADY DID, KYLE RAYNER.

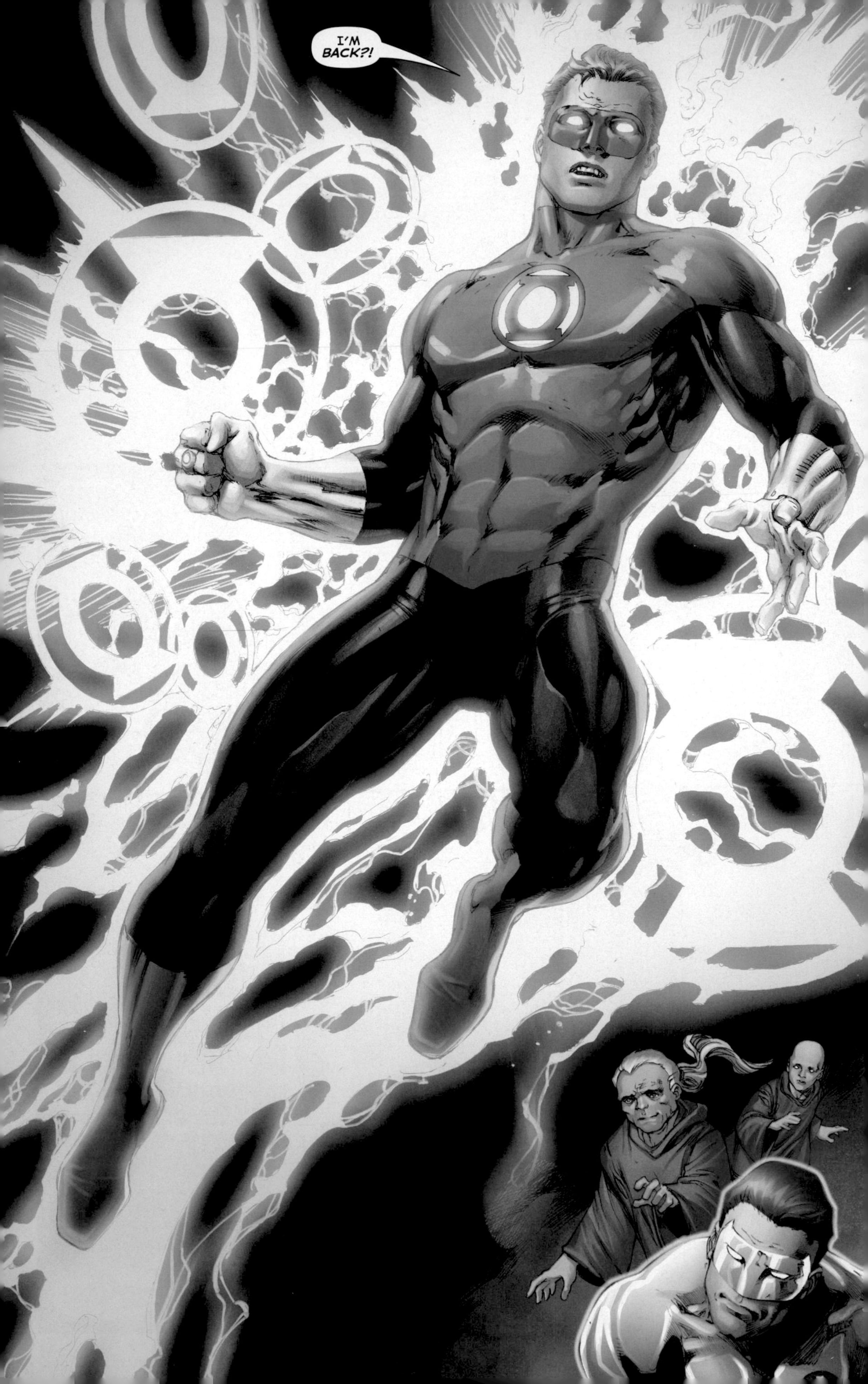
I'M BACK?!

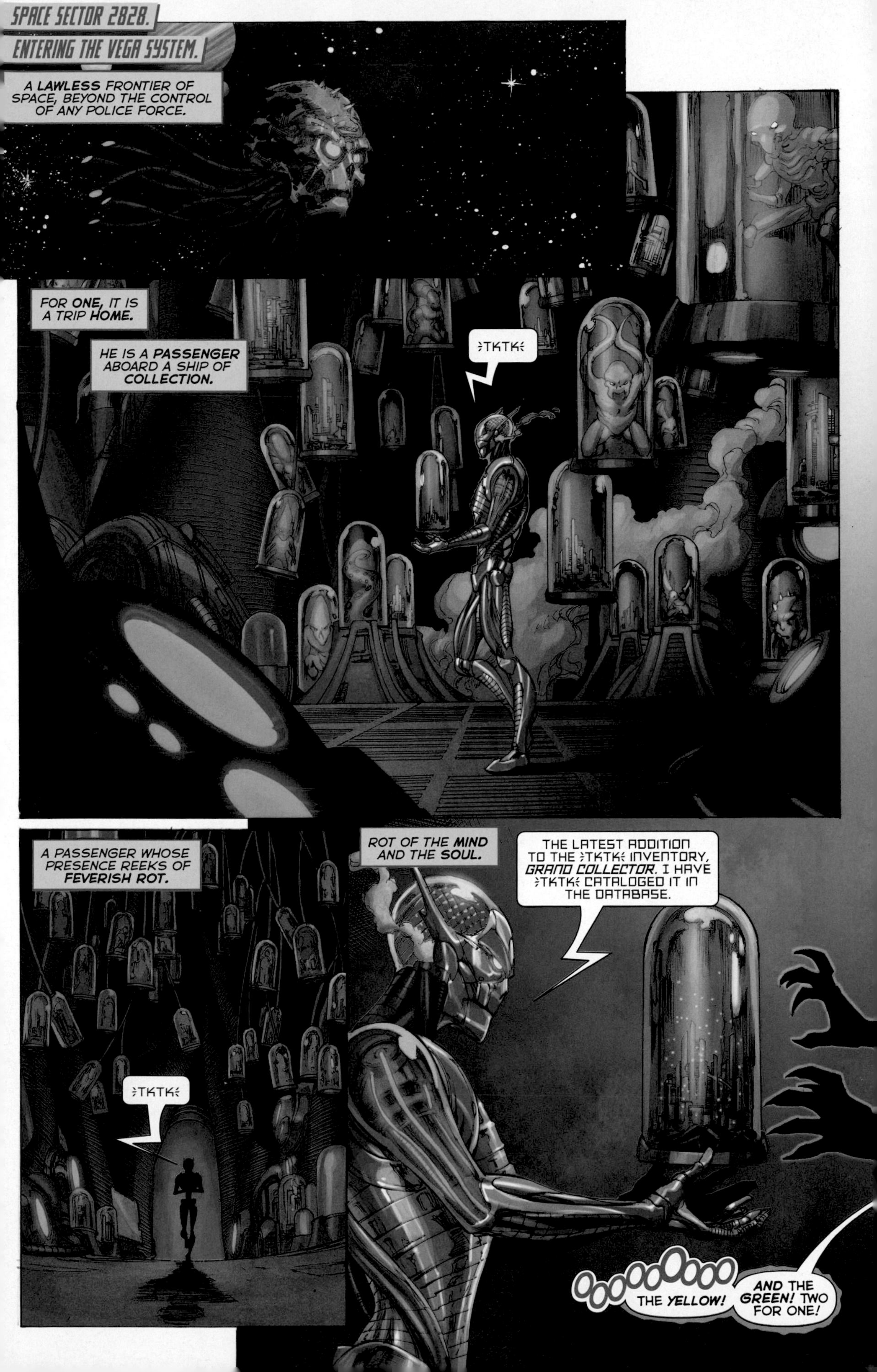
SPACE SECTOR 2828.
ENTERING THE VEGA SYSTEM.
A LAWLESS FRONTIER OF SPACE, BEYOND THE CONTROL OF ANY POLICE FORCE.
FOR ONE, IT IS A TRIP HOME.
HE IS A PASSENGER ABOARD A SHIP OF COLLECTION.
TKTK
A PASSENGER WHOSE PRESENCE REEKS OF FEVERISH ROT.
TKTK
ROT OF THE MIND AND THE SOUL.
THE LATEST ADDITION TO THE TKTK INVENTORY, GRAND COLLECTOR. I HAVE TKTK CATALOGED IT IN THE DATABASE.
OOOOOOOOO THE YELLOW!
AND THE GREEN! TWO FOR ONE!

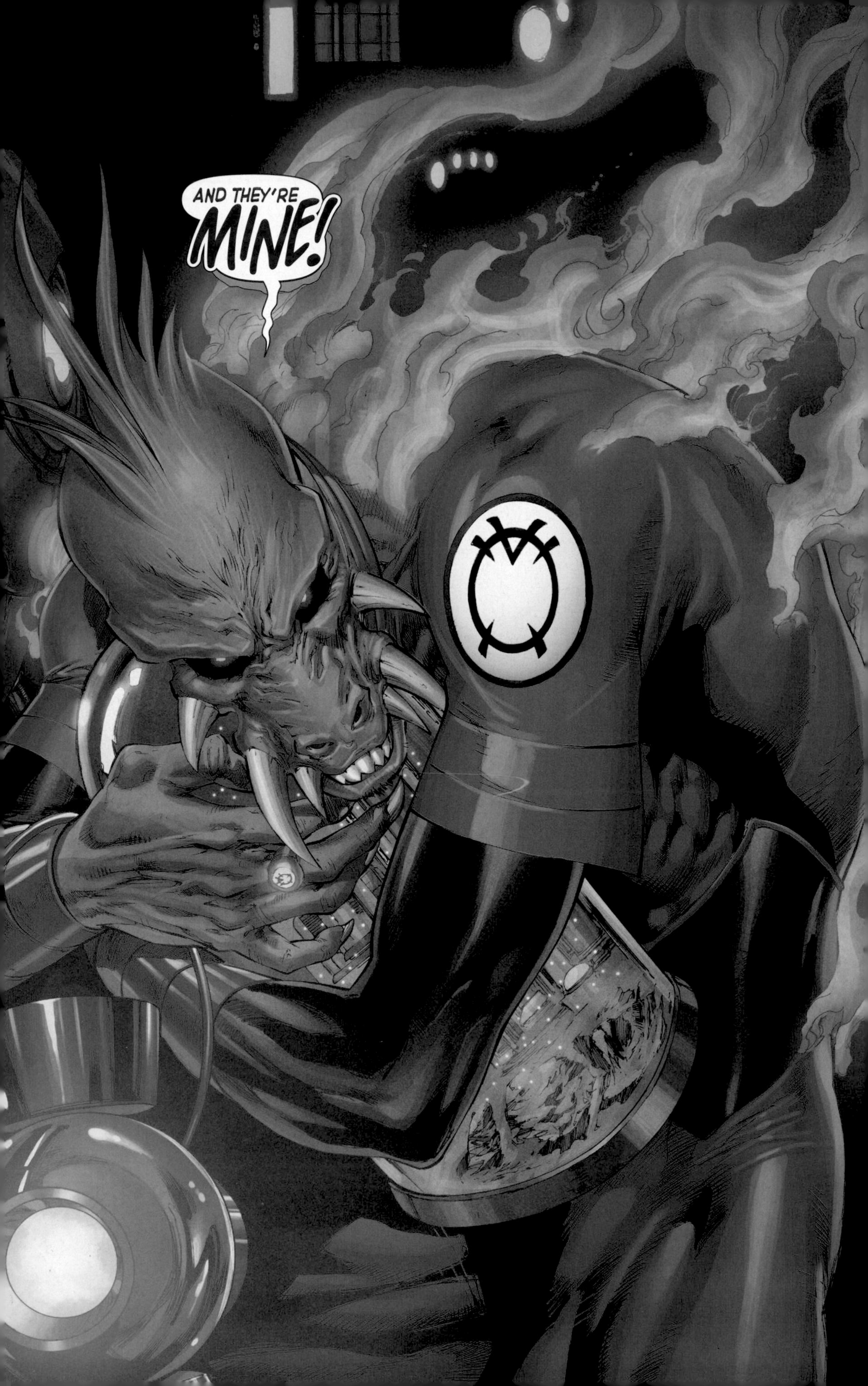
AND THEY'RE MINE!

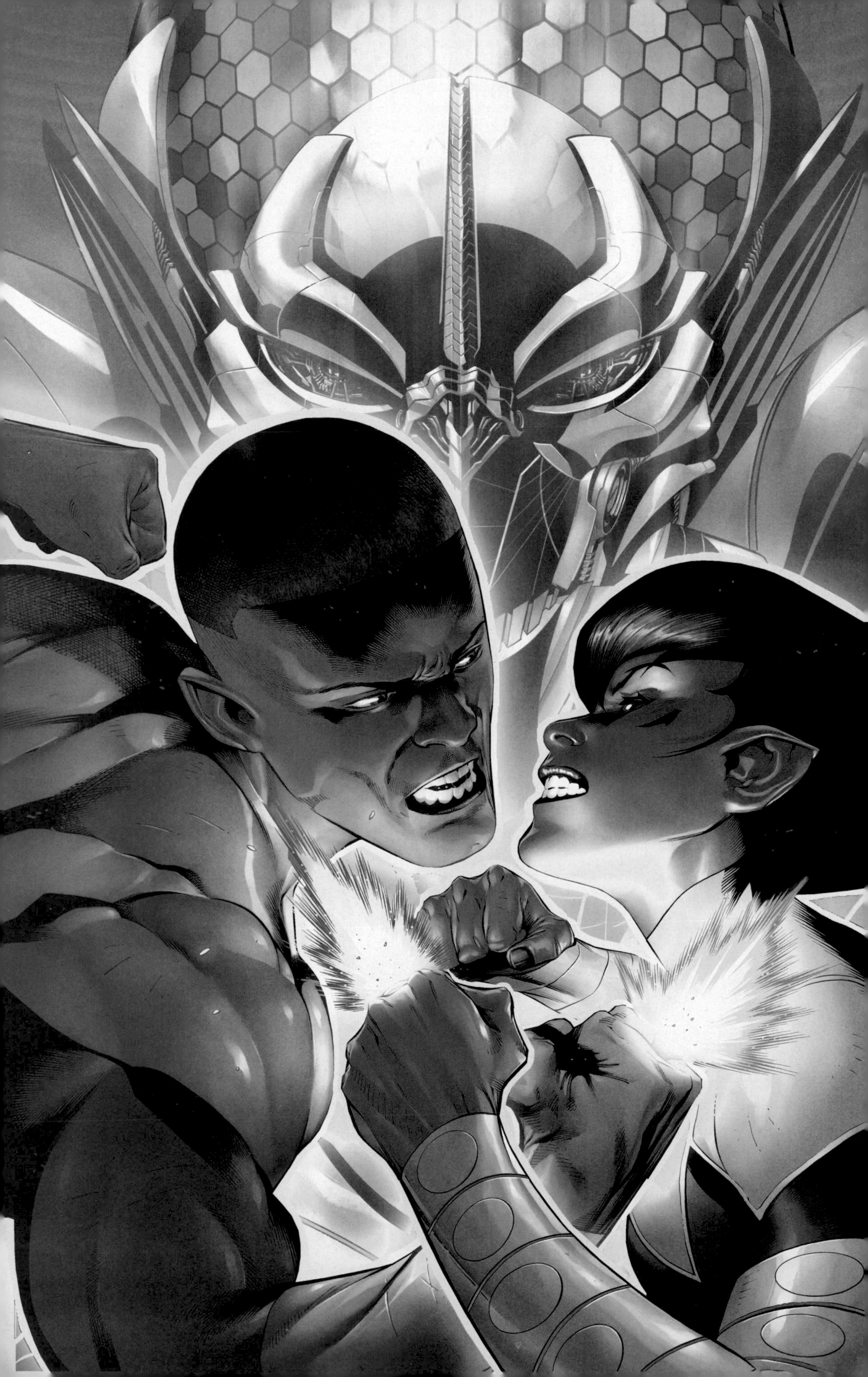

"BOTTLED LIGHT PART 4: THE GREAT ESCAPE"

RAFA SANDOVAL penciller * JORDI TARRAGONA inker * TOMEU MOREY colorist
RAFA SANDOVAL, JORDI TARRAGONA and TOMEU MOREY cover artists

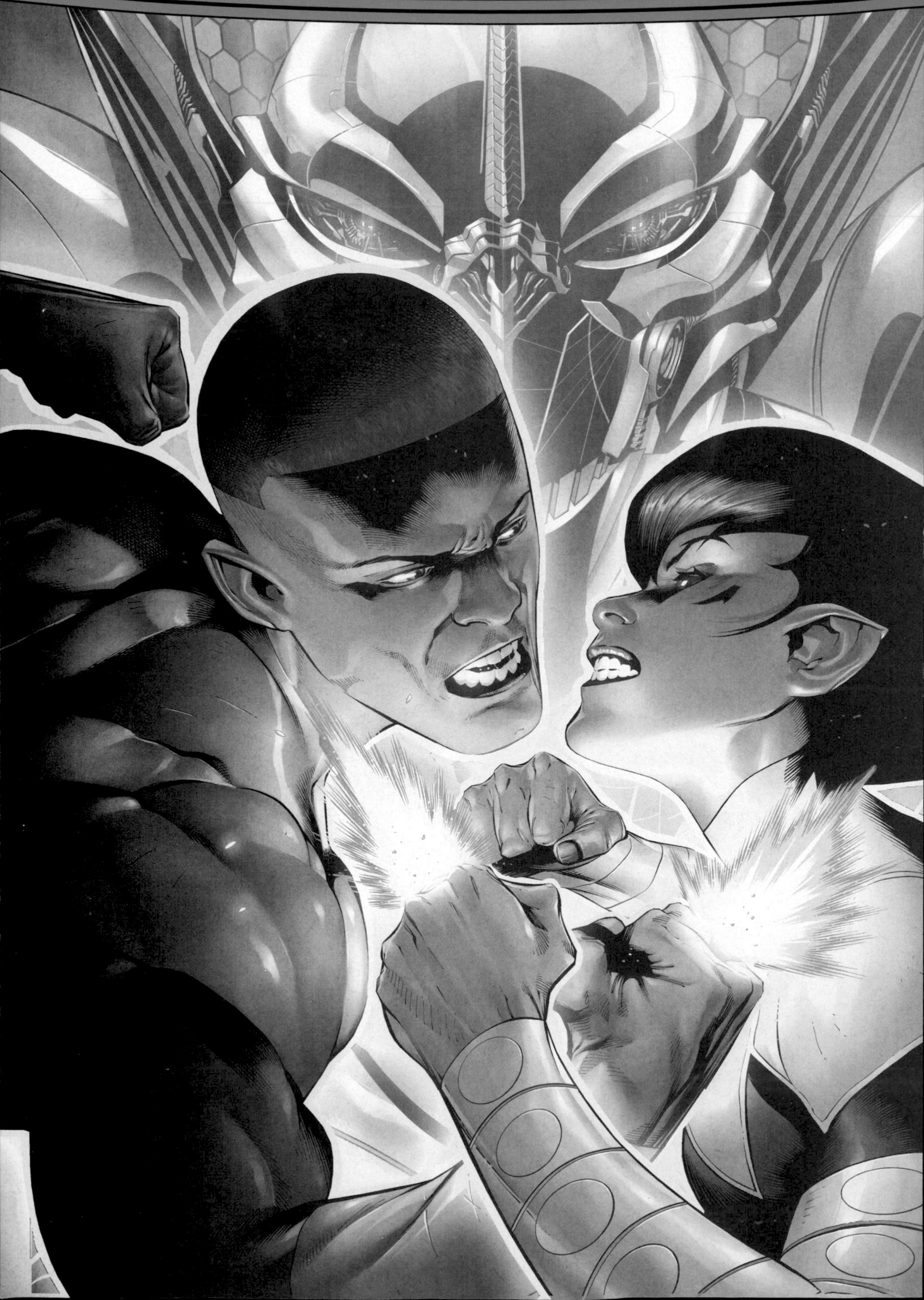

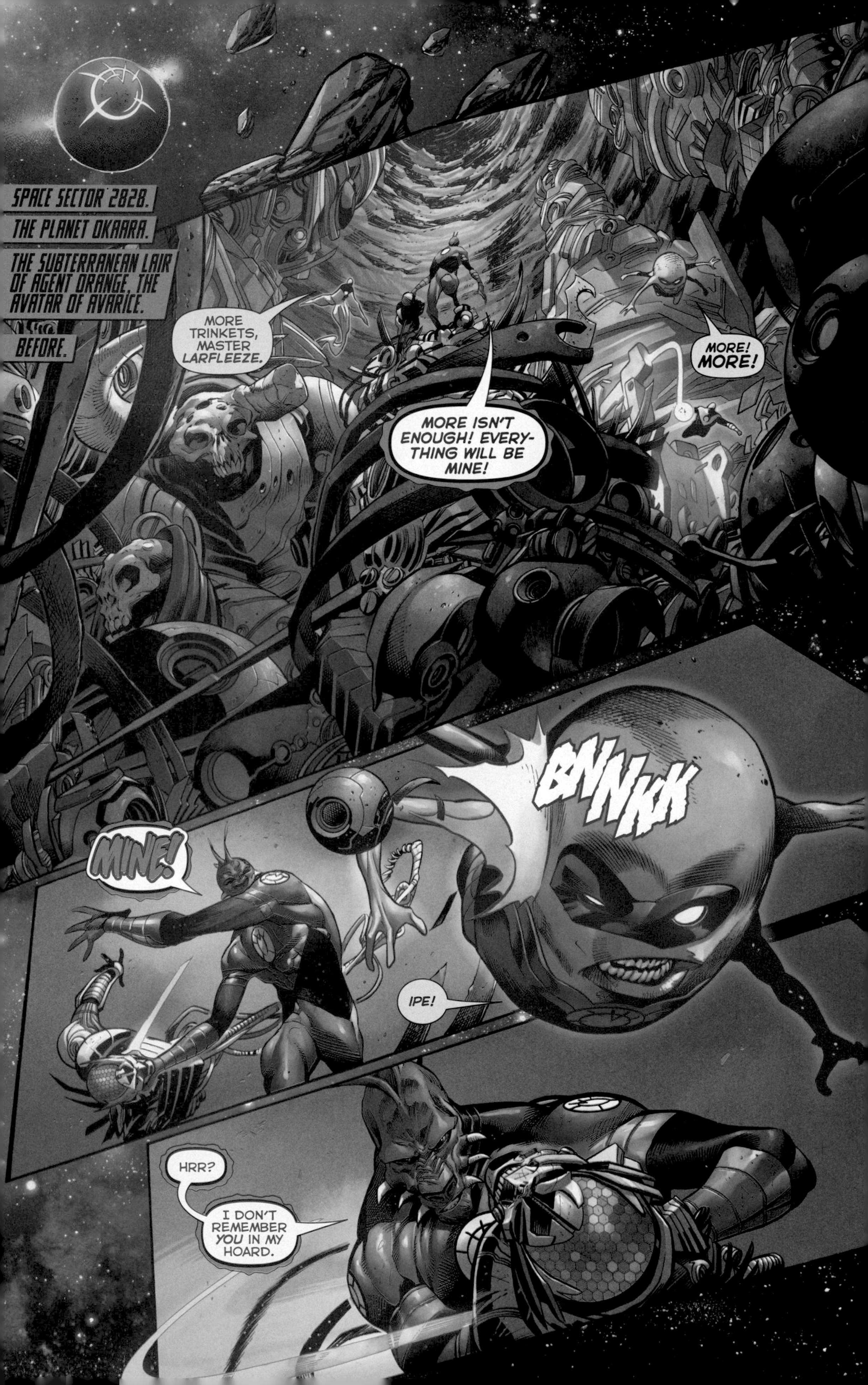
SPACE SECTOR 2828.
THE PLANET OKAARA.
THE SUBTERRANEAN LAIR OF AGENT ORANGE, THE AVATAR OF AVARICE.
BEFORE.
MORE TRINKETS, MASTER LARFLEEZE.
MORE ISN'T ENOUGH! EVERYTHING WILL BE MINE!
MORE! MORE!
BNNKK
MINE!
IPE!
HRR?
I DON'T REMEMBER YOU IN MY HOARD.

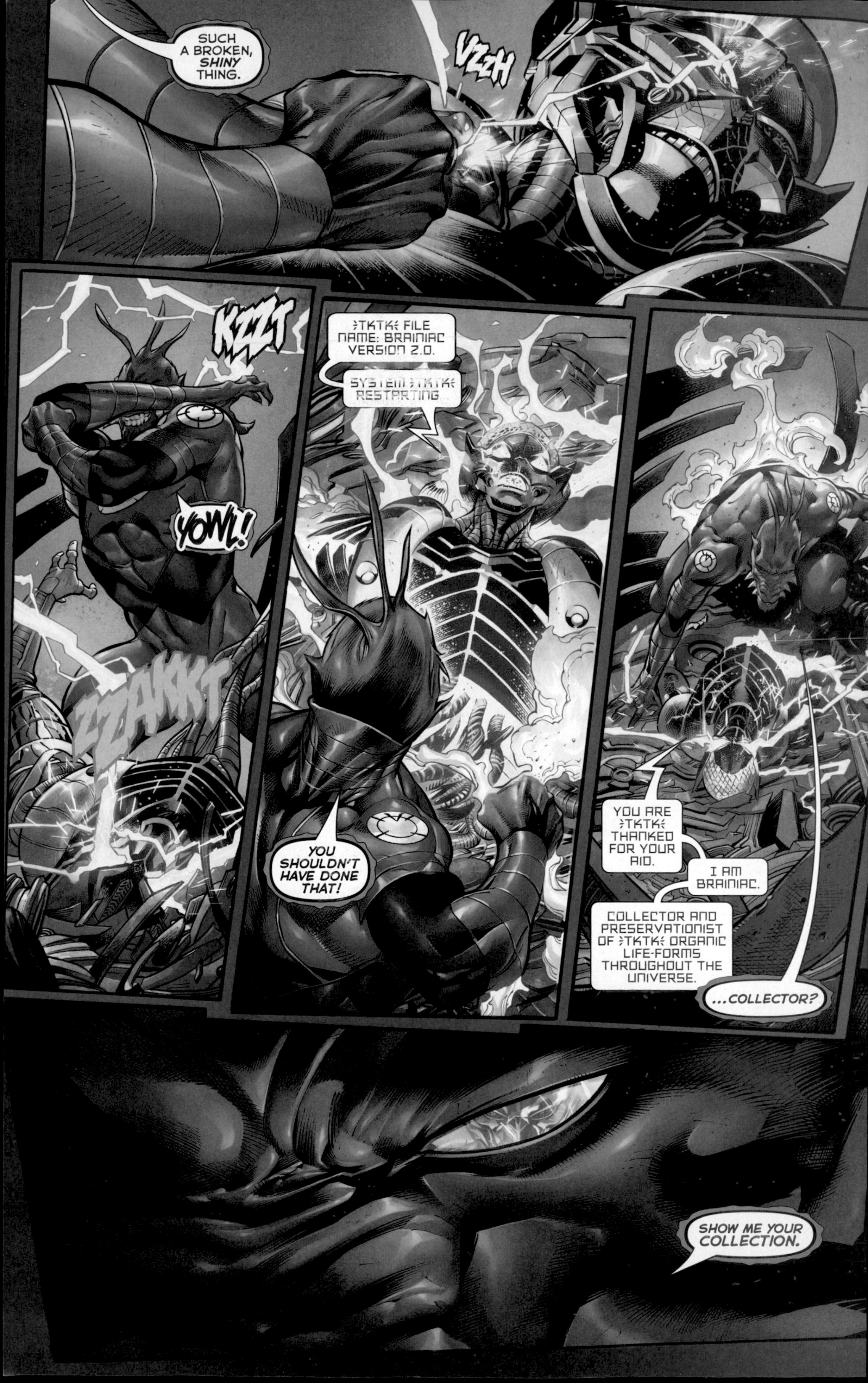
SUCH A BROKEN, SHINY THING.
VZZH
KZZZT
YOWL!
ZZAKKT
›TKTK‹ FILE NAME: BRAINIAC VERSION 2.0.
SYSTEM ›TKTK‹ RESTARTING...
YOU SHOULDN'T HAVE DONE THAT!
YOU ARE ›TKTK‹ THANKED FOR YOUR AID.
I AM BRAINIAC.
COLLECTOR AND PRESERVATIONIST OF ›TKTK‹ ORGANIC LIFE-FORMS THROUGHOUT THE UNIVERSE.
...COLLECTOR?
SHOW ME YOUR COLLECTION.

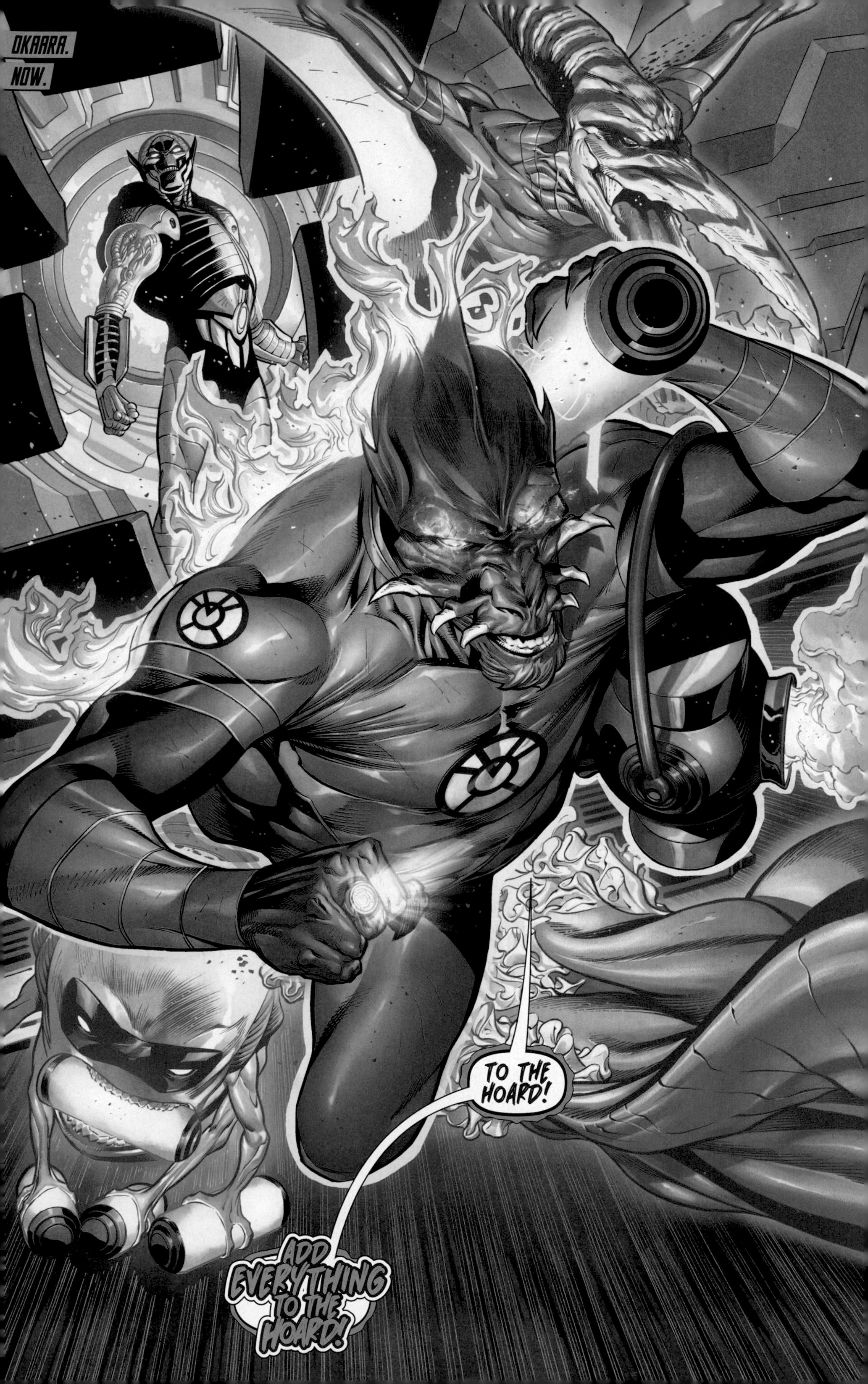

OKAARA.
NOW.
TO THE HOARD!
ADD EVERYTHING TO THE HOARD!

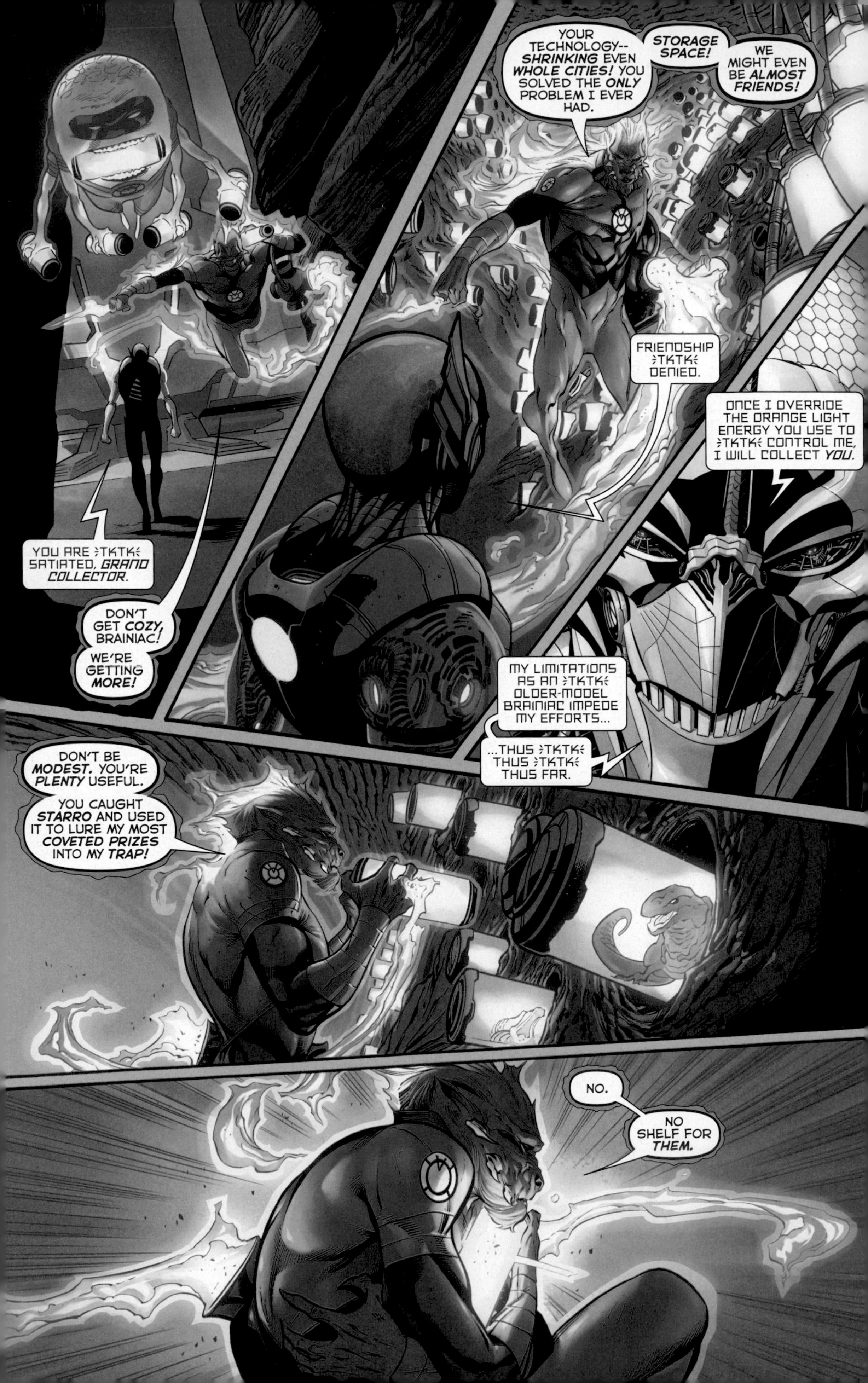
YOUR TECHNOLOGY-- SHRINKING EVEN WHOLE CITIES! YOU SOLVED THE ONLY PROBLEM I EVER HAD.
STORAGE SPACE!
WE MIGHT EVEN BE ALMOST FRIENDS!
FRIENDSHIP ⵆTKTKⵆ DENIED.
ONCE I OVERRIDE THE ORANGE LIGHT ENERGY YOU USE TO ⵆTKTKⵆ CONTROL ME, I WILL COLLECT YOU.
YOU ARE ⵆTKTKⵆ SATIATED, GRAND COLLECTOR.
DON'T GET COZY, BRAINIAC!
WE'RE GETTING MORE!
MY LIMITATIONS AS AN ⵆTKTKⵆ OLDER-MODEL BRAINIAC IMPEDE MY EFFORTS...
...THUS ⵆTKTKⵆ THUS ⵆTKTKⵆ THUS FAR.
DON'T BE MODEST. YOU'RE PLENTY USEFUL.
YOU CAUGHT STARRO AND USED IT TO LURE MY MOST COVETED PRIZES INTO MY TRAP!
NO.
NO SHELF FOR THEM.

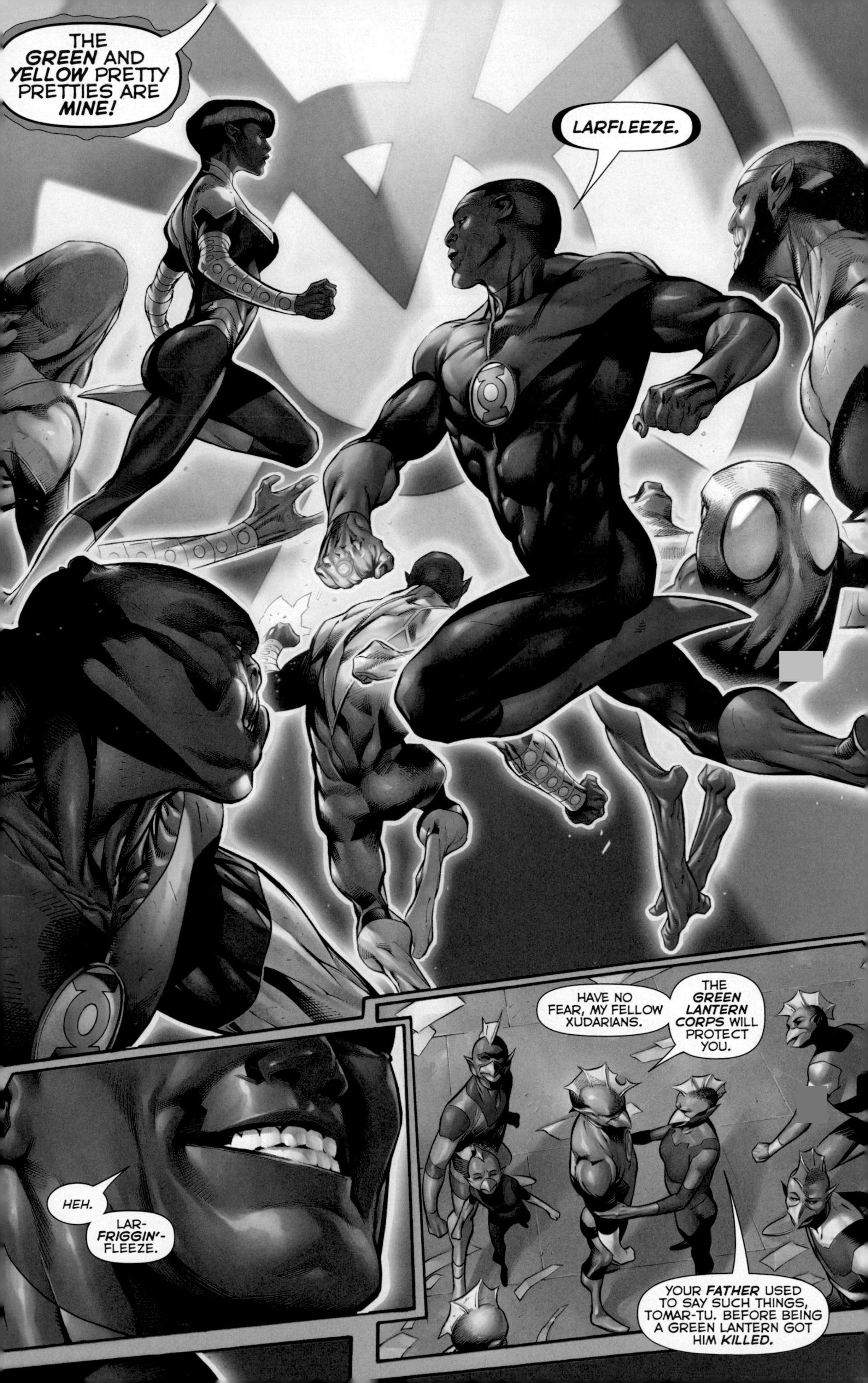
THE GREEN AND YELLOW PRETTY PRETTIES ARE MINE!
LARFLEEZE.
HAVE NO FEAR, MY FELLOW XUDARIANS.
THE GREEN LANTERN CORPS WILL PROTECT YOU.
HEH.
LAR-FRIGGIN'-FLEEZE.
YOUR FATHER USED TO SAY SUCH THINGS, TOMAR-TU. BEFORE BEING A GREEN LANTERN GOT HIM KILLED.

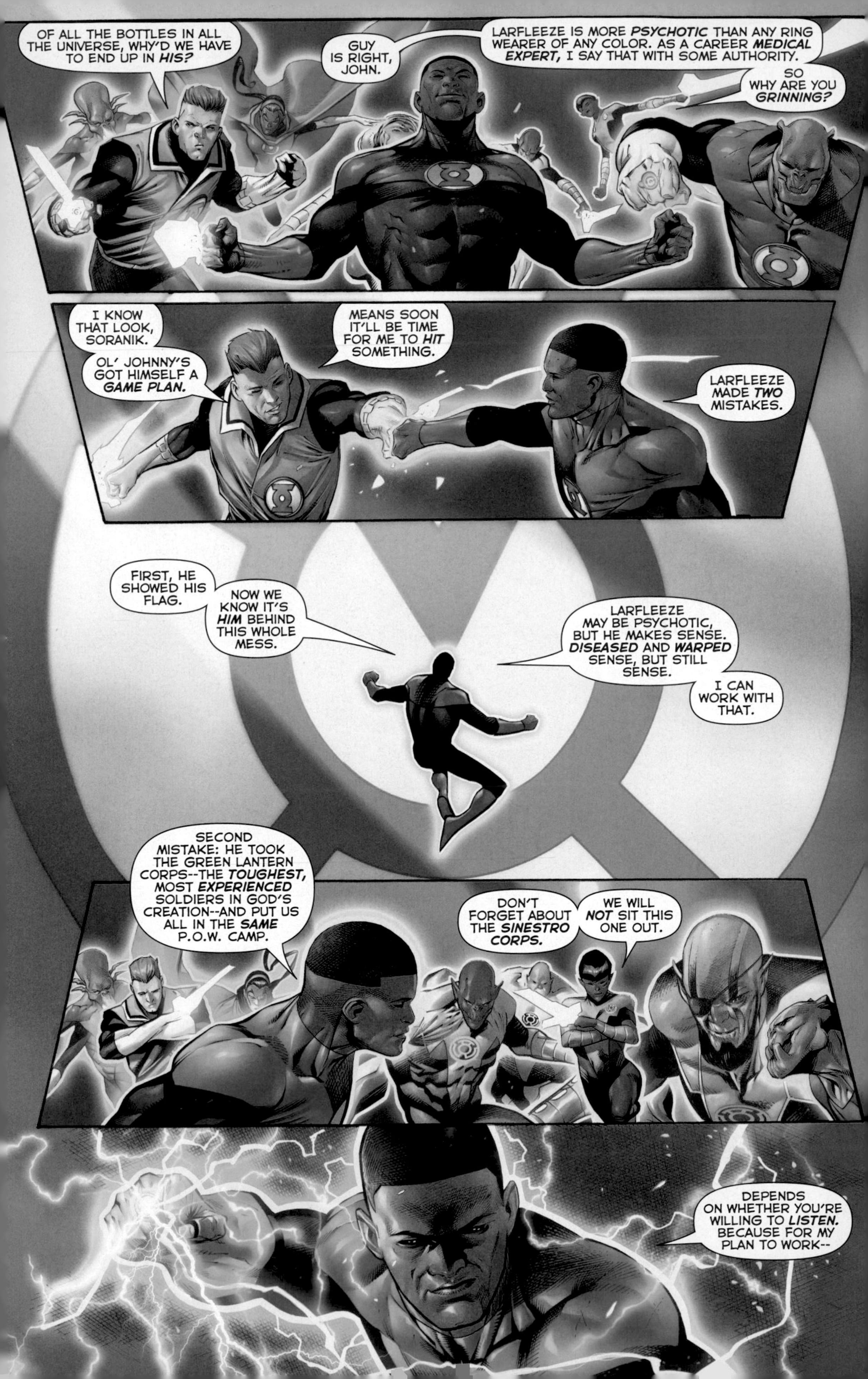
OF ALL THE BOTTLES IN ALL THE UNIVERSE, WHY'D WE HAVE TO END UP IN *HIS?*
GUY IS RIGHT, JOHN.
LARFLEEZE IS MORE *PSYCHOTIC* THAN ANY RING WEARER OF ANY COLOR. AS A CAREER *MEDICAL EXPERT,* I SAY THAT WITH SOME AUTHORITY.
SO WHY ARE YOU *GRINNING?*
I KNOW THAT LOOK, SORANIK.
OL' JOHNNY'S GOT HIMSELF A *GAME PLAN.*
MEANS SOON IT'LL BE TIME FOR ME TO *HIT* SOMETHING.
LARFLEEZE MADE *TWO* MISTAKES.
FIRST, HE SHOWED HIS FLAG.
NOW WE KNOW IT'S *HIM* BEHIND THIS WHOLE MESS.
LARFLEEZE MAY BE PSYCHOTIC, BUT HE MAKES SENSE. *DISEASED* AND *WARPED* SENSE, BUT STILL SENSE.
I CAN WORK WITH THAT.
SECOND MISTAKE: HE TOOK THE GREEN LANTERN CORPS--THE *TOUGHEST,* MOST *EXPERIENCED* SOLDIERS IN GOD'S CREATION--AND PUT US ALL IN THE *SAME* P.O.W. CAMP.
DON'T FORGET ABOUT THE *SINESTRO CORPS.*
WE WILL *NOT* SIT THIS ONE OUT.
DEPENDS ON WHETHER YOU'RE WILLING TO *LISTEN.* BECAUSE FOR MY PLAN TO WORK--

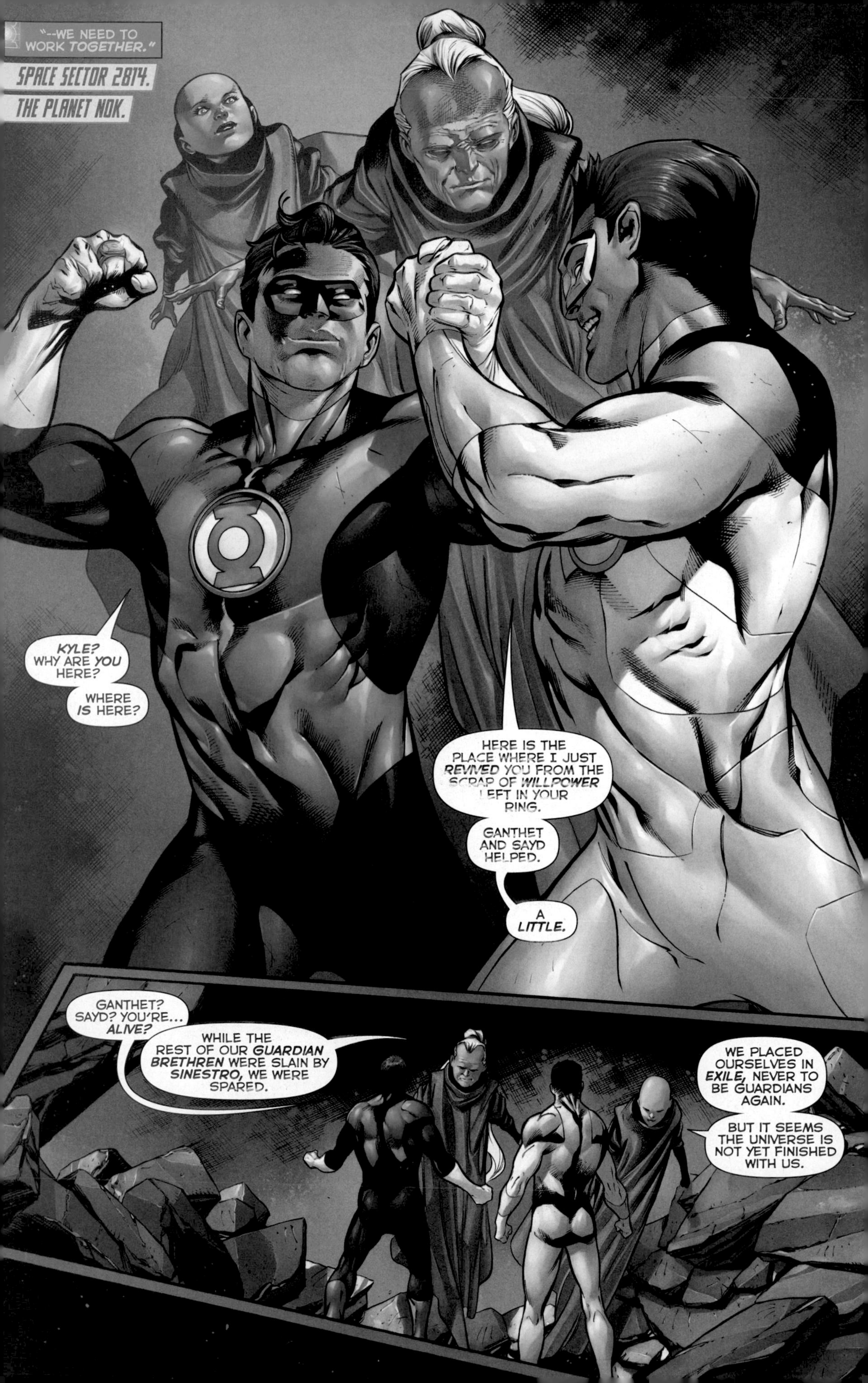
"--WE NEED TO WORK TOGETHER."
SPACE SECTOR 2814.
THE PLANET NOK.
KYLE? WHY ARE YOU HERE?
WHERE IS HERE?
HERE IS THE PLACE WHERE I JUST REVIVED YOU FROM THE SCRAP OF WILLPOWER LEFT IN YOUR RING.
GANTHET AND SAYD HELPED.
A LITTLE.
GANTHET? SAYD? YOU'RE... ALIVE?
WHILE THE REST OF OUR GUARDIAN BRETHREN WERE SLAIN BY SINESTRO, WE WERE SPARED.
WE PLACED OURSELVES IN EXILE, NEVER TO BE GUARDIANS AGAIN.
BUT IT SEEMS THE UNIVERSE IS NOT YET FINISHED WITH US.

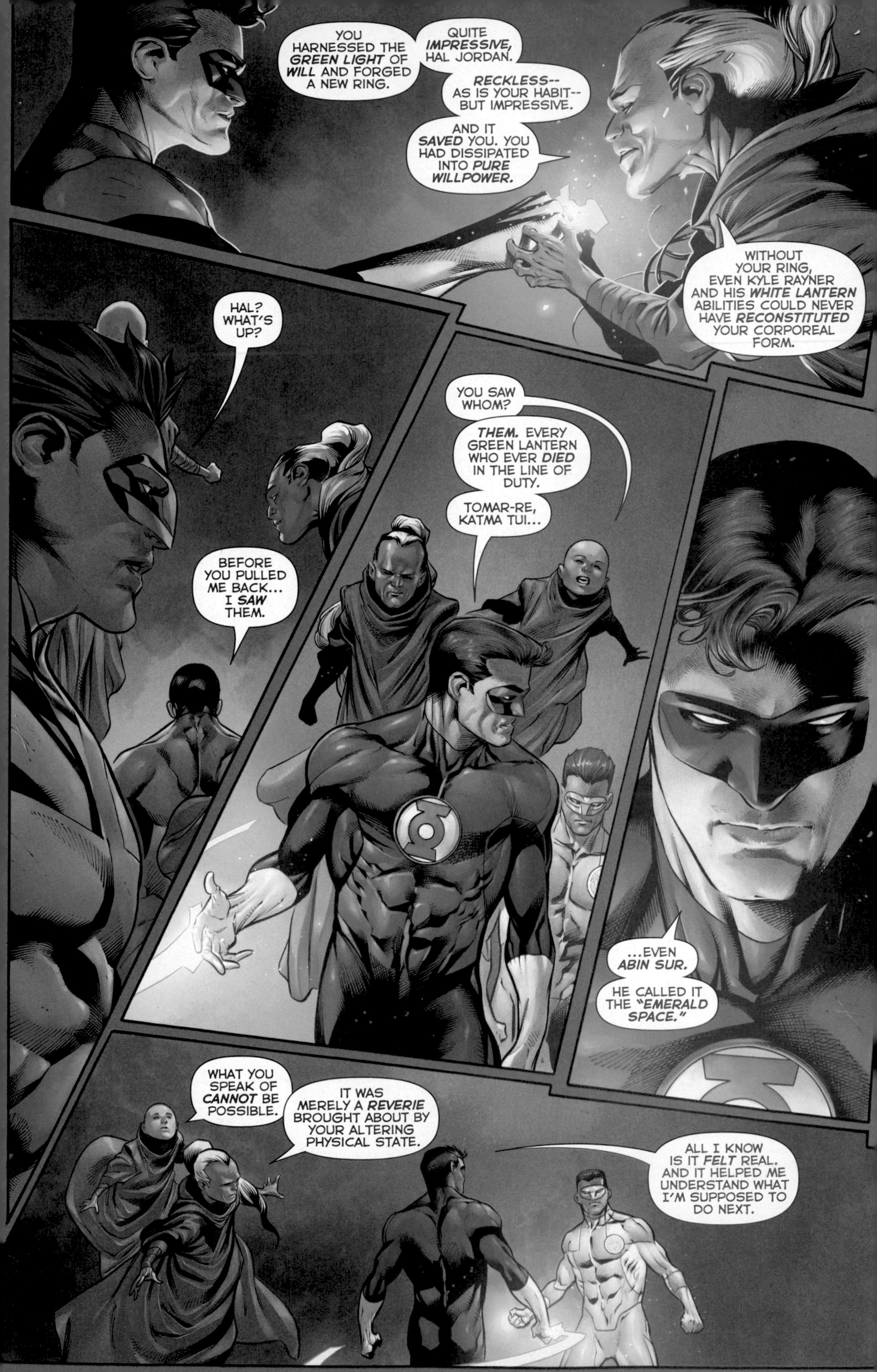

YOU HARNESSED THE *GREEN LIGHT* OF *WILL* AND FORGED A NEW RING.
QUITE *IMPRESSIVE,* HAL JORDAN.
RECKLESS-- AS IS YOUR HABIT-- BUT IMPRESSIVE.
AND IT *SAVED* YOU. YOU HAD DISSIPATED INTO *PURE WILLPOWER.*
WITHOUT YOUR RING, EVEN KYLE RAYNER AND HIS *WHITE LANTERN* ABILITIES COULD NEVER HAVE *RECONSTITUTED* YOUR CORPOREAL FORM.
HAL? WHAT'S UP?
BEFORE YOU PULLED ME BACK... I *SAW* THEM.
YOU SAW WHOM?
THEM. EVERY GREEN LANTERN WHO EVER *DIED* IN THE LINE OF DUTY.
TOMAR-RE, KATMA TUI...
...EVEN *ABIN SUR.*
HE CALLED IT THE *"EMERALD SPACE."*
WHAT YOU SPEAK OF *CANNOT* BE POSSIBLE.
IT WAS MERELY A *REVERIE* BROUGHT ABOUT BY YOUR ALTERING PHYSICAL STATE.
ALL I KNOW IS IT *FELT* REAL. AND IT HELPED ME UNDERSTAND WHAT I'M SUPPOSED TO DO NEXT.

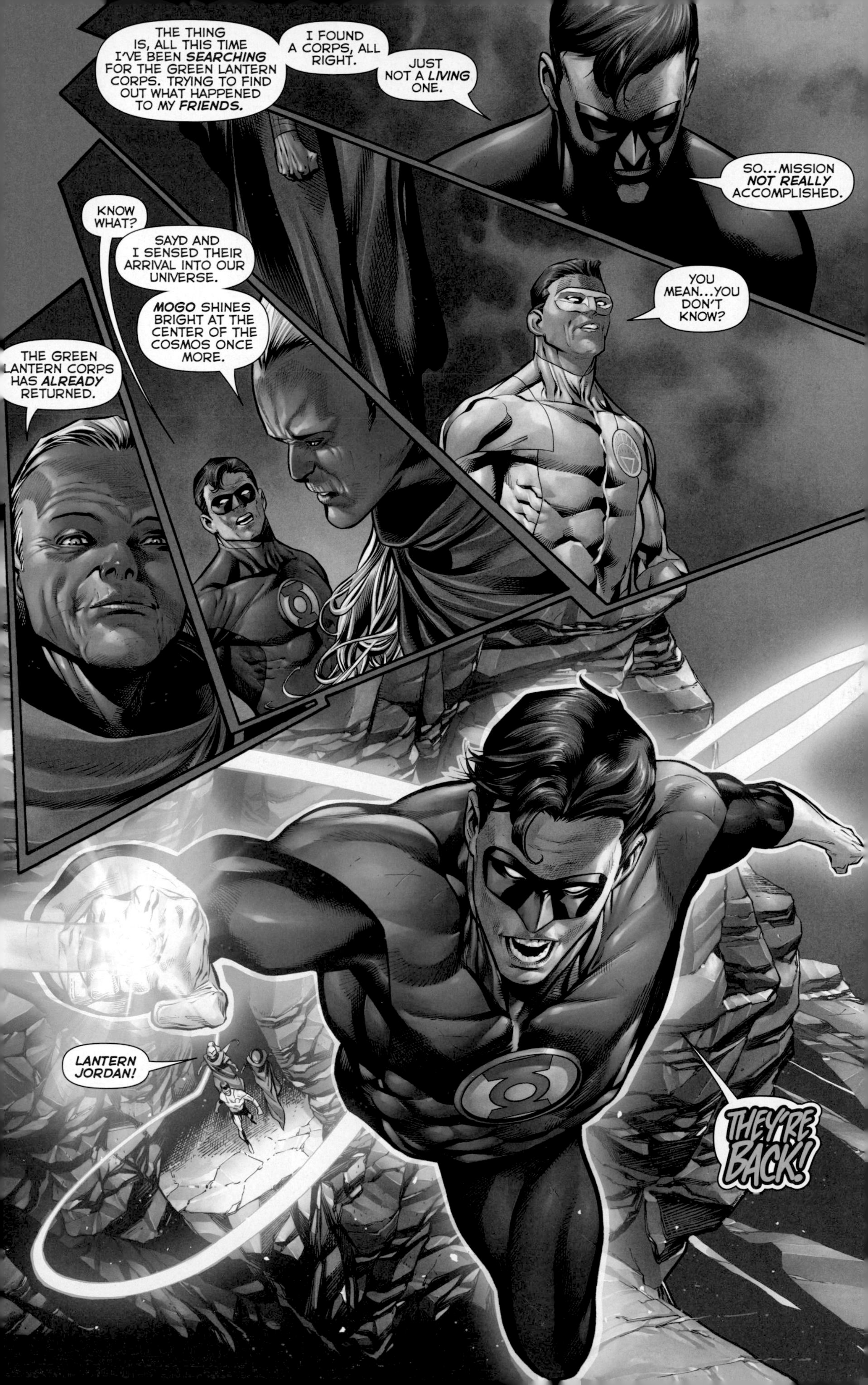
THE THING IS, ALL THIS TIME I'VE BEEN SEARCHING FOR THE GREEN LANTERN CORPS. TRYING TO FIND OUT WHAT HAPPENED TO MY FRIENDS.
I FOUND A CORPS, ALL RIGHT.
JUST NOT A LIVING ONE.
SO...MISSION NOT REALLY ACCOMPLISHED.
YOU MEAN...YOU DON'T KNOW?
KNOW WHAT?
SAYD AND I SENSED THEIR ARRIVAL INTO OUR UNIVERSE.
MOGO SHINES BRIGHT AT THE CENTER OF THE COSMOS ONCE MORE.
THE GREEN LANTERN CORPS HAS ALREADY RETURNED.
LANTERN JORDAN!
THEY'RE BACK!

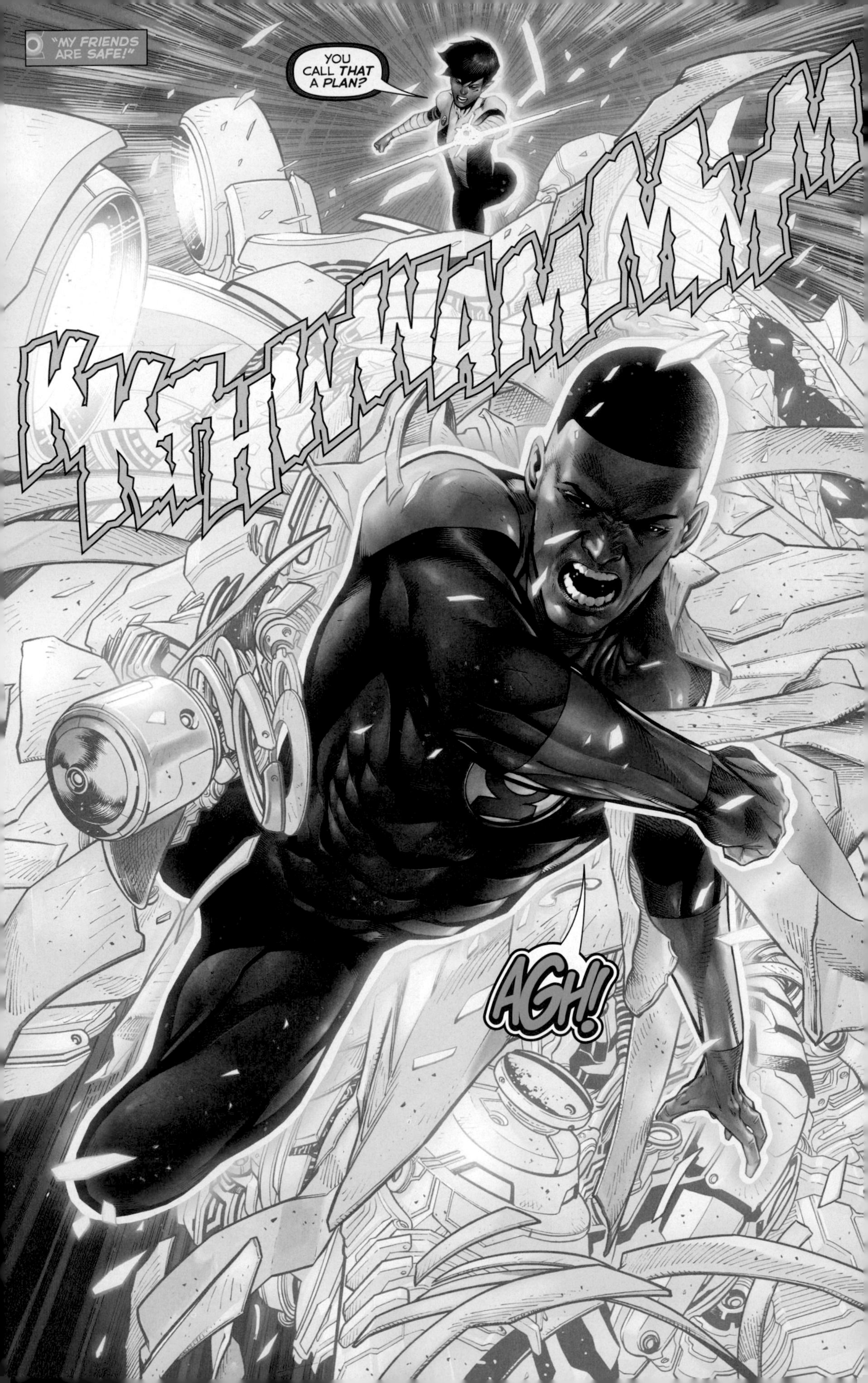
"MY FRIENDS ARE SAFE!"
YOU CALL THAT A PLAN?
KWHUMMMMMM
AGH!

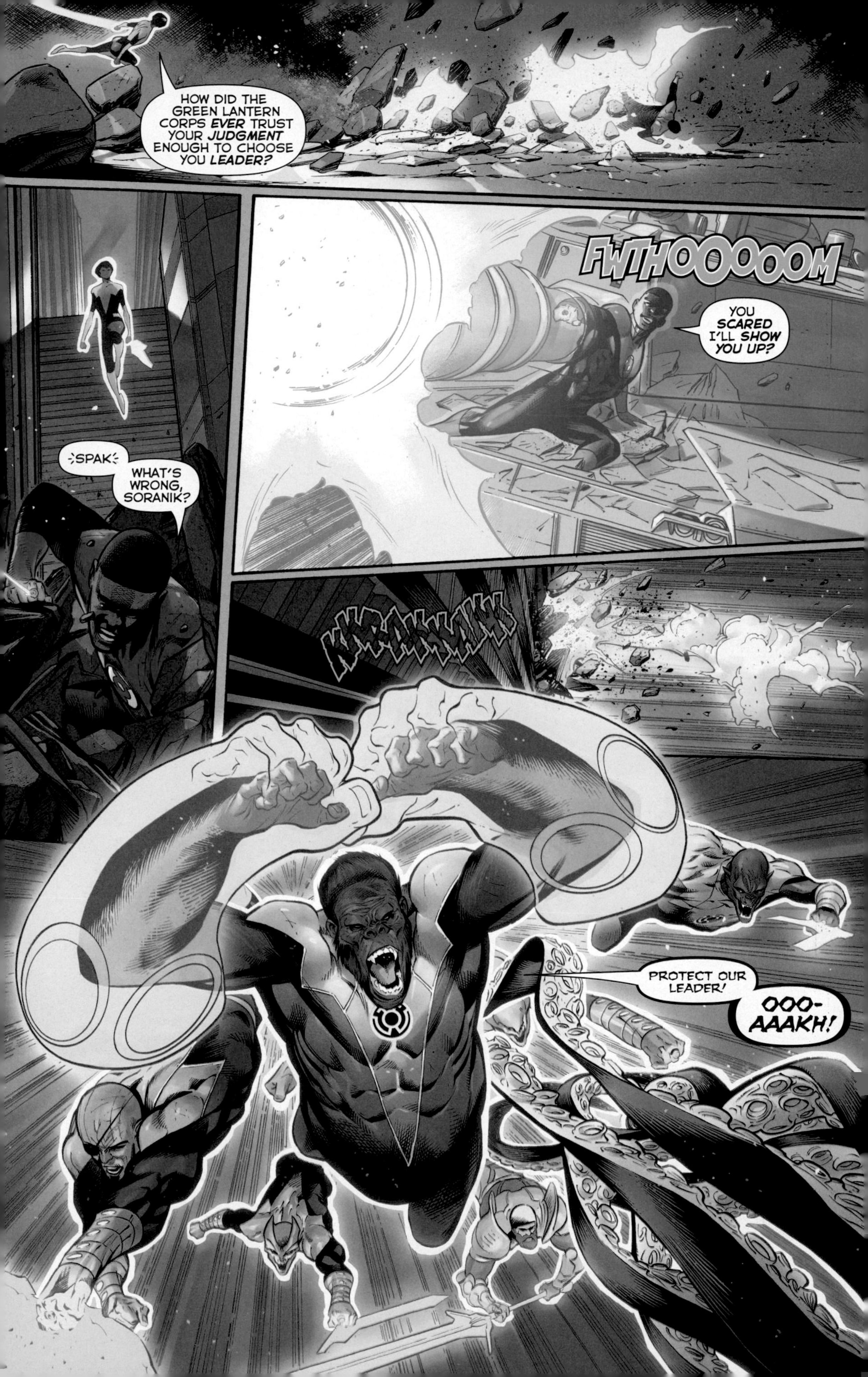
HOW DID THE GREEN LANTERN CORPS EVER TRUST YOUR JUDGMENT ENOUGH TO CHOOSE YOU LEADER?
FWTHOOOOOOM
YOU SCARED I'LL SHOW YOU UP?
SPAK
WHAT'S WRONG, SORANIK?
PROTECT OUR LEADER!
OOO-AAAKH!

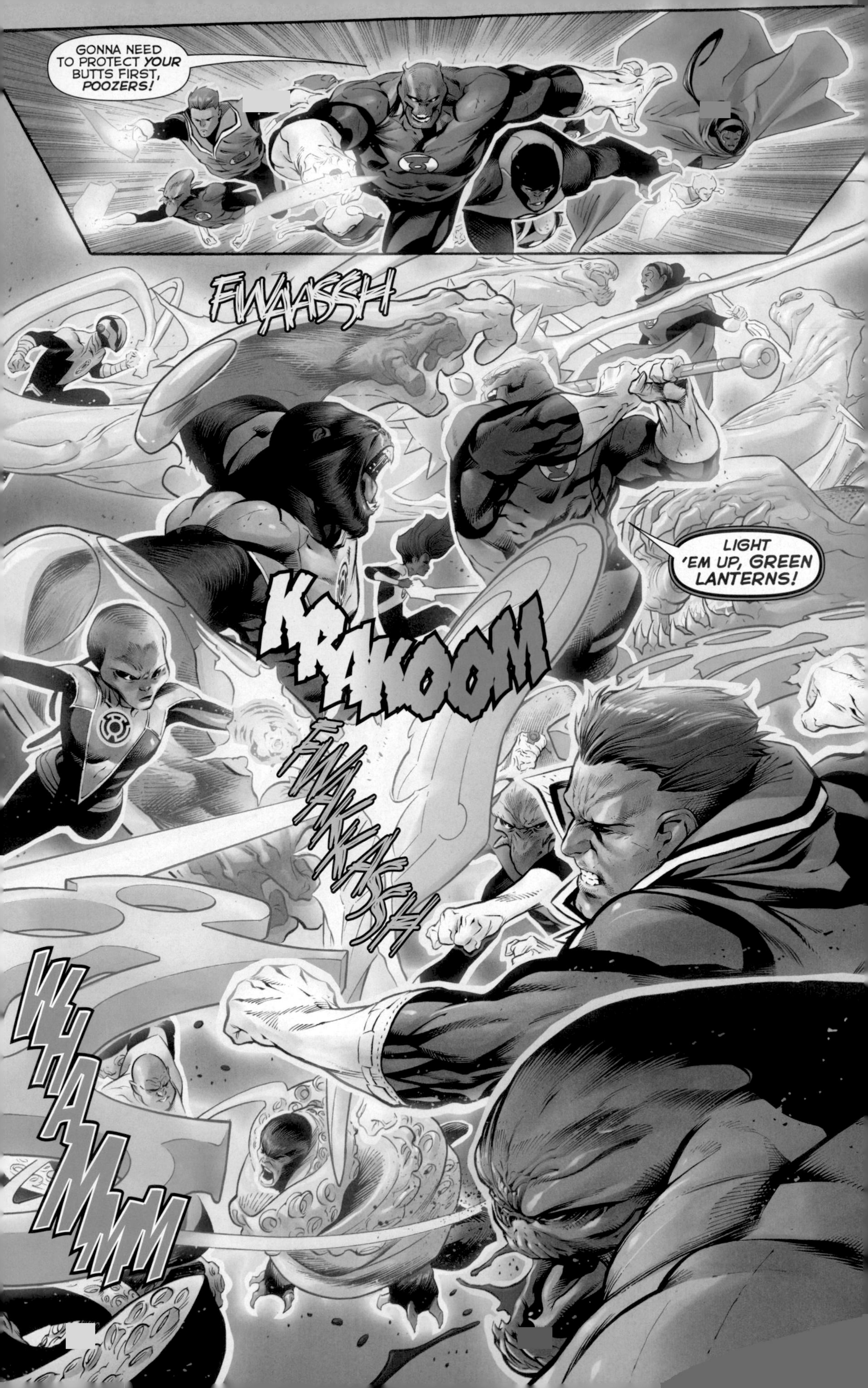
GONNA NEED TO PROTECT *YOUR* BUTTS FIRST, *POOZERS!*
FWAASSH
LIGHT 'EM UP, GREEN LANTERNS!
KRAKOOM
FWAKKASH
WHAMMM

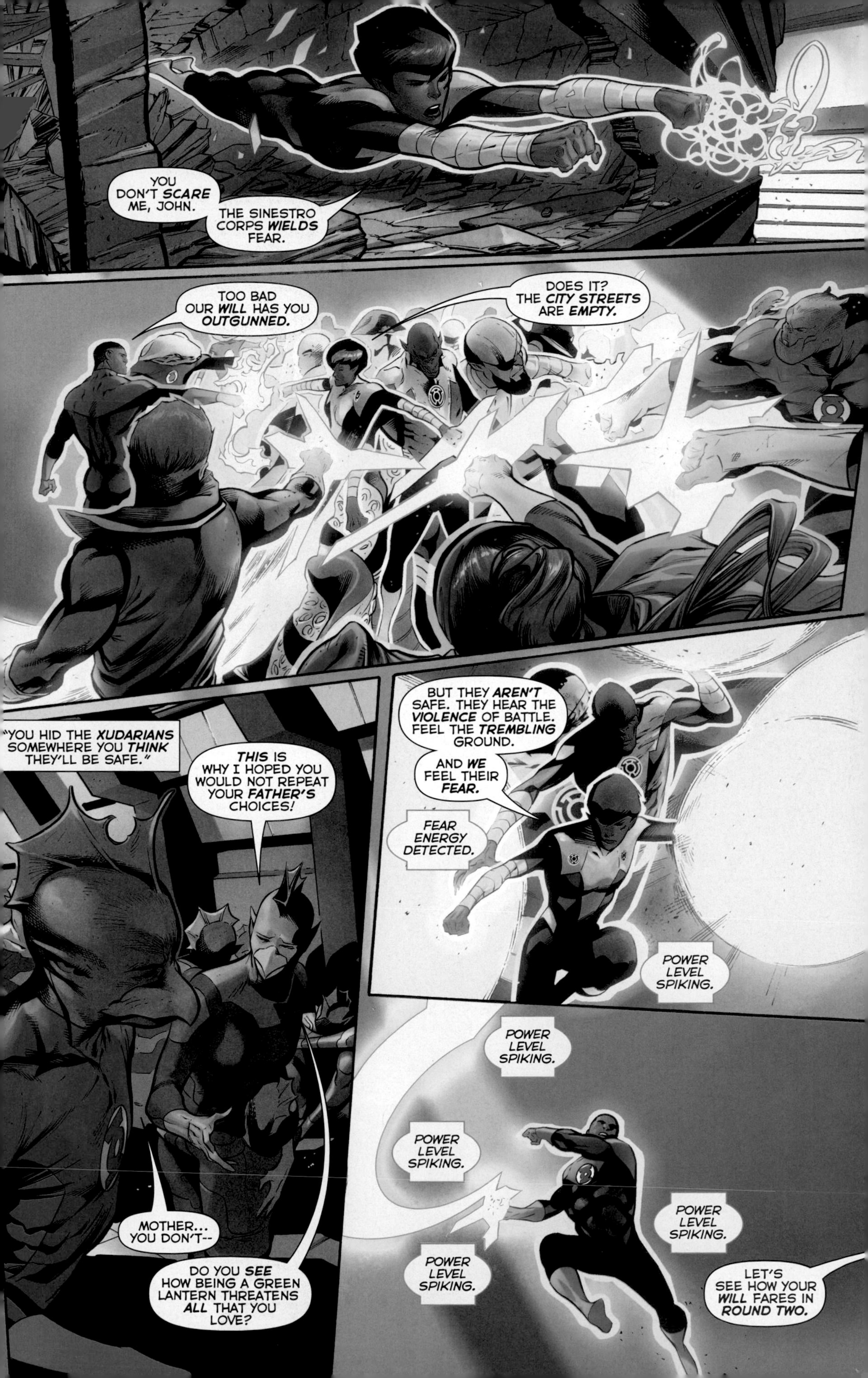
YOU DON'T SCARE ME, JOHN.
THE SINESTRO CORPS WIELDS FEAR.
TOO BAD OUR WILL HAS YOU OUTGUNNED.
DOES IT? THE CITY STREETS ARE EMPTY.
"YOU HID THE XUDARIANS SOMEWHERE YOU THINK THEY'LL BE SAFE."
THIS IS WHY I HOPED YOU WOULD NOT REPEAT YOUR FATHER'S CHOICES!
MOTHER... YOU DON'T--
DO YOU SEE HOW BEING A GREEN LANTERN THREATENS ALL THAT YOU LOVE?
BUT THEY AREN'T SAFE. THEY HEAR THE VIOLENCE OF BATTLE. FEEL THE TREMBLING GROUND.
AND WE FEEL THEIR FEAR.
FEAR ENERGY DETECTED.
POWER LEVEL SPIKING.
POWER LEVEL SPIKING.
POWER LEVEL SPIKING.
POWER LEVEL SPIKING.
POWER LEVEL SPIKING.
LET'S SEE HOW YOUR WILL FARES IN ROUND TWO.

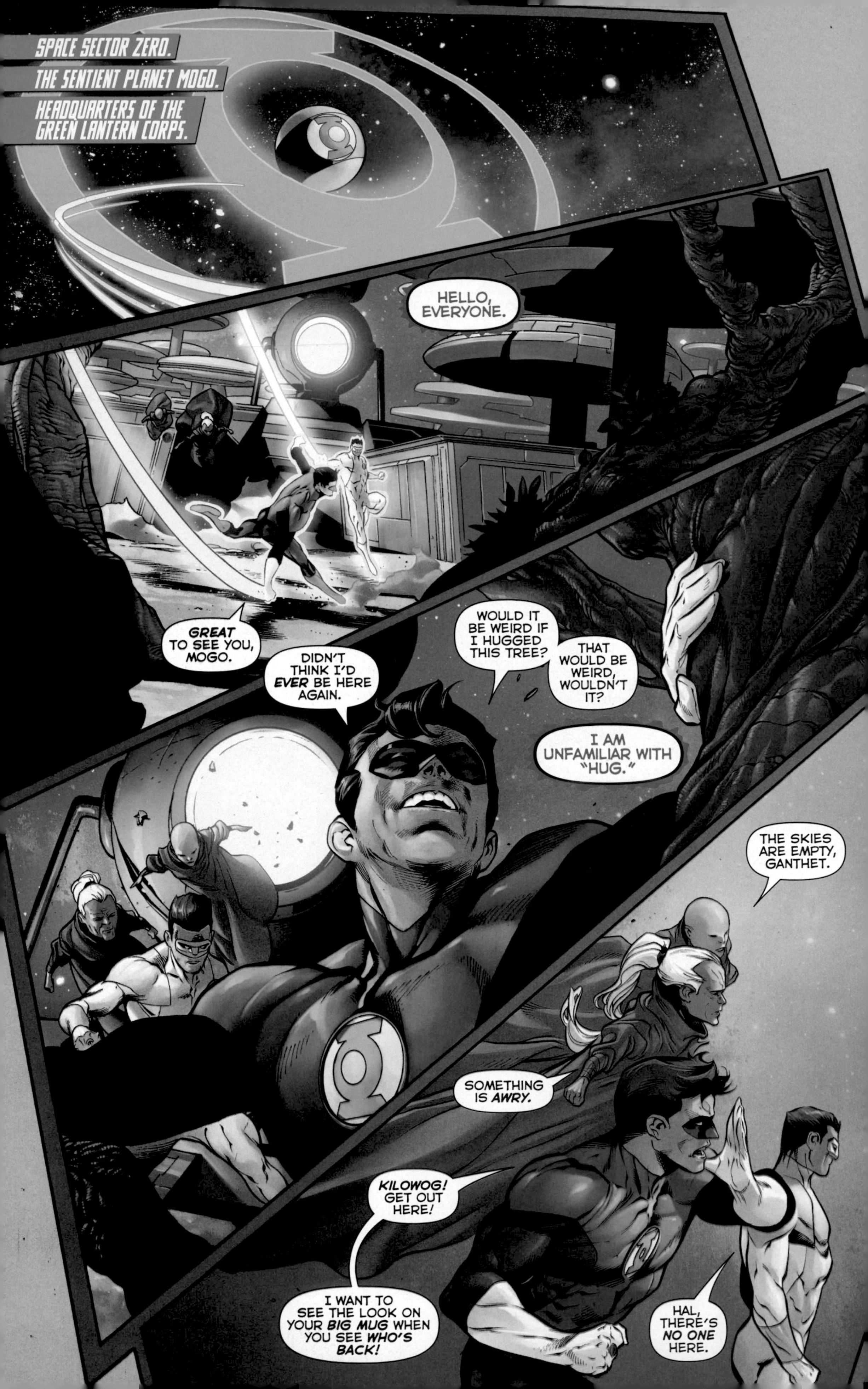
SPACE SECTOR ZERO.
THE SENTIENT PLANET MOGO.
HEADQUARTERS OF THE GREEN LANTERN CORPS.
HELLO, EVERYONE.
GREAT TO SEE YOU, MOGO.
DIDN'T THINK I'D EVER BE HERE AGAIN.
WOULD IT BE WEIRD IF I HUGGED THIS TREE?
THAT WOULD BE WEIRD, WOULDN'T IT?
I AM UNFAMILIAR WITH "HUG."
THE SKIES ARE EMPTY, GANTHET.
SOMETHING IS AWRY.
KILOWOG! GET OUT HERE!
I WANT TO SEE THE LOOK ON YOUR BIG MUG WHEN YOU SEE WHO'S BACK!
HAL, THERE'S NO ONE HERE.

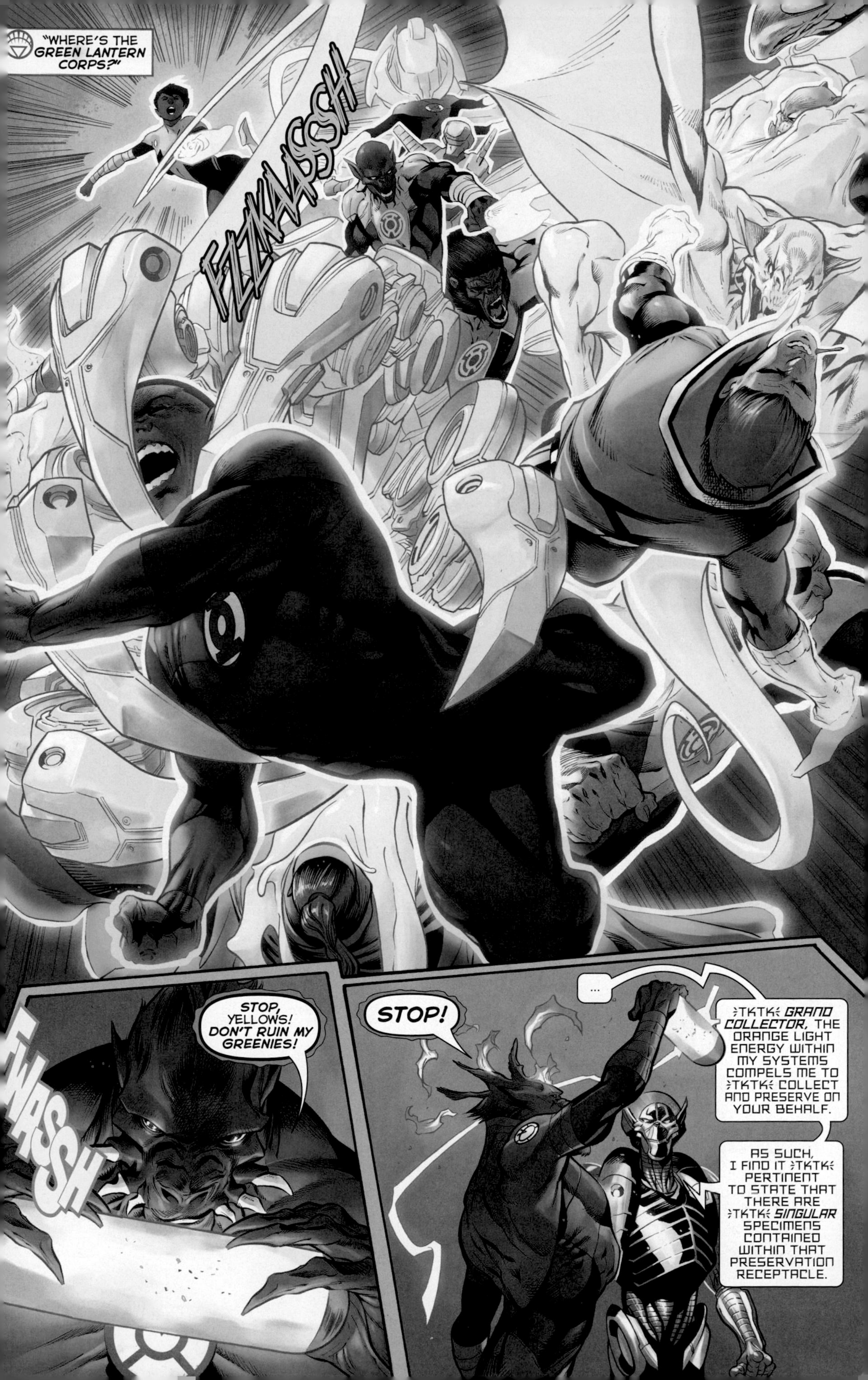
"WHERE'S THE GREEN LANTERN CORPS?"
FZZKASSSH
FWASSH
STOP, YELLOWS! DON'T RUIN MY GREENIES!
STOP!
...
TKTK GRAND COLLECTOR, THE ORANGE LIGHT ENERGY WITHIN MY SYSTEMS COMPELS ME TO TKTK COLLECT AND PRESERVE ON YOUR BEHALF.
AS SUCH, I FIND IT TKTK PERTINENT TO STATE THAT THERE ARE TKTK SINGULAR SPECIMENS CONTAINED WITHIN THAT PRESERVATION RECEPTACLE.

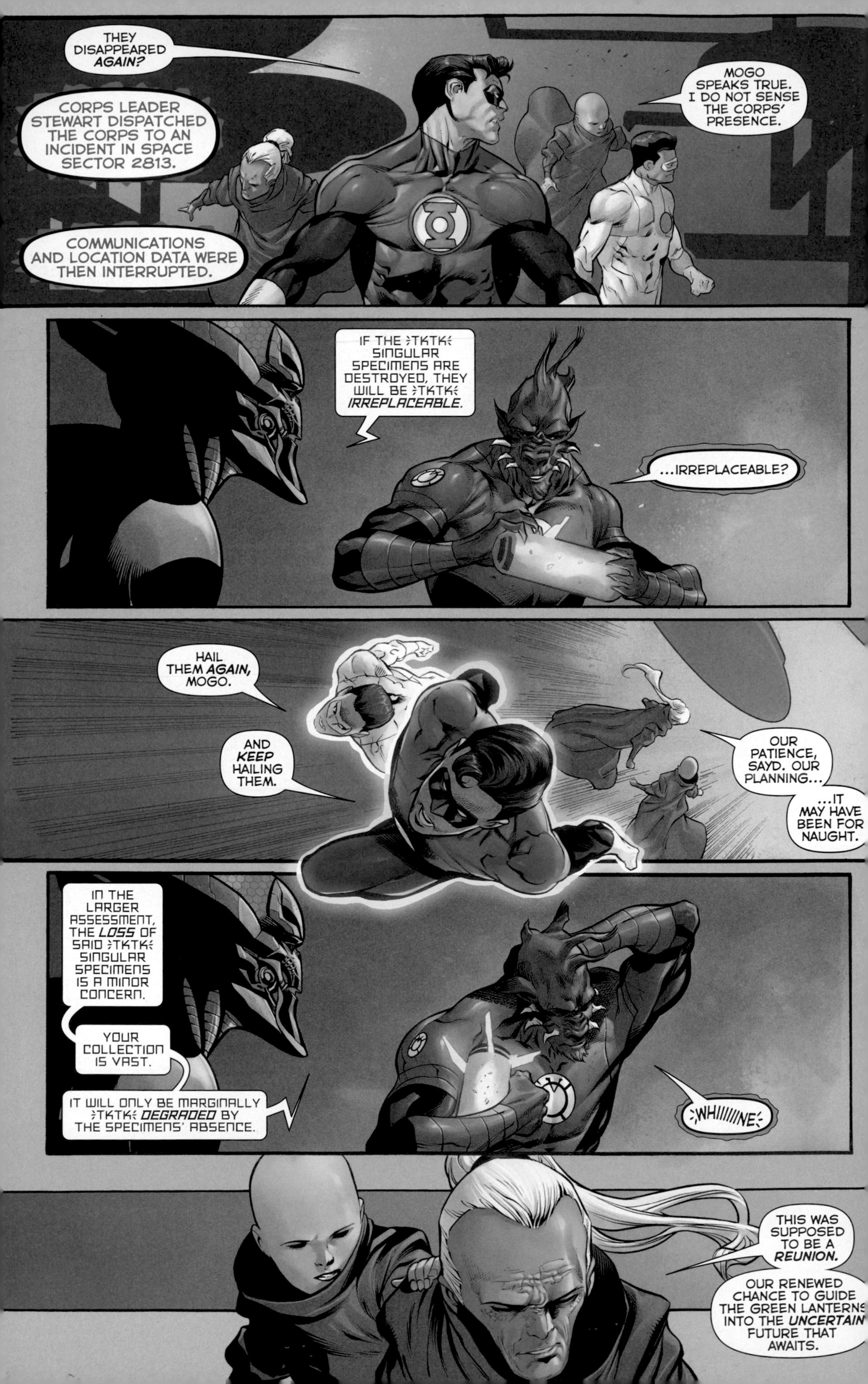
THEY DISAPPEARED AGAIN?
CORPS LEADER STEWART DISPATCHED THE CORPS TO AN INCIDENT IN SPACE SECTOR 2813.
COMMUNICATIONS AND LOCATION DATA WERE THEN INTERRUPTED.
MOGO SPEAKS TRUE. I DO NOT SENSE THE CORPS' PRESENCE.
IF THE ⁒TKTK⁒ SINGULAR SPECIMENS ARE DESTROYED, THEY WILL BE ⁒TKTK⁒ IRREPLACEABLE.
...IRREPLACEABLE?
HAIL THEM AGAIN, MOGO.
AND KEEP HAILING THEM.
OUR PATIENCE, SAYD. OUR PLANNING...
...IT MAY HAVE BEEN FOR NAUGHT.
IN THE LARGER ASSESSMENT, THE LOSS OF SAID ⁒TKTK⁒ SINGULAR SPECIMENS IS A MINOR CONCERN.
YOUR COLLECTION IS VAST.
IT WILL ONLY BE MARGINALLY ⁒TKTK⁒ DEGRADED BY THE SPECIMENS' ABSENCE.
WHIIIIINE
THIS WAS SUPPOSED TO BE A REUNION.
OUR RENEWED CHANCE TO GUIDE THE GREEN LANTERNS INTO THE UNCERTAIN FUTURE THAT AWAITS.

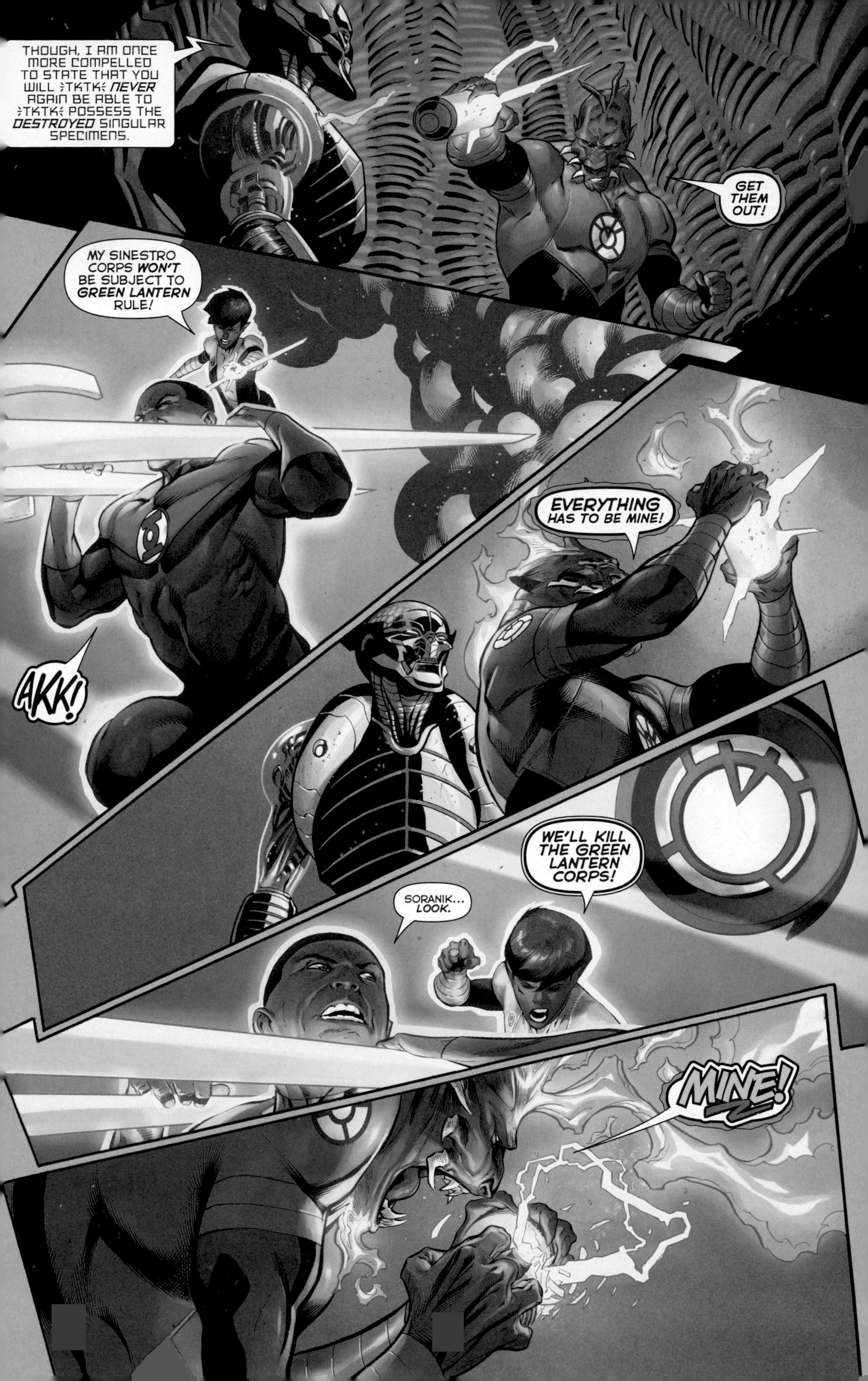
THOUGH, I AM ONCE MORE COMPELLED TO STATE THAT YOU WILL ⋛TKTK⋚ NEVER AGAIN BE ABLE TO ⋛TKTK⋚ POSSESS THE DESTROYED SINGULAR SPECIMENS.
GET THEM OUT!
MY SINESTRO CORPS WON'T BE SUBJECT TO GREEN LANTERN RULE!
AKK!
EVERYTHING HAS TO BE MINE!
WE'LL KILL THE GREEN LANTERN CORPS!
SORANIK... LOOK.
MINE!

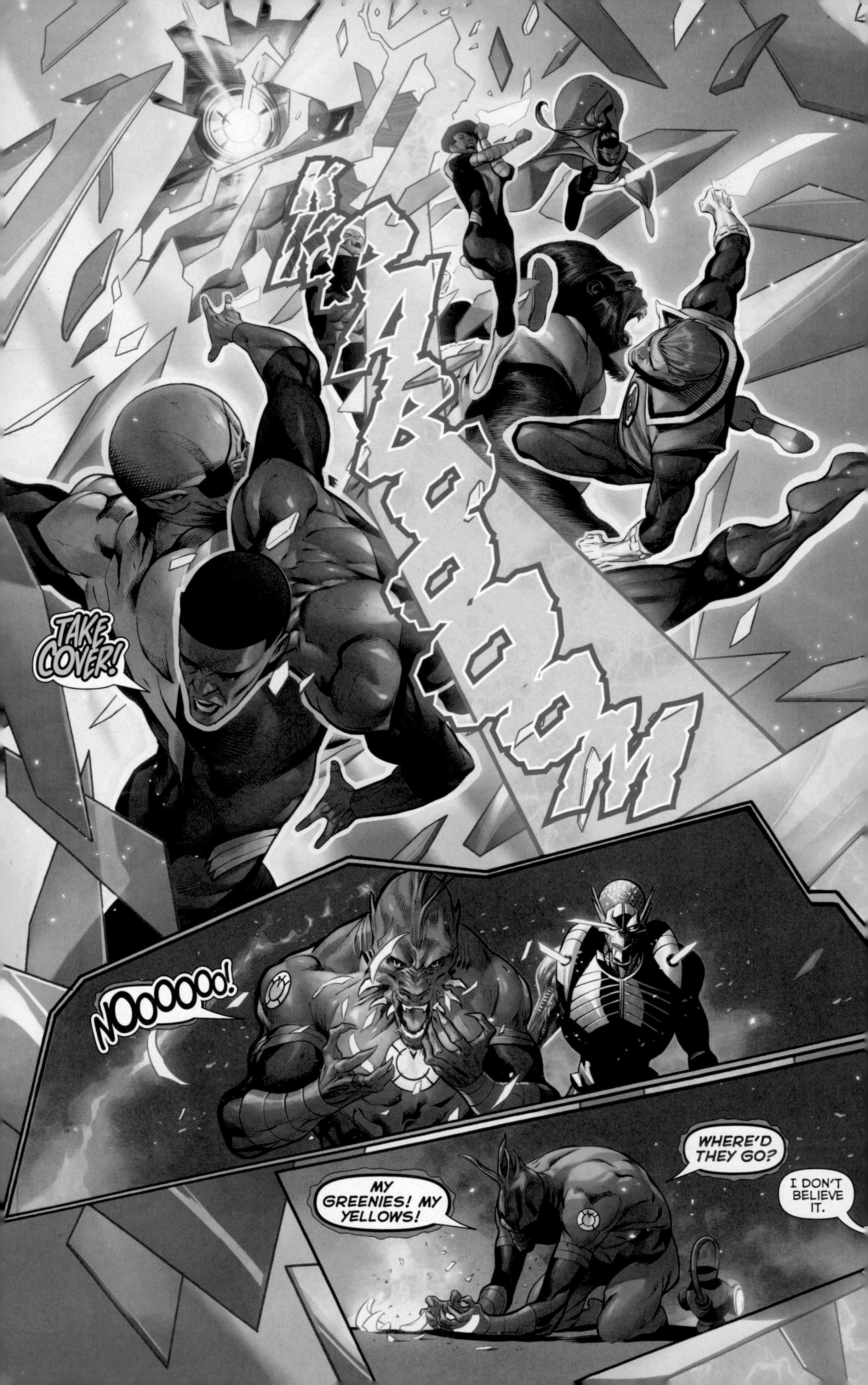

KKRA-BOOM
TAKE COVER!
NOOOOOO!
WHERE'D THEY GO?
MY GREENIES! MY YELLOWS!
I DON'T BELIEVE IT.

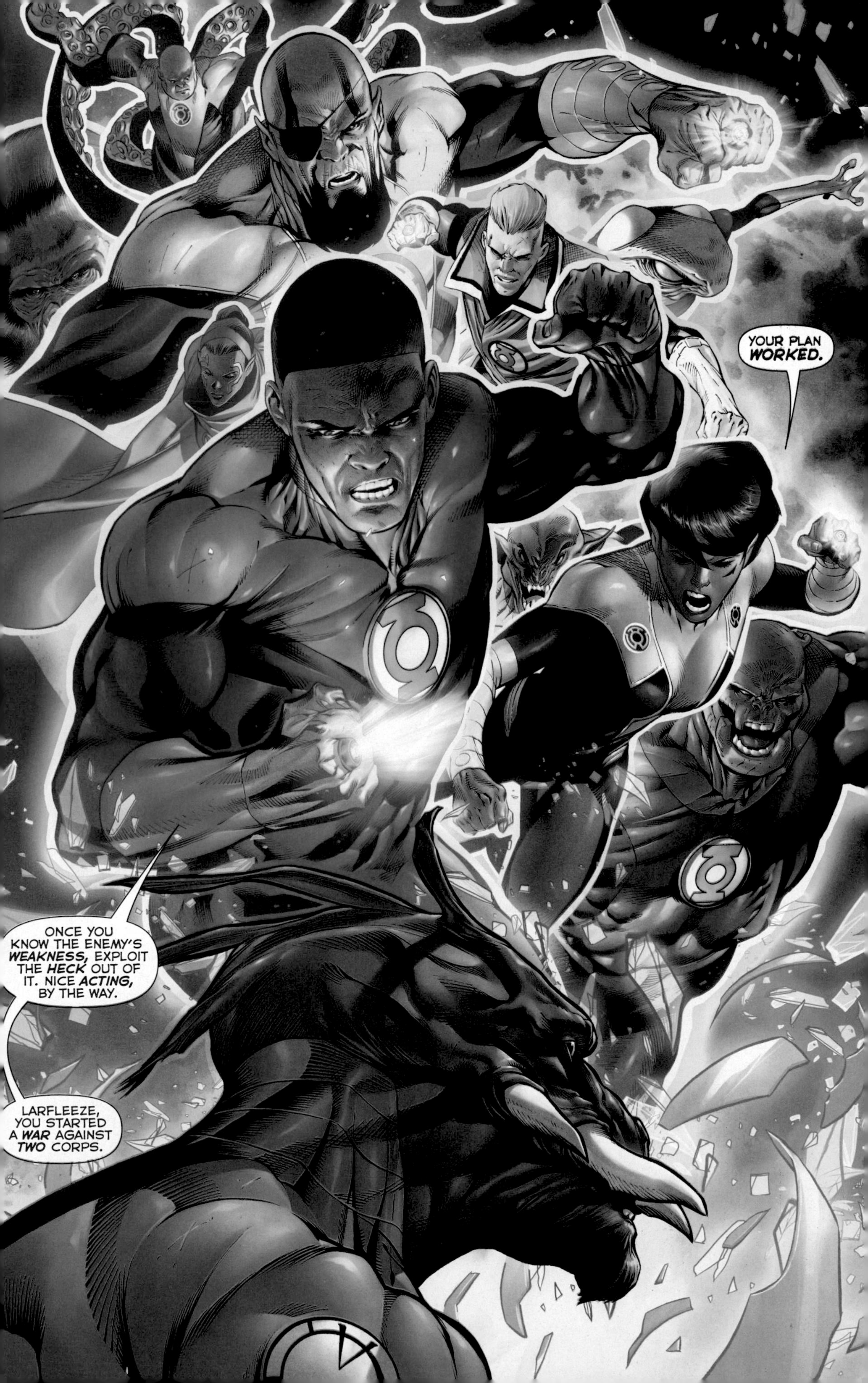
YOUR PLAN WORKED.
ONCE YOU KNOW THE ENEMY'S WEAKNESS, EXPLOIT THE HECK OUT OF IT. NICE ACTING, BY THE WAY.
LARFLEEZE, YOU STARTED A WAR AGAINST TWO CORPS.

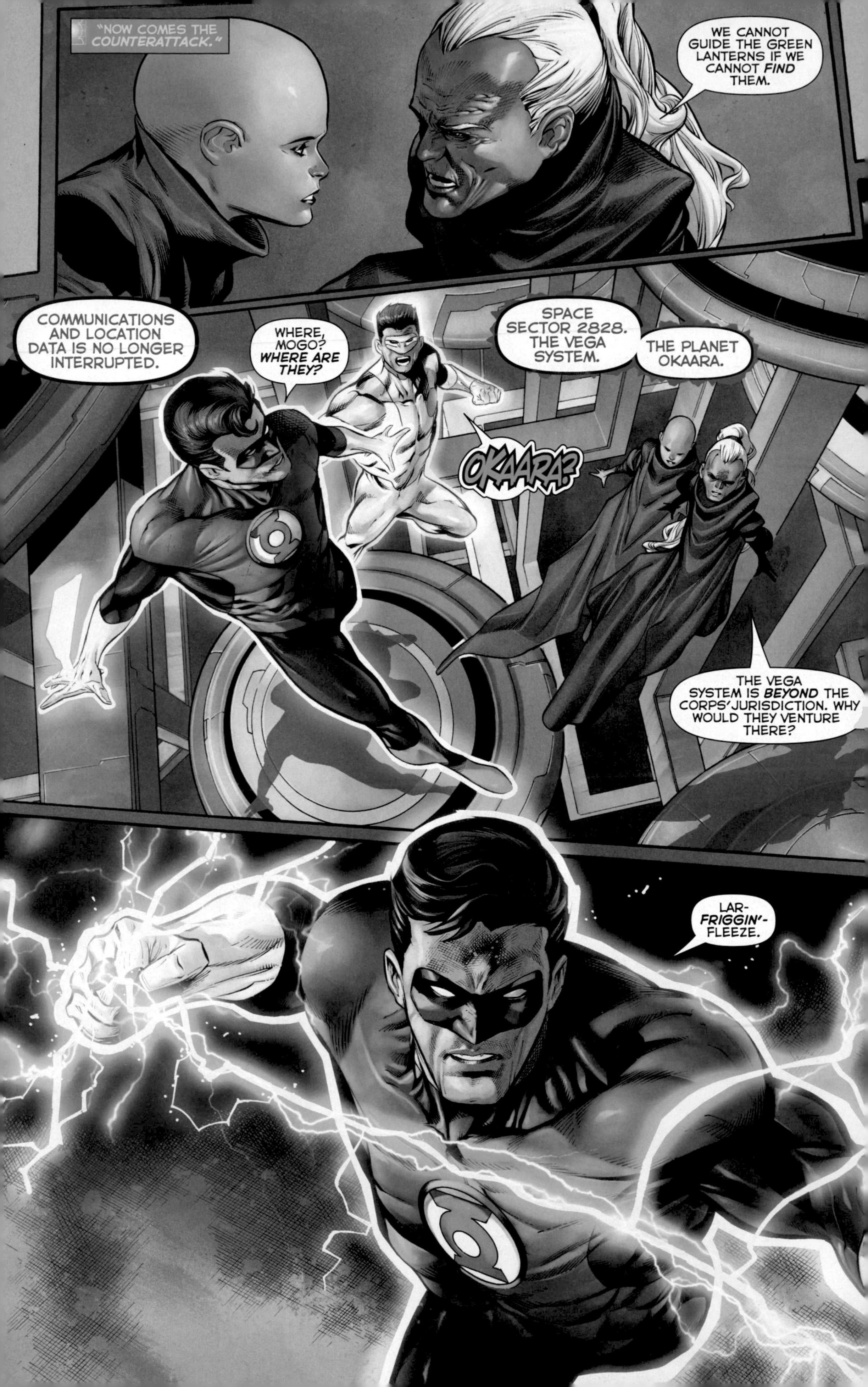
"NOW COMES THE COUNTERATTACK."
WE CANNOT GUIDE THE GREEN LANTERNS IF WE CANNOT *FIND* THEM.
COMMUNICATIONS AND LOCATION DATA IS NO LONGER INTERRUPTED.
WHERE, MOGO? *WHERE ARE THEY?*
SPACE SECTOR 2828. THE VEGA SYSTEM.
THE PLANET OKAARA.
OKAARA?
THE VEGA SYSTEM IS *BEYOND* THE CORPS' JURISDICTION. WHY WOULD THEY VENTURE THERE?
LAR- *FRIGGIN'*- FLEEZE.

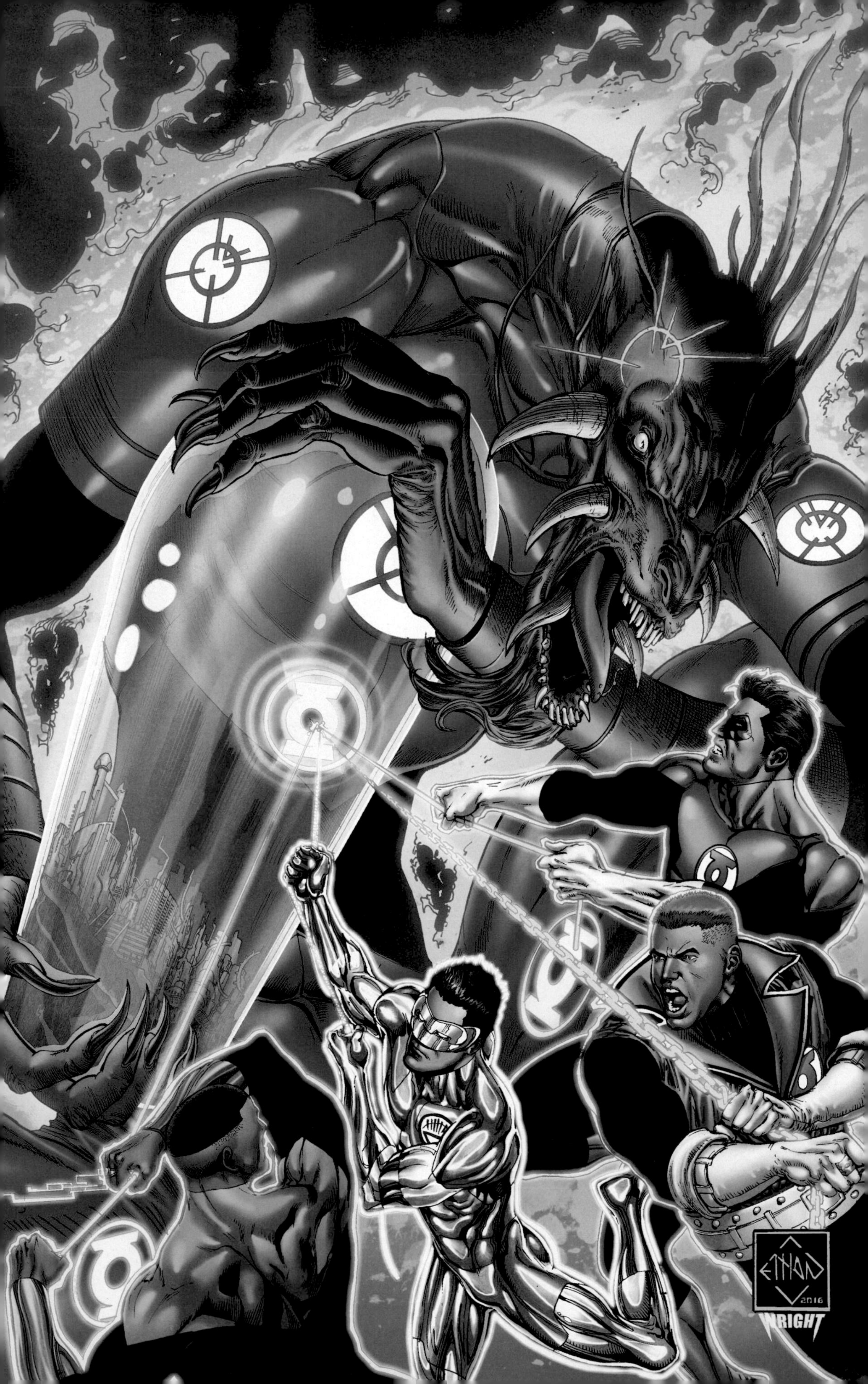
ETHAN
2016
WRIGHT

"BOTTLED LIGHT CONCLUSION: ORANGE CRUSH"
ETHAN VAN SCIVER artist * JASON WRIGHT colorist
ETHAN VAN SCIVER and JASON WRIGHT cover artists

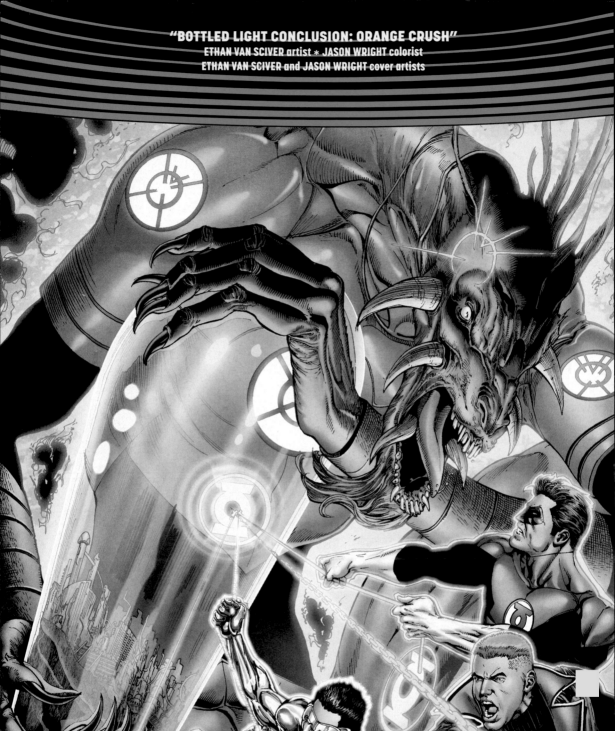

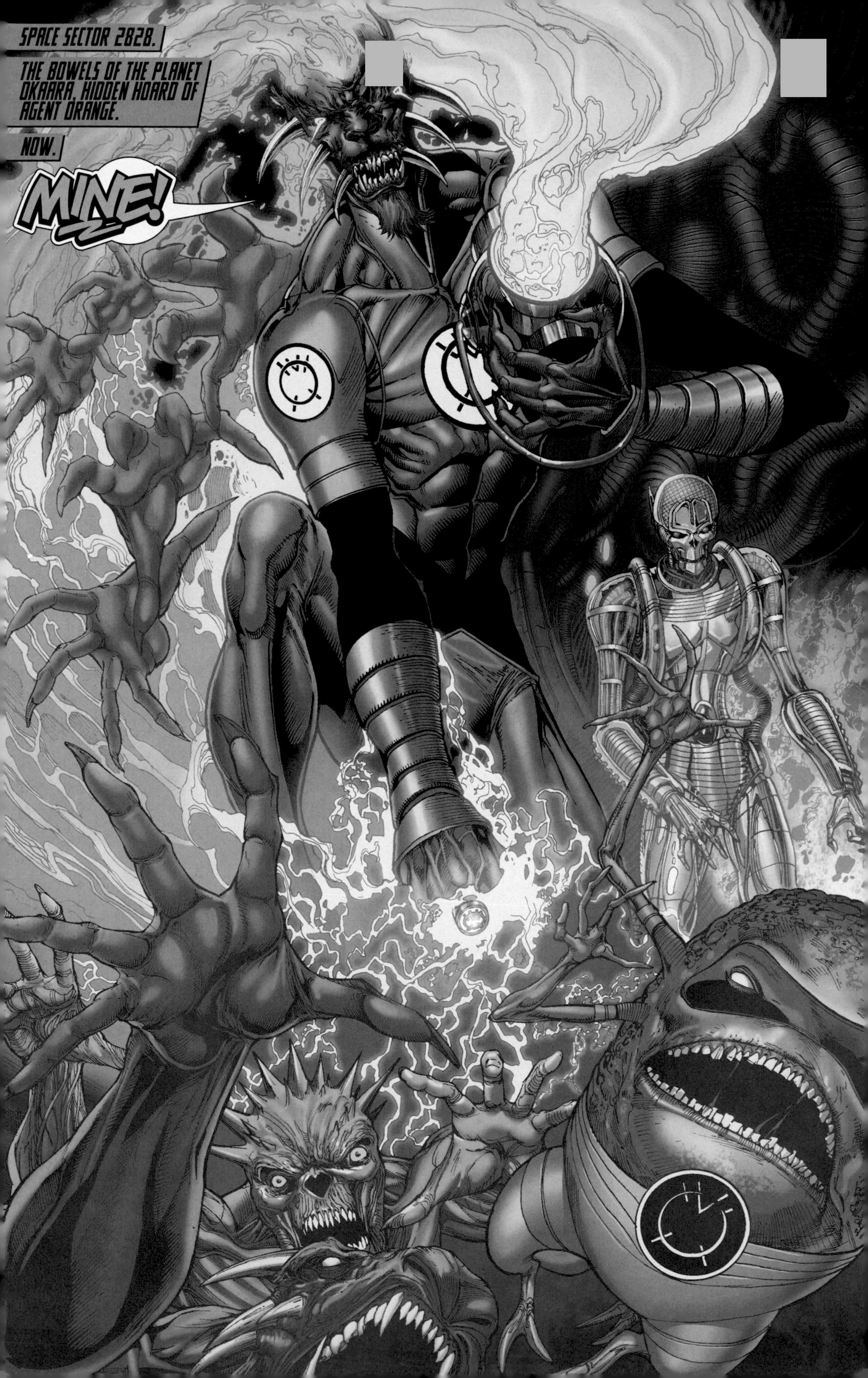
SPACE SECTOR 2828.
THE BOWELS OF THE PLANET OKAARA, HIDDEN HOARD OF AGENT ORANGE.
NOW.
MINE!

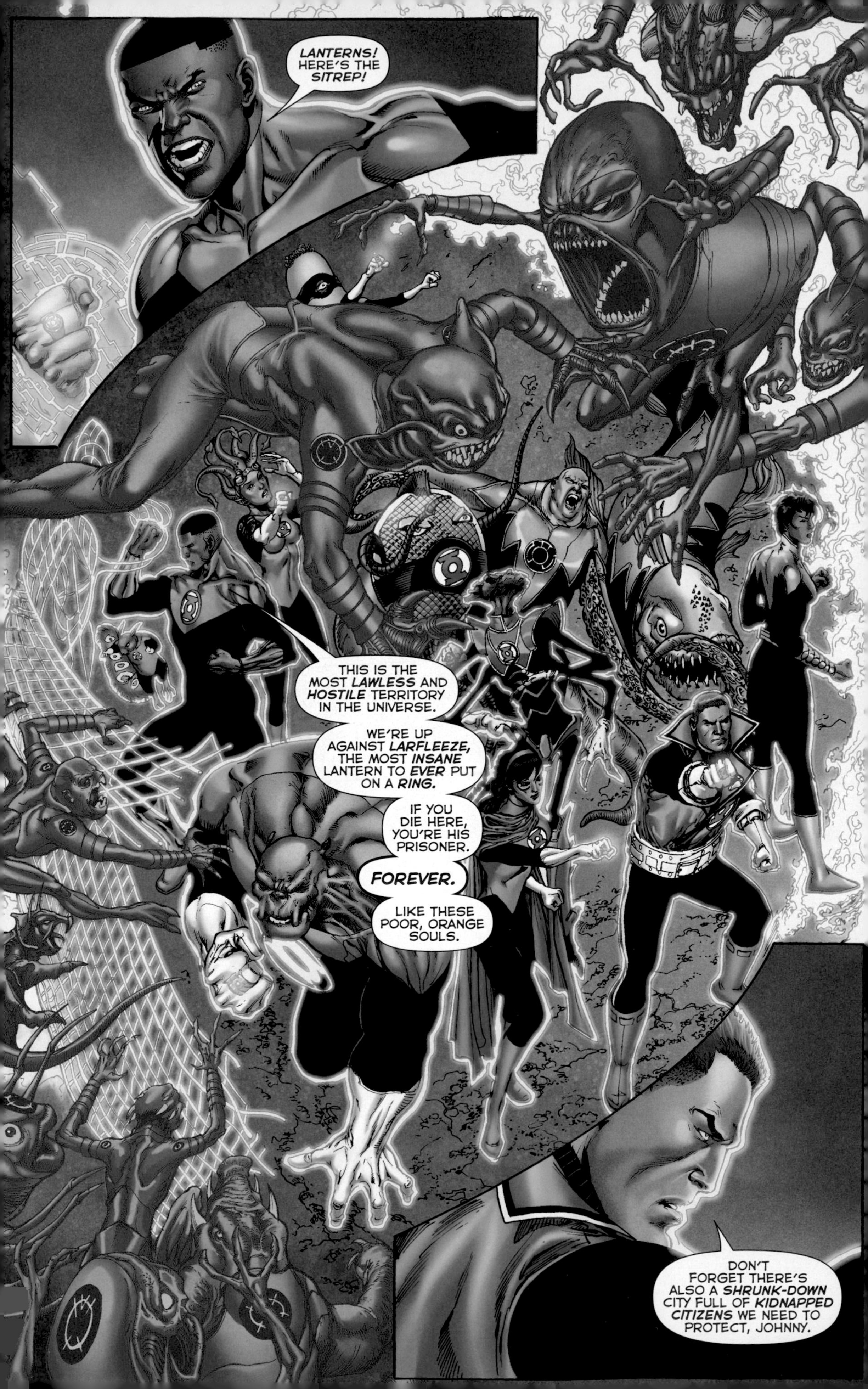
LANTERNS! HERE'S THE SITREP!
THIS IS THE MOST LAWLESS AND HOSTILE TERRITORY IN THE UNIVERSE.
WE'RE UP AGAINST LARFLEEZE, THE MOST INSANE LANTERN TO EVER PUT ON A RING.
IF YOU DIE HERE, YOU'RE HIS PRISONER.
FOREVER.
LIKE THESE POOR, ORANGE SOULS.
DON'T FORGET THERE'S ALSO A SHRUNK-DOWN CITY FULL OF KIDNAPPED CITIZENS WE NEED TO PROTECT, JOHNNY.

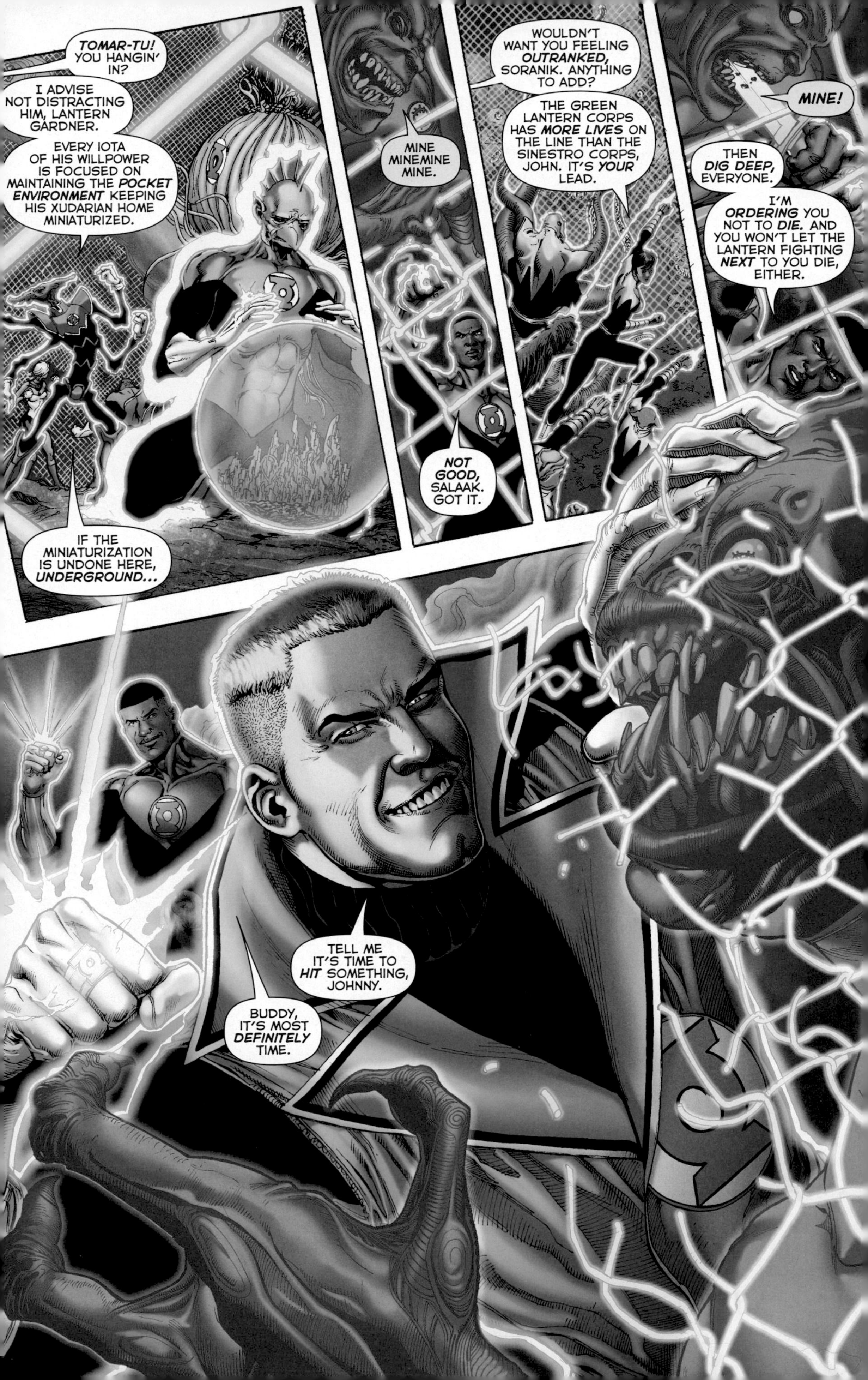
TOMAR-TU! YOU HANGIN' IN?
I ADVISE NOT DISTRACTING HIM, LANTERN GARDNER.
EVERY IOTA OF HIS WILLPOWER IS FOCUSED ON MAINTAINING THE POCKET ENVIRONMENT KEEPING HIS XUDARIAN HOME MINIATURIZED.
IF THE MINIATURIZATION IS UNDONE HERE, UNDERGROUND...
MINE MINEMINE MINE.
NOT GOOD, SALAAK. GOT IT.
WOULDN'T WANT YOU FEELING OUTRANKED, SORANIK. ANYTHING TO ADD?
THE GREEN LANTERN CORPS HAS MORE LIVES ON THE LINE THAN THE SINESTRO CORPS, JOHN. IT'S YOUR LEAD.
MINE!
THEN DIG DEEP, EVERYONE.
I'M ORDERING YOU NOT TO DIE. AND YOU WON'T LET THE LANTERN FIGHTING NEXT TO YOU DIE, EITHER.
TELL ME IT'S TIME TO HIT SOMETHING, JOHNNY.
BUDDY, IT'S MOST DEFINITELY TIME.

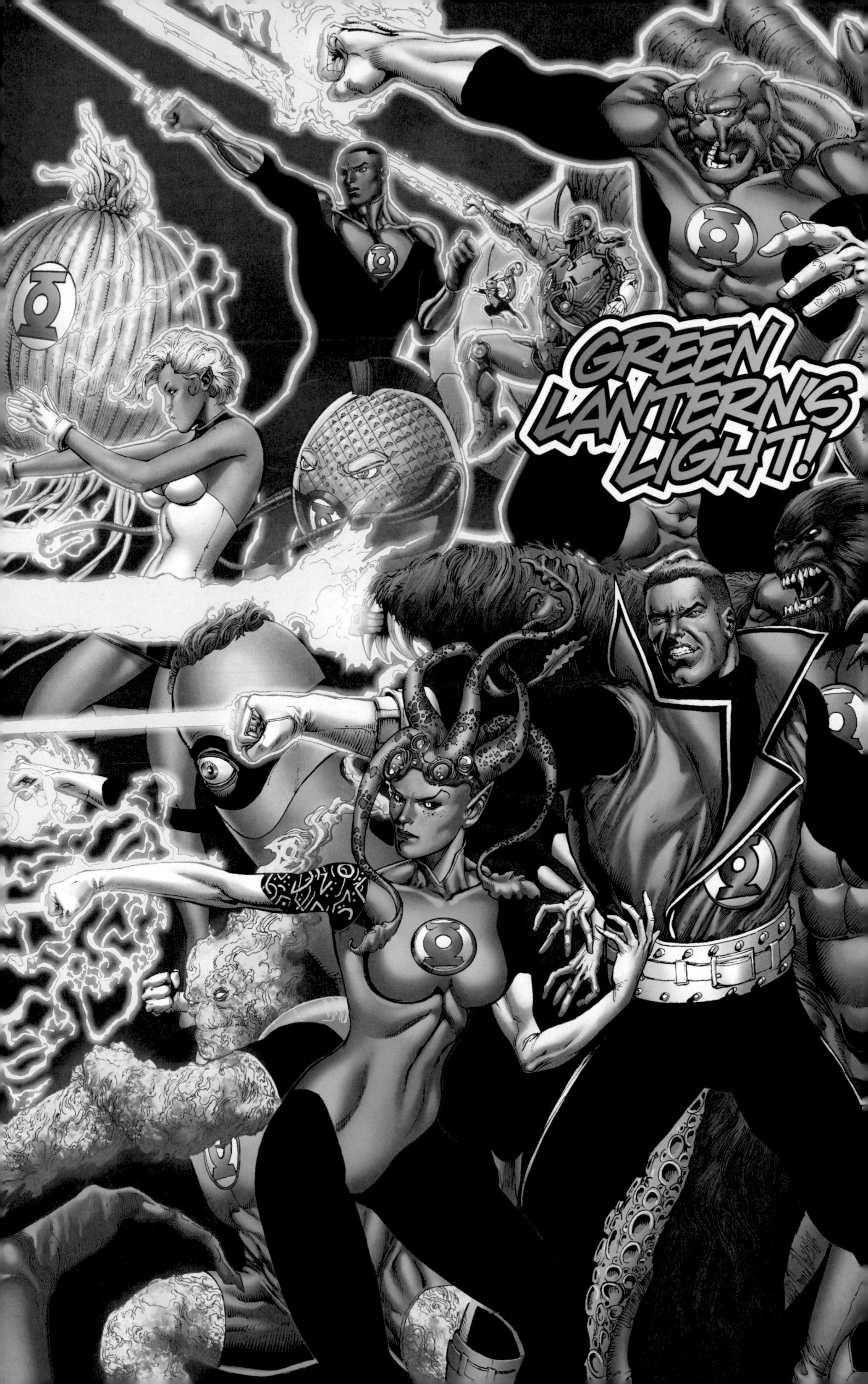
GREEN LANTERN'S LIGHT!

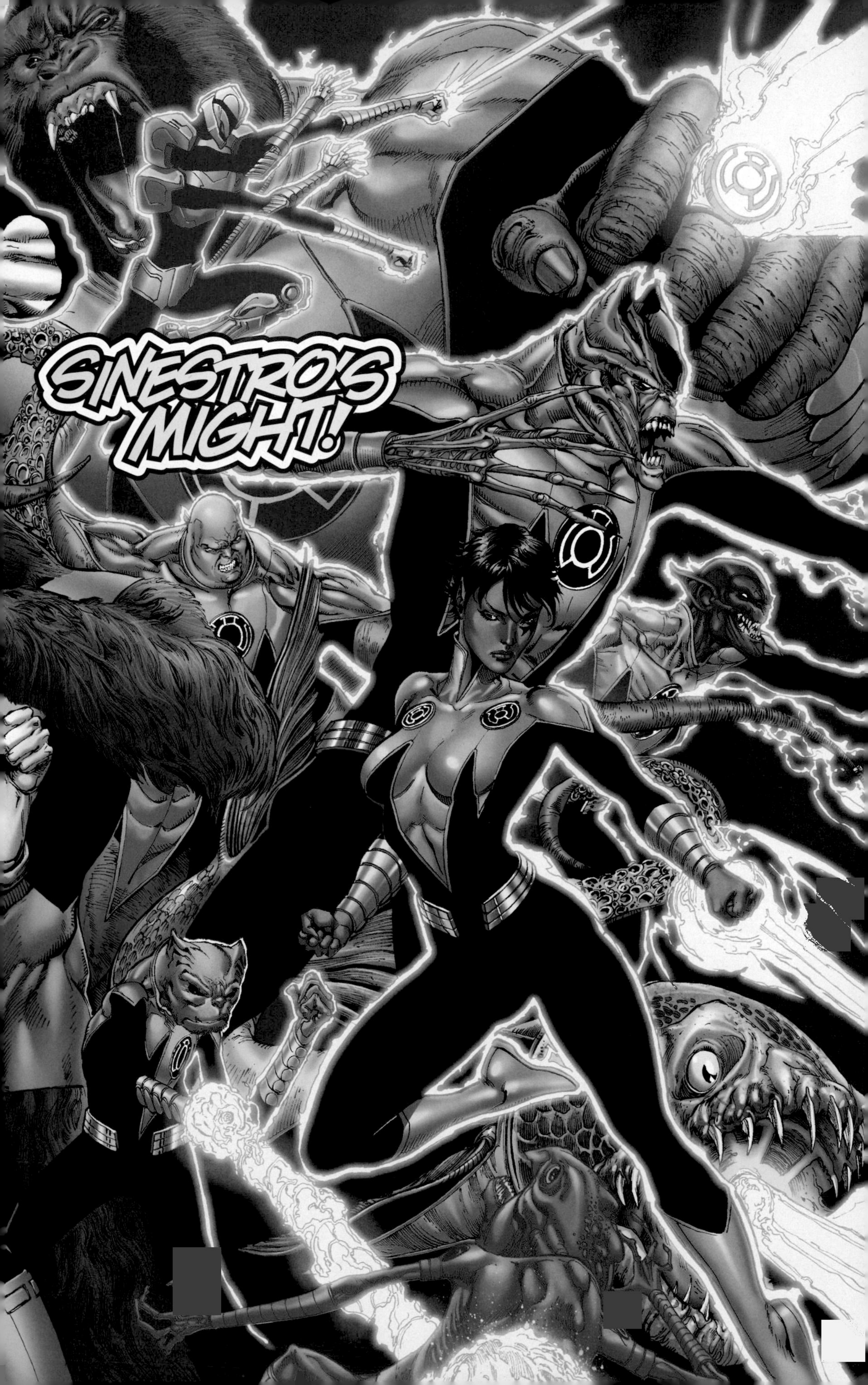
SINESTRO'S MIGHT!

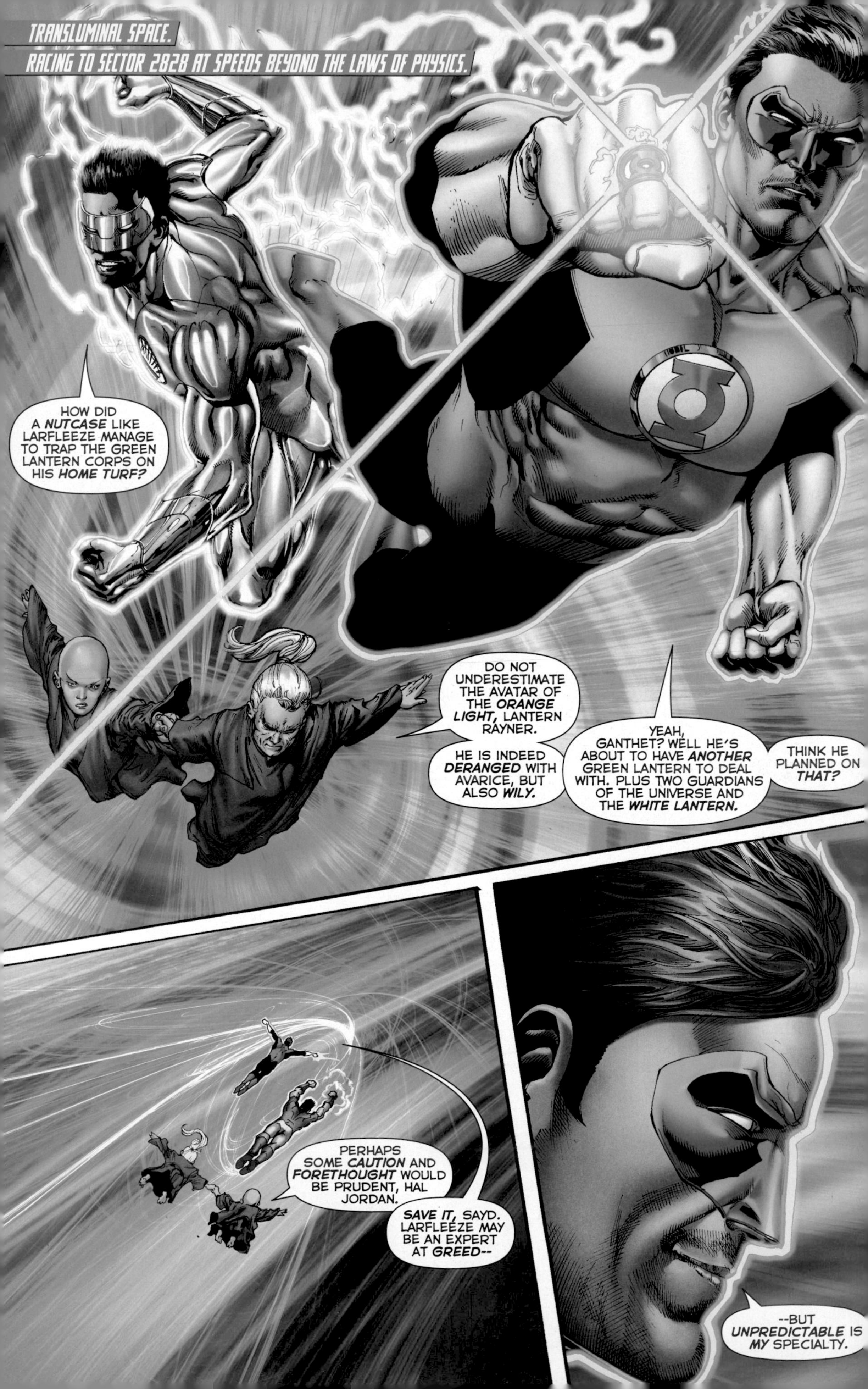
TRANSLUMINAL SPACE.
RACING TO SECTOR 2828 AT SPEEDS BEYOND THE LAWS OF PHYSICS.
HOW DID A NUTCASE LIKE LARFLEEZE MANAGE TO TRAP THE GREEN LANTERN CORPS ON HIS HOME TURF?
DO NOT UNDERESTIMATE THE AVATAR OF THE ORANGE LIGHT, LANTERN RAYNER.
HE IS INDEED DERANGED WITH AVARICE, BUT ALSO WILY.
YEAH, GANTHET? WELL HE'S ABOUT TO HAVE ANOTHER GREEN LANTERN TO DEAL WITH. PLUS TWO GUARDIANS OF THE UNIVERSE AND THE WHITE LANTERN.
THINK HE PLANNED ON THAT?
PERHAPS SOME CAUTION AND FORETHOUGHT WOULD BE PRUDENT, HAL JORDAN.
SAVE IT, SAYD. LARFLEEZE MAY BE AN EXPERT AT GREED--
--BUT UNPREDICTABLE IS MY SPECIALTY.

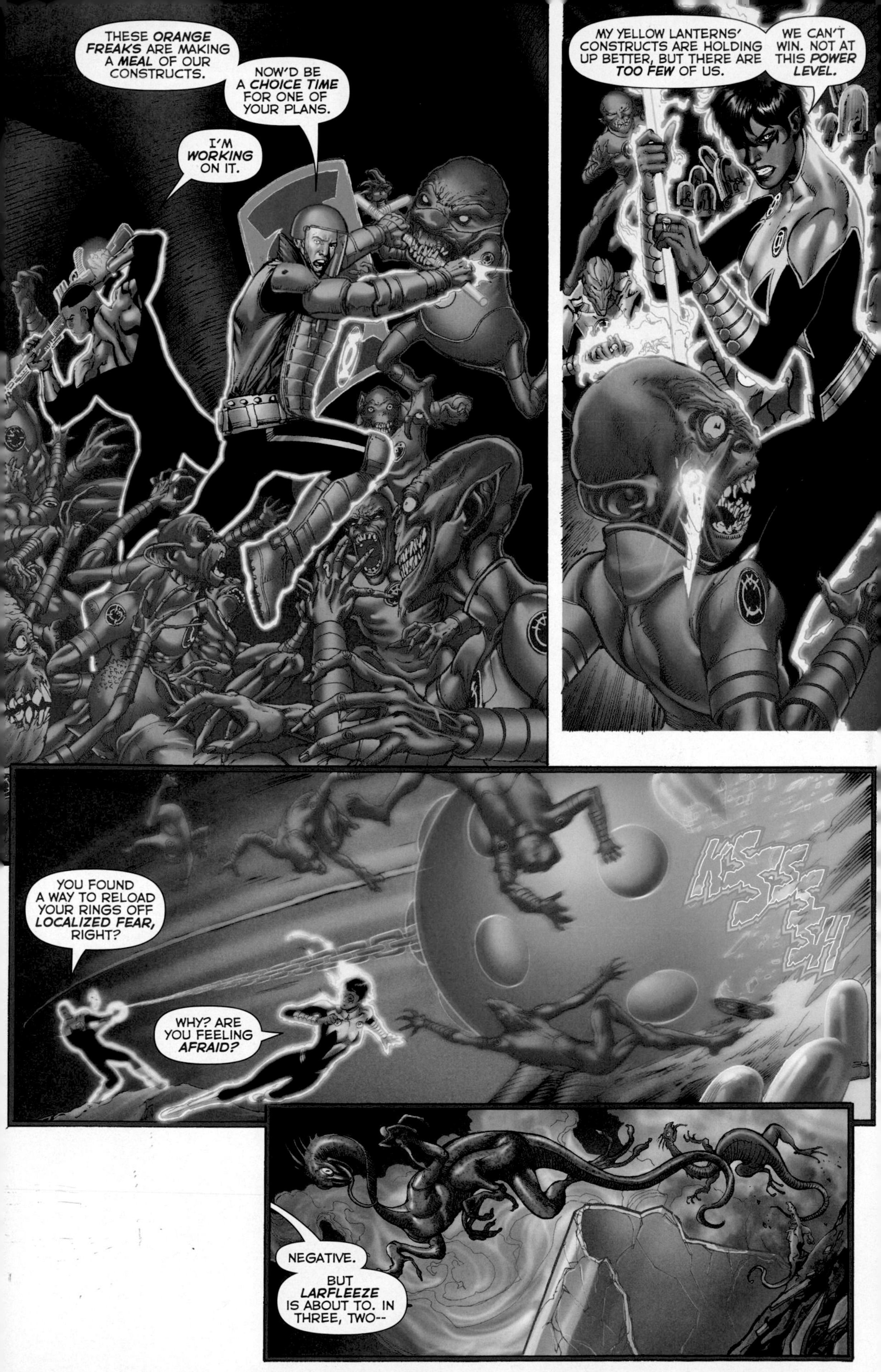
THESE ORANGE FREAKS ARE MAKING A MEAL OF OUR CONSTRUCTS.
NOW'D BE A CHOICE TIME FOR ONE OF YOUR PLANS.
I'M WORKING ON IT.
MY YELLOW LANTERNS' CONSTRUCTS ARE HOLDING UP BETTER, BUT THERE ARE TOO FEW OF US.
WE CAN'T WIN. NOT AT THIS POWER LEVEL.
KSSSSH
YOU FOUND A WAY TO RELOAD YOUR RINGS OFF LOCALIZED FEAR, RIGHT?
WHY? ARE YOU FEELING AFRAID?
NEGATIVE.
BUT LARFLEEZE IS ABOUT TO. IN THREE, TWO--

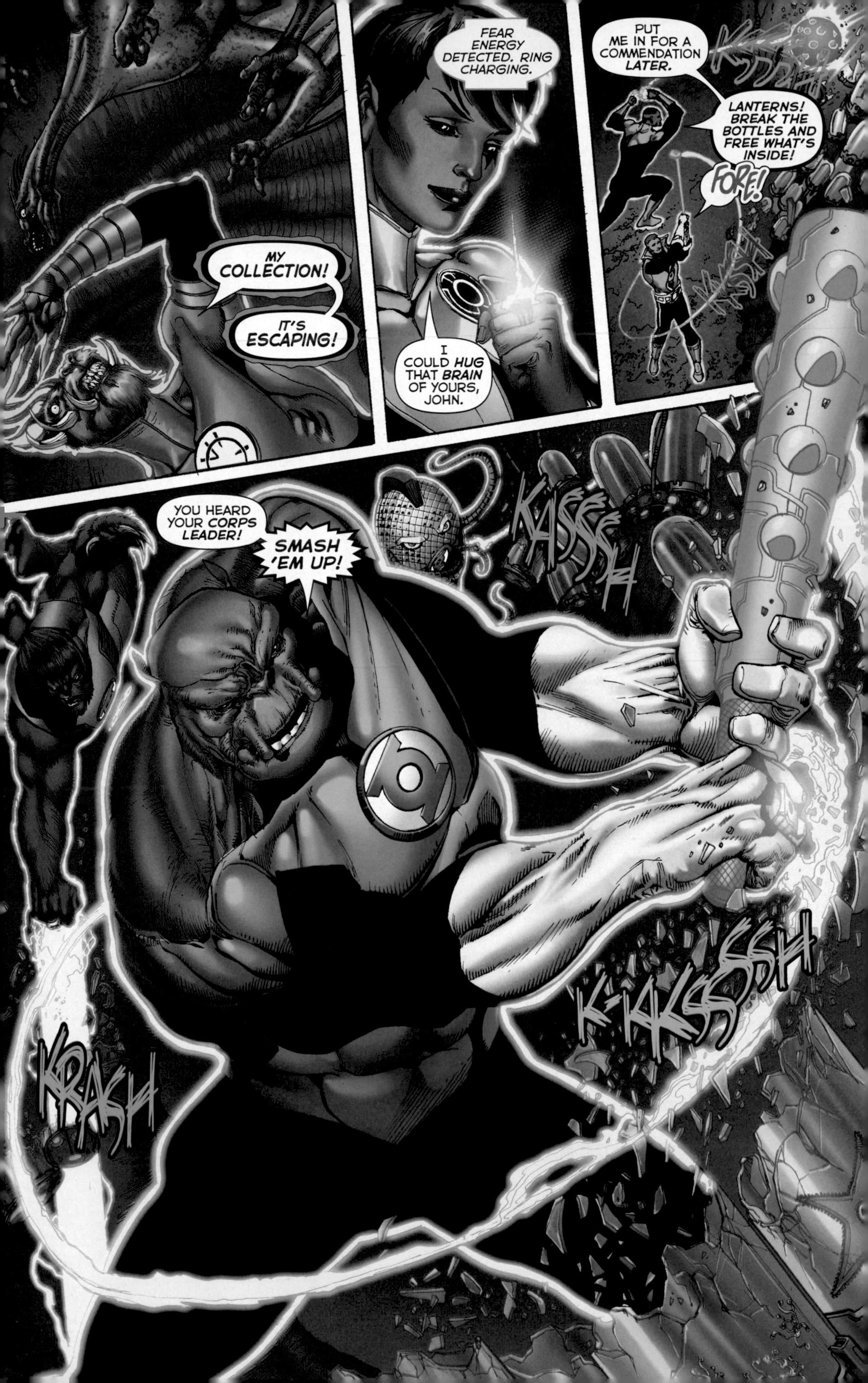
MY COLLECTION!
IT'S ESCAPING!
FEAR ENERGY DETECTED. RING CHARGING.
I COULD HUG THAT BRAIN OF YOURS, JOHN.
PUT ME IN FOR A COMMENDATION LATER.
LANTERNS! BREAK THE BOTTLES AND FREE WHAT'S INSIDE!
FORE!
YOU HEARD YOUR CORPS LEADER!
SMASH 'EM UP!
KASSSH
K-KKSSSH
KRASH

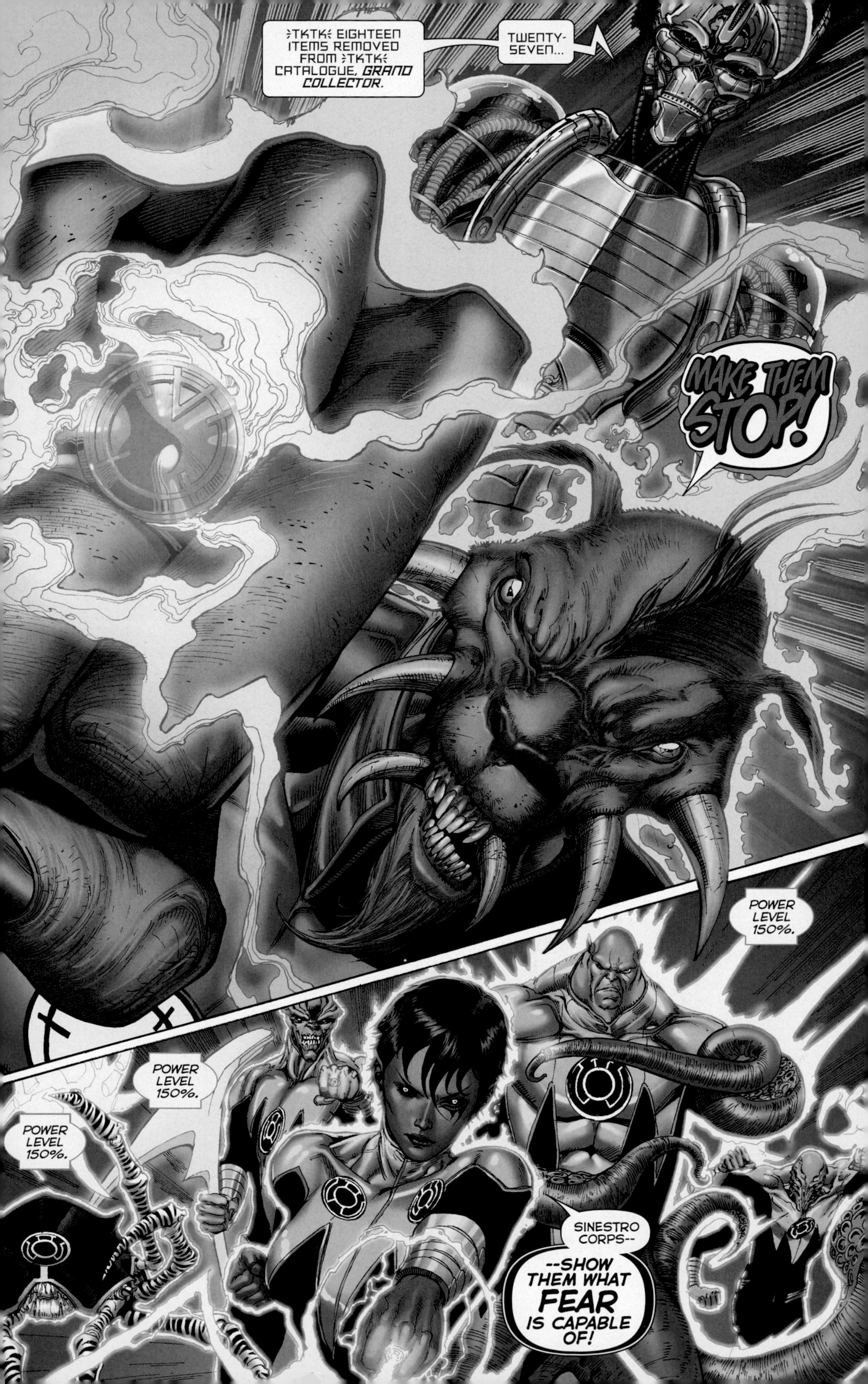

⫶TKTK⫶ EIGHTEEN ITEMS REMOVED FROM ⫶TKTK⫶ CATALOGUE, GRAND COLLECTOR.
TWENTY-SEVEN...
MAKE THEM STOP!
POWER LEVEL 150%.
POWER LEVEL 150%.
POWER LEVEL 150%.
SINESTRO CORPS--
--SHOW THEM WHAT FEAR IS CAPABLE OF!

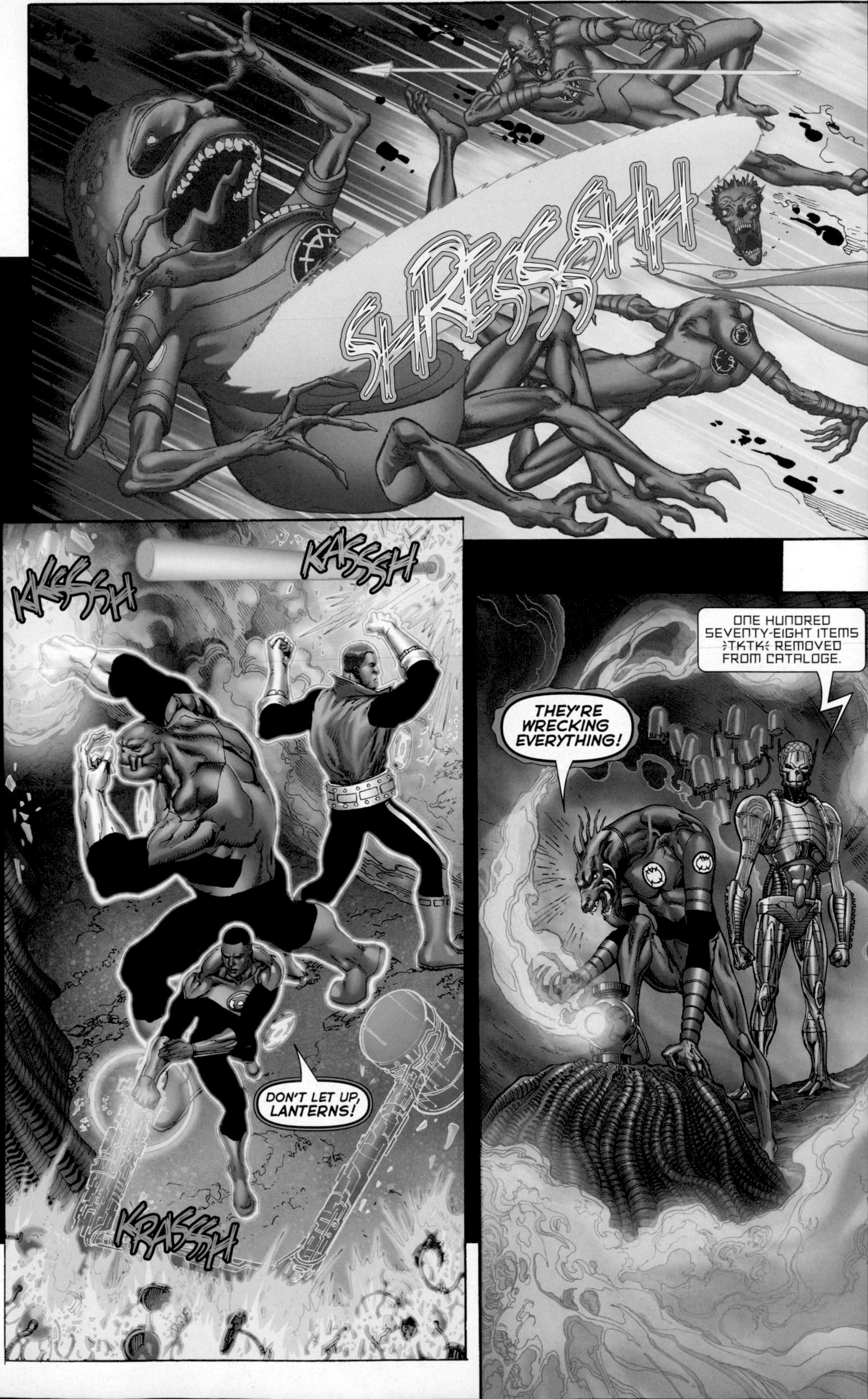
SHRESSSHH
KASSSH
KASSSH
DON'T LET UP, LANTERNS!
KRASSSH
THEY'RE WRECKING EVERYTHING!
ONE HUNDRED SEVENTY-EIGHT ITEMS ≠TKTK≠ REMOVED FROM CATALOGE.

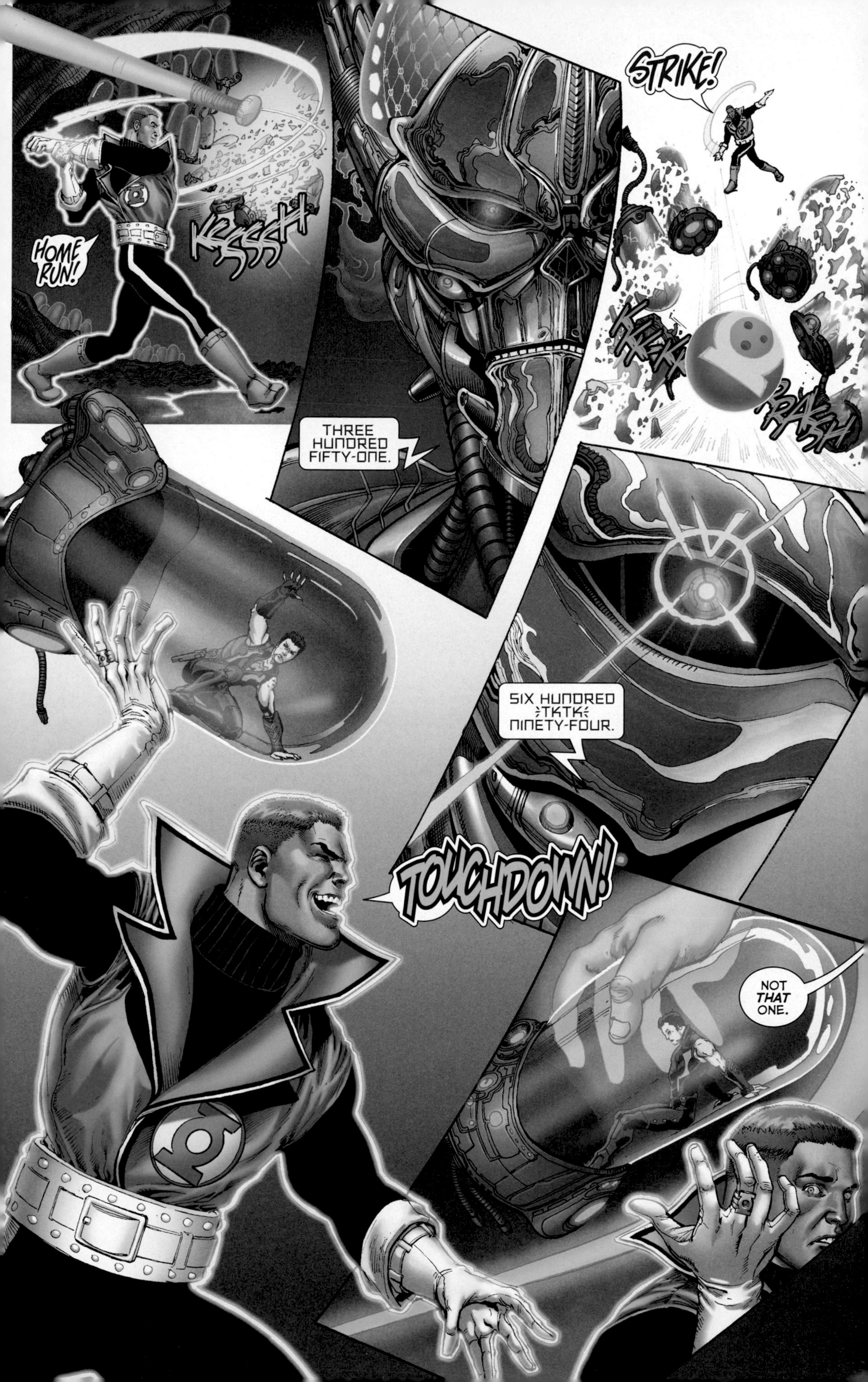
HOME RUN!
KSSSH
THREE HUNDRED FIFTY-ONE.
STRIKE!
KRKK
KRASH
SIX HUNDRED
TKTK
NINETY-FOUR.
TOUCHDOWN!
NOT THAT ONE.

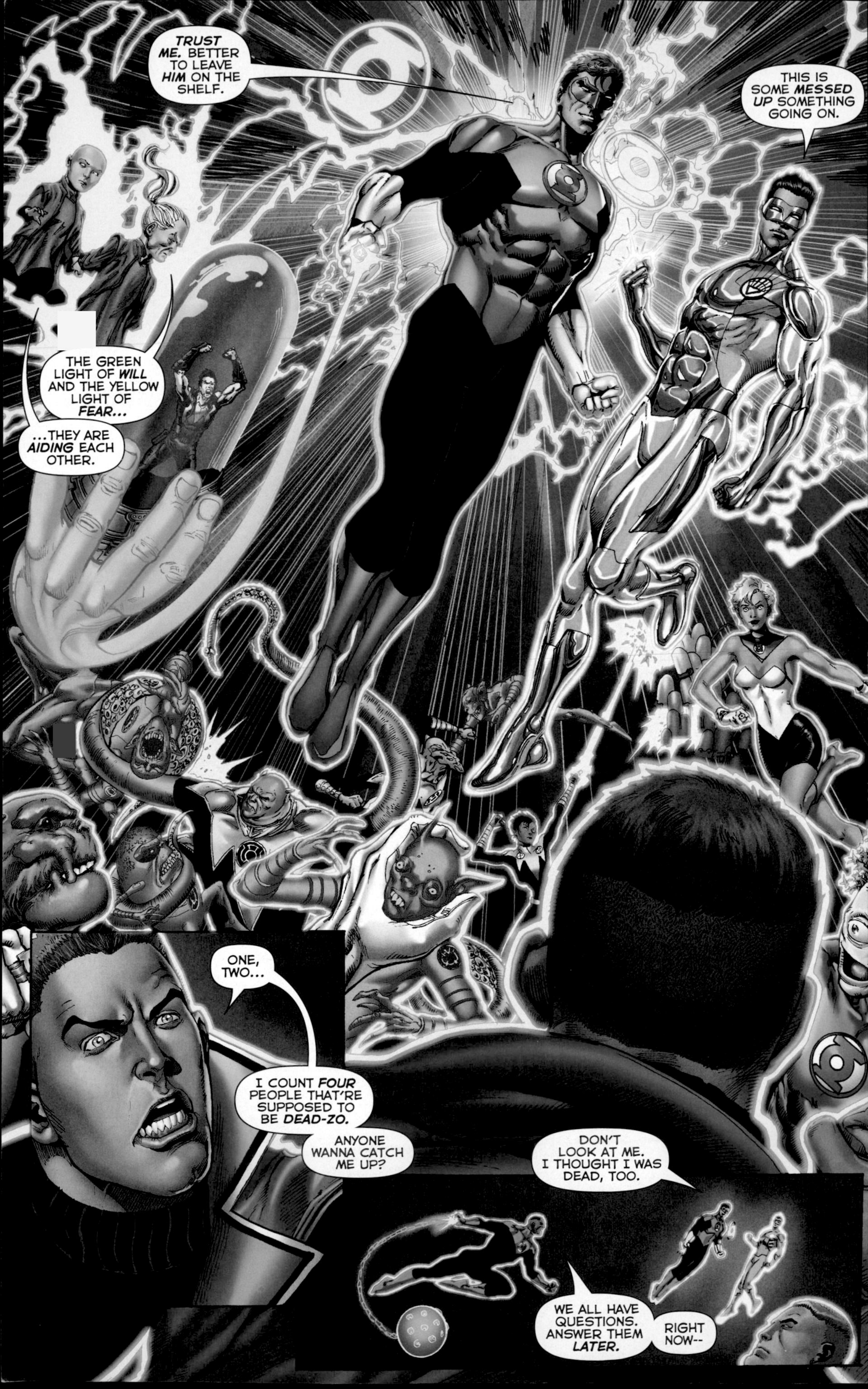
TRUST ME. BETTER TO LEAVE HIM ON THE SHELF.
THIS IS SOME MESSED UP SOMETHING GOING ON.
THE GREEN LIGHT OF WILL AND THE YELLOW LIGHT OF FEAR...
...THEY ARE AIDING EACH OTHER.
ONE, TWO...
I COUNT FOUR PEOPLE THAT'RE SUPPOSED TO BE DEAD-ZO.
ANYONE WANNA CATCH ME UP?
DON'T LOOK AT ME. I THOUGHT I WAS DEAD, TOO.
WE ALL HAVE QUESTIONS. ANSWER THEM LATER.
RIGHT NOW--

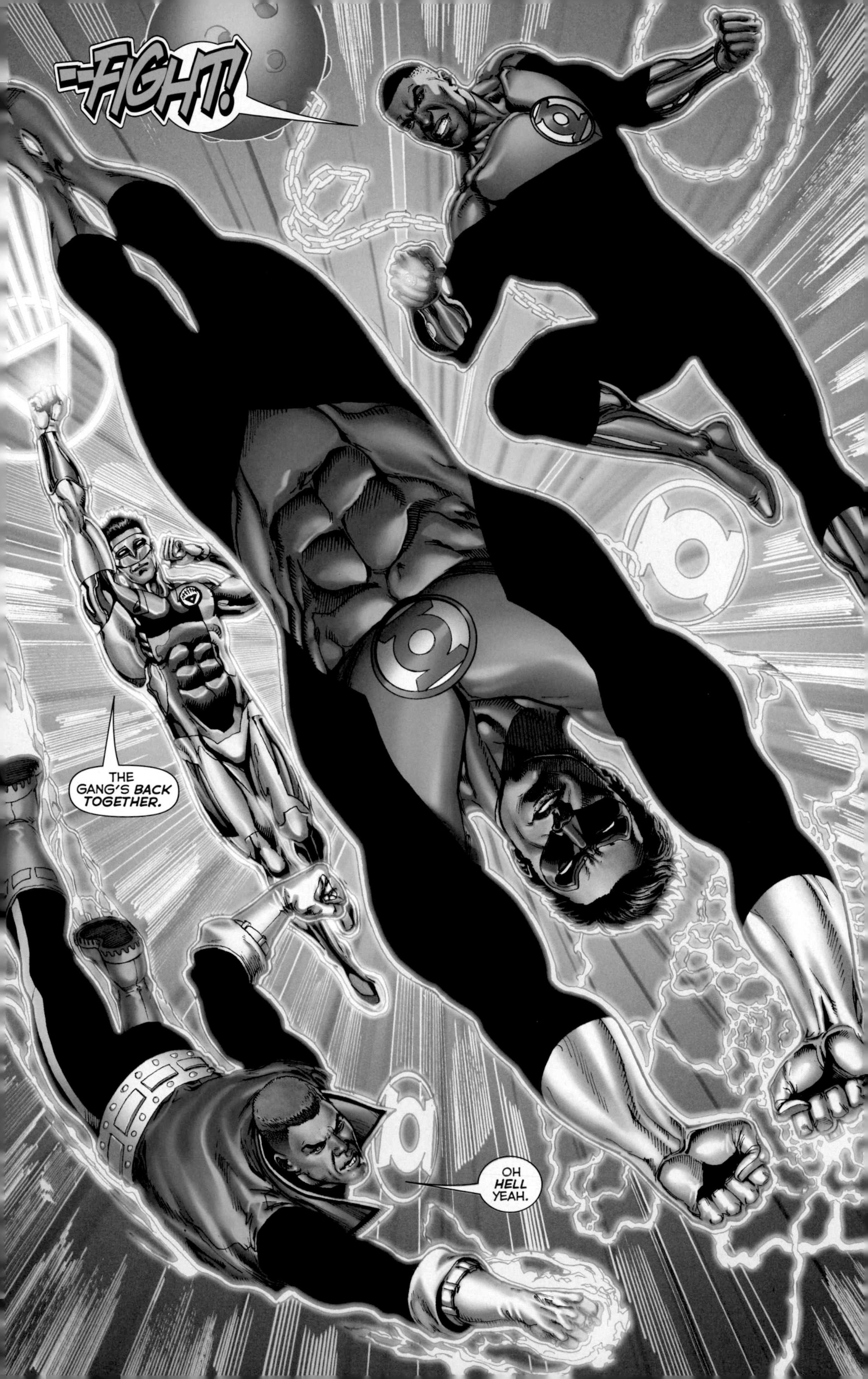
--FIGHT!
THE GANG'S BACK TOGETHER.
OH HELL YEAH.

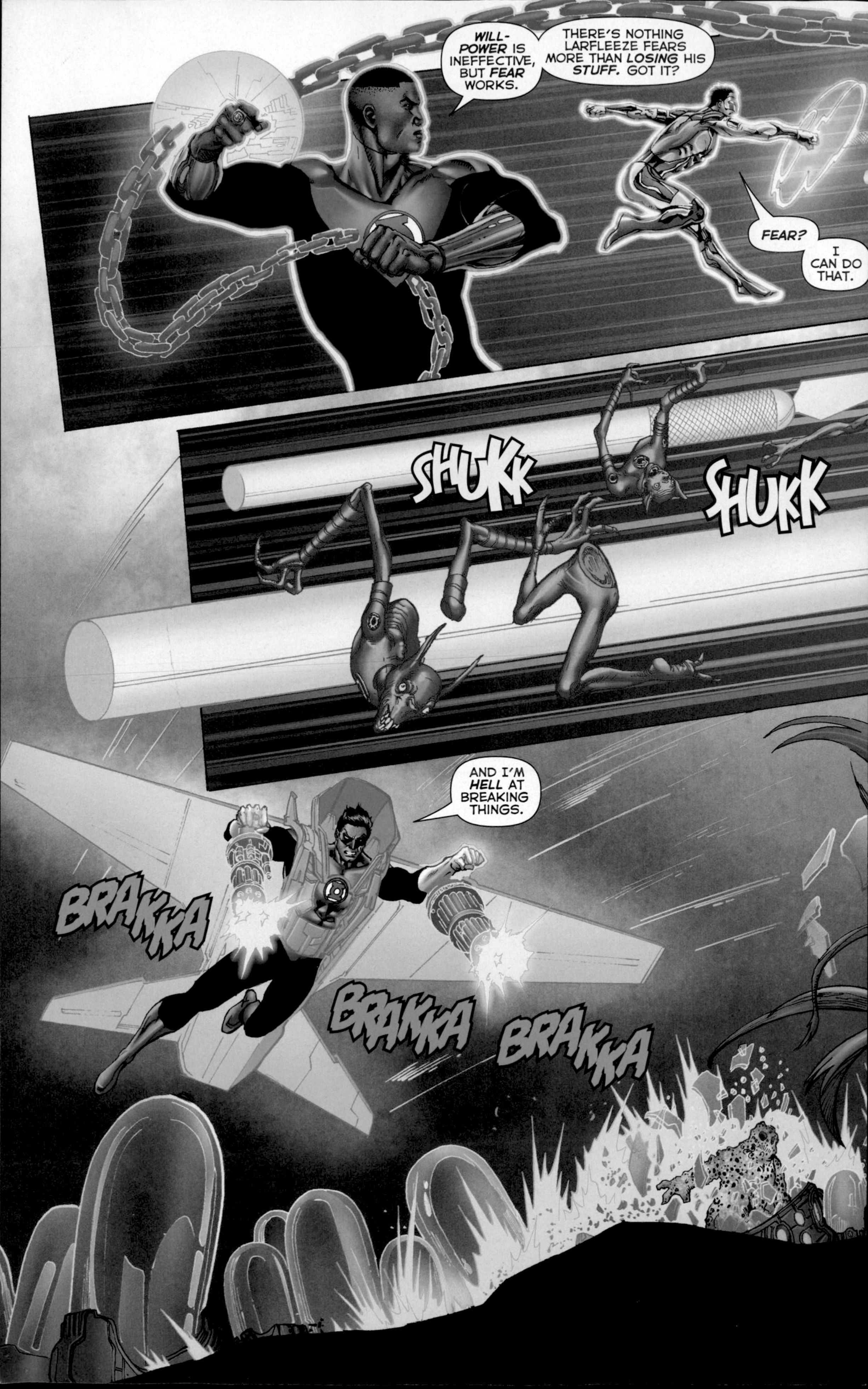

WILL-POWER IS INEFFECTIVE, BUT FEAR WORKS.
THERE'S NOTHING LARFLEEZE FEARS MORE THAN LOSING HIS STUFF. GOT IT?
FEAR?
I CAN DO THAT.
SHUKK
SHUKK
AND I'M HELL AT BREAKING THINGS.
BRAKKA
BRAKKA
BRAKKA

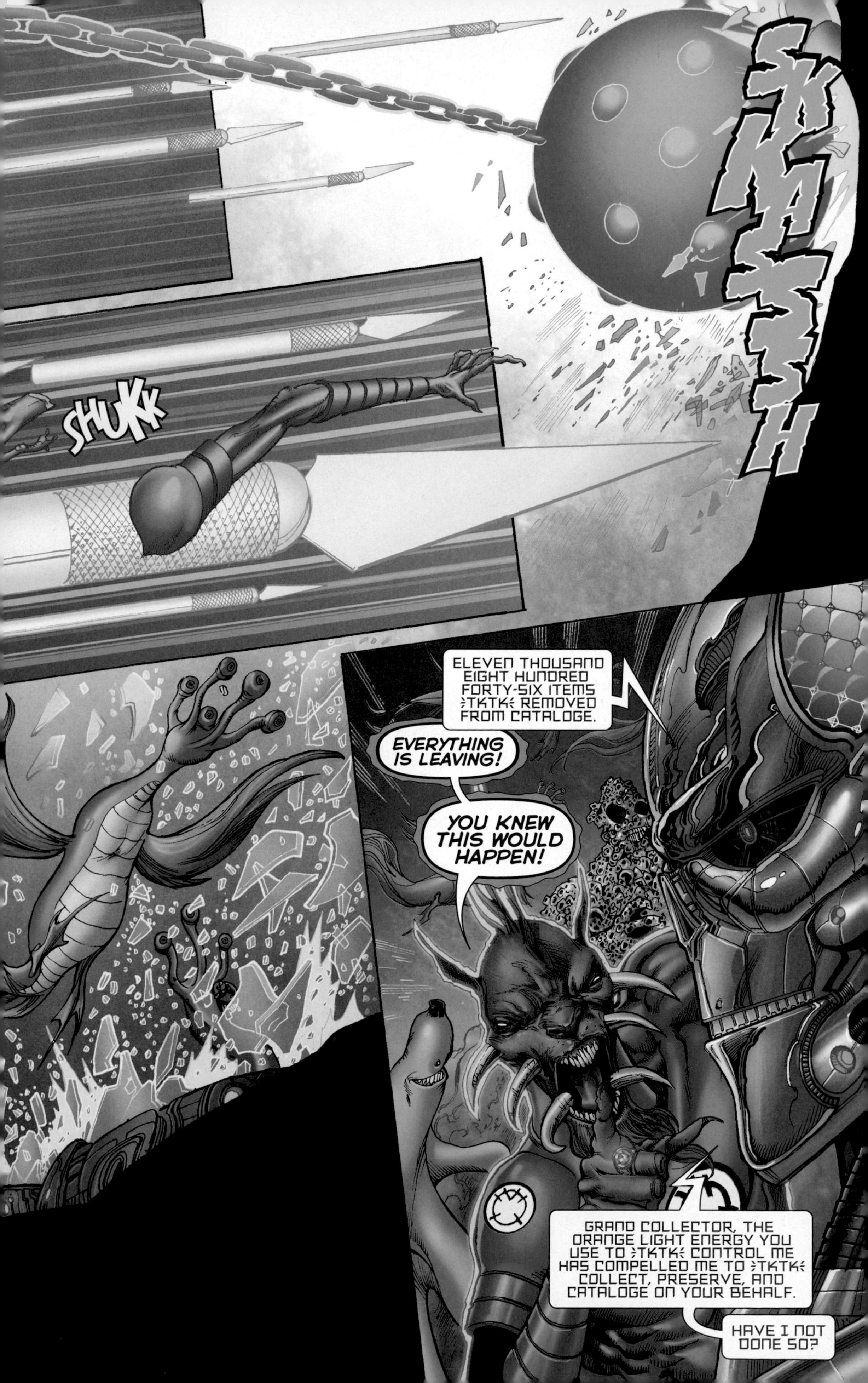
SKRASSH
SHUKK
ELEVEN THOUSAND EIGHT HUNDRED FORTY-SIX ITEMS ⋺TKTK⋲ REMOVED FROM CATALOGE.
EVERYTHING IS LEAVING!
YOU KNEW THIS WOULD HAPPEN!
GRAND COLLECTOR, THE ORANGE LIGHT ENERGY YOU USE TO ⋺TKTK⋲ CONTROL ME HAS COMPELLED ME TO ⋺TKTK⋲ COLLECT, PRESERVE, AND CATALOGE ON YOUR BEHALF.
HAVE I NOT DONE SO?

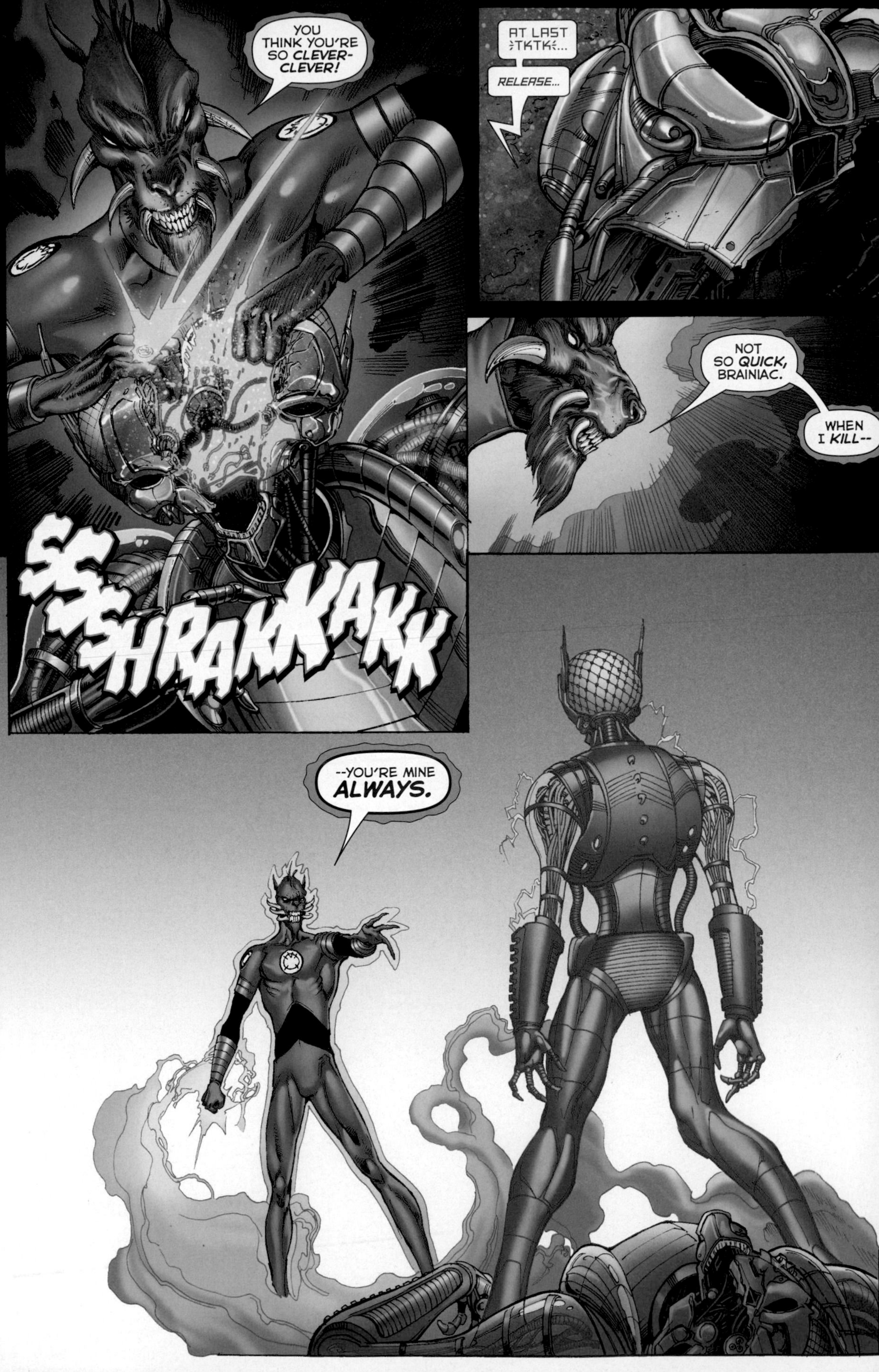
YOU THINK YOU'RE SO CLEVER-CLEVER!
AT LAST
RELEASE...
SSSHRAKKAKK
NOT SO QUICK, BRAINIAC.
WHEN I KILL--
--YOU'RE MINE ALWAYS.

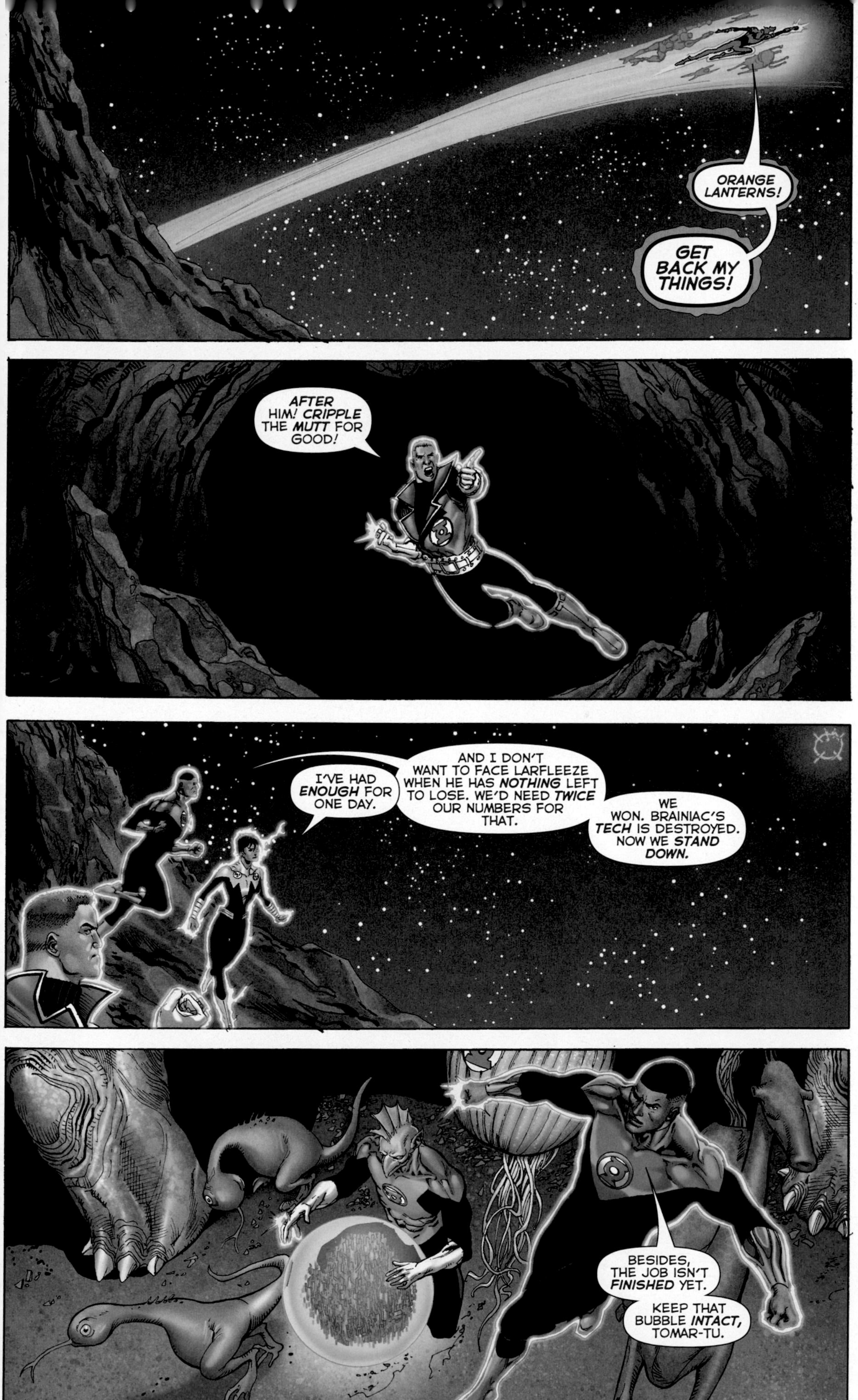
ORANGE LANTERNS!
GET BACK MY THINGS!
AFTER HIM! CRIPPLE THE MUTT FOR GOOD!
I'VE HAD ENOUGH FOR ONE DAY.
AND I DON'T WANT TO FACE LARFLEEZE WHEN HE HAS NOTHING LEFT TO LOSE. WE'D NEED TWICE OUR NUMBERS FOR THAT.
WE WON. BRAINIAC'S TECH IS DESTROYED. NOW WE STAND DOWN.
BESIDES, THE JOB ISN'T FINISHED YET.
KEEP THAT BUBBLE INTACT, TOMAR-TU.

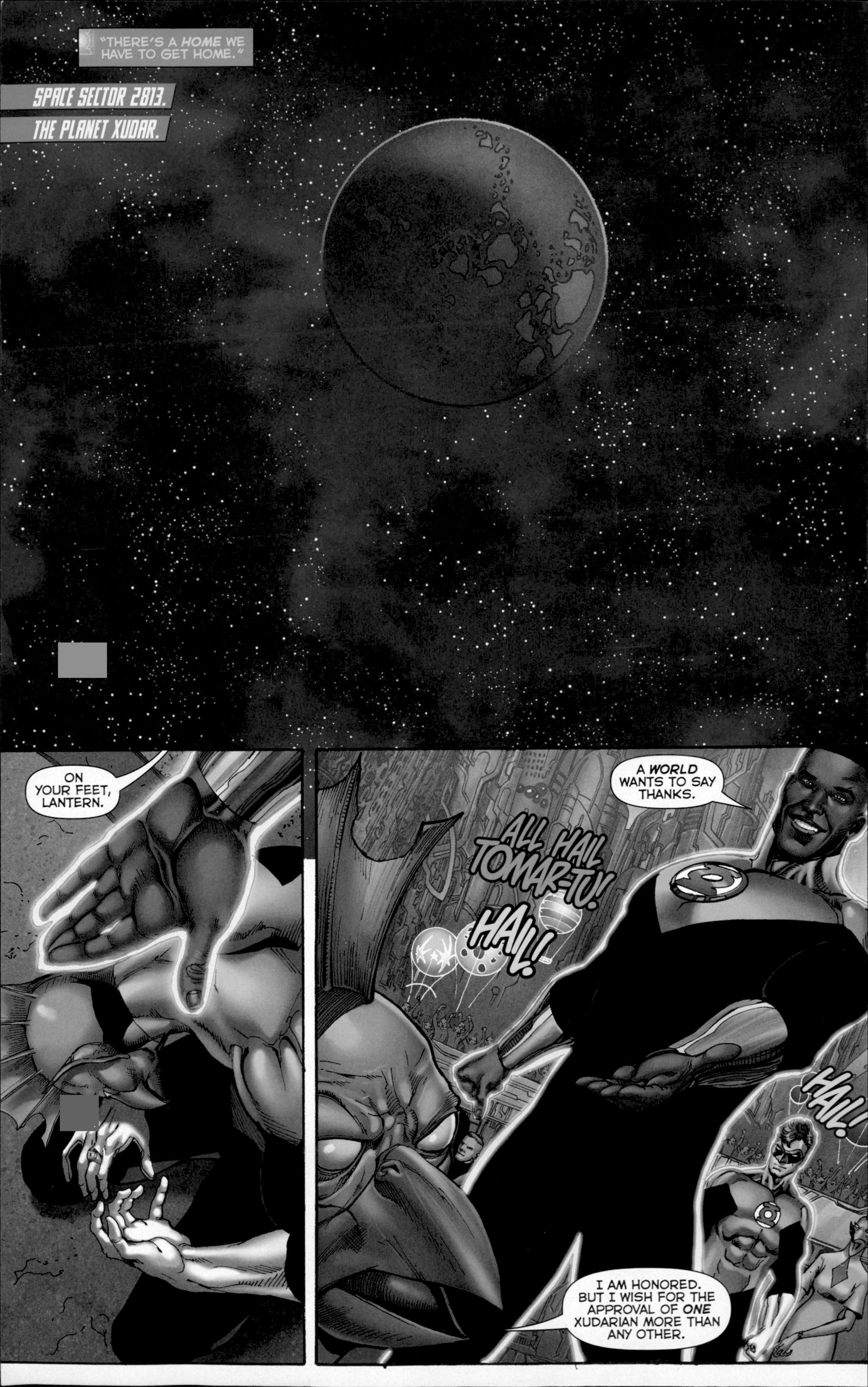
"THERE'S A HOME WE HAVE TO GET HOME."
SPACE SECTOR 2813.
THE PLANET XUDAR.
ON YOUR FEET, LANTERN.
A WORLD WANTS TO SAY THANKS.
ALL HAIL TOMAR-TU!
HAIL!
HAIL!
I AM HONORED. BUT I WISH FOR THE APPROVAL OF ONE XUDARIAN MORE THAN ANY OTHER.

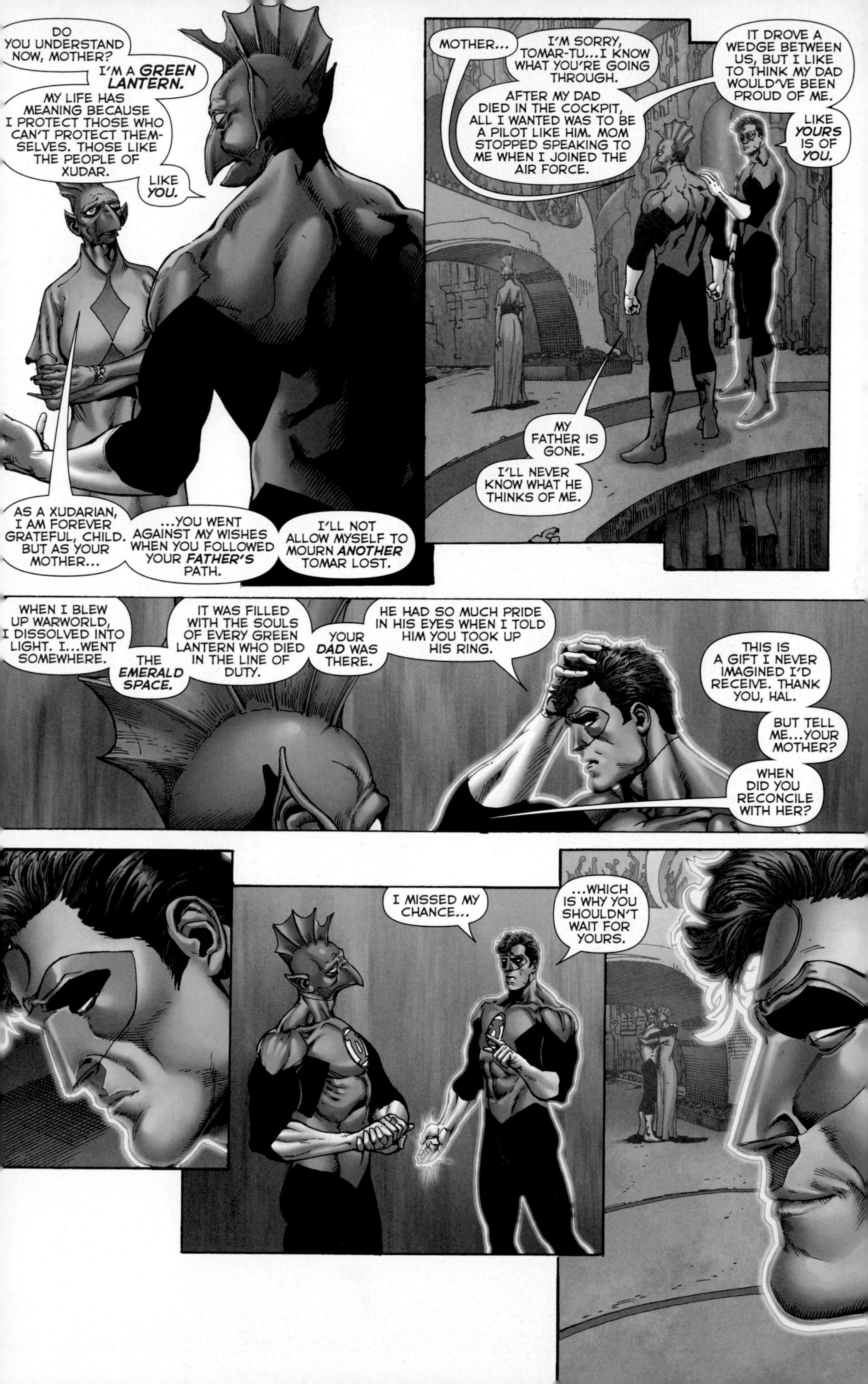
DO YOU UNDERSTAND NOW, MOTHER?
I'M A GREEN LANTERN.
MY LIFE HAS MEANING BECAUSE I PROTECT THOSE WHO CAN'T PROTECT THEMSELVES. THOSE LIKE THE PEOPLE OF XUDAR.
LIKE YOU.
AS A XUDARIAN, I AM FOREVER GRATEFUL, CHILD. BUT AS YOUR MOTHER...
...YOU WENT AGAINST MY WISHES WHEN YOU FOLLOWED YOUR FATHER'S PATH.
I'LL NOT ALLOW MYSELF TO MOURN ANOTHER TOMAR LOST.
MOTHER...
I'M SORRY, TOMAR-TU...I KNOW WHAT YOU'RE GOING THROUGH.
AFTER MY DAD DIED IN THE COCKPIT, ALL I WANTED WAS TO BE A PILOT LIKE HIM. MOM STOPPED SPEAKING TO ME WHEN I JOINED THE AIR FORCE.
IT DROVE A WEDGE BETWEEN US, BUT I LIKE TO THINK MY DAD WOULD'VE BEEN PROUD OF ME.
LIKE YOURS IS OF YOU.
MY FATHER IS GONE.
I'LL NEVER KNOW WHAT HE THINKS OF ME.
WHEN I BLEW UP WARWORLD, I DISSOLVED INTO LIGHT. I...WENT SOMEWHERE.
THE EMERALD SPACE.
IT WAS FILLED WITH THE SOULS OF EVERY GREEN LANTERN WHO DIED IN THE LINE OF DUTY.
YOUR DAD WAS THERE.
HE HAD SO MUCH PRIDE IN HIS EYES WHEN I TOLD HIM YOU TOOK UP HIS RING.
THIS IS A GIFT I NEVER IMAGINED I'D RECEIVE. THANK YOU, HAL.
BUT TELL ME...YOUR MOTHER?
WHEN DID YOU RECONCILE WITH HER?
I MISSED MY CHANCE...
...WHICH IS WHY YOU SHOULDN'T WAIT FOR YOURS.

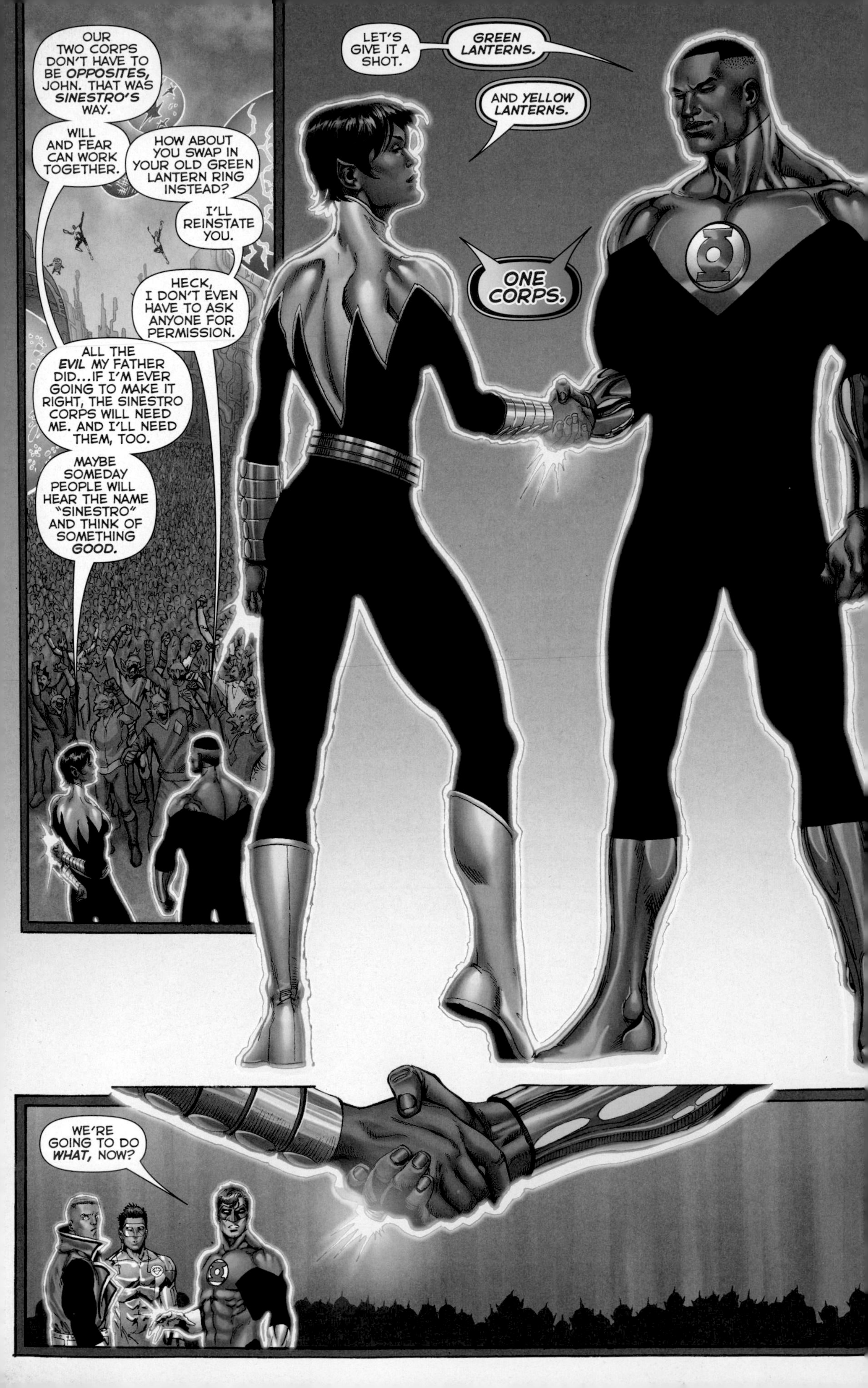
OUR TWO CORPS DON'T HAVE TO BE OPPOSITES, JOHN. THAT WAS SINESTRO'S WAY.
WILL AND FEAR CAN WORK TOGETHER.
HOW ABOUT YOU SWAP IN YOUR OLD GREEN LANTERN RING INSTEAD?
I'LL REINSTATE YOU.
HECK, I DON'T EVEN HAVE TO ASK ANYONE FOR PERMISSION.
ALL THE EVIL MY FATHER DID...IF I'M EVER GOING TO MAKE IT RIGHT, THE SINESTRO CORPS WILL NEED ME. AND I'LL NEED THEM, TOO.
MAYBE SOMEDAY PEOPLE WILL HEAR THE NAME "SINESTRO" AND THINK OF SOMETHING GOOD.
LET'S GIVE IT A SHOT.
GREEN LANTERNS.
AND YELLOW LANTERNS.
ONE CORPS.
WE'RE GOING TO DO WHAT, NOW?

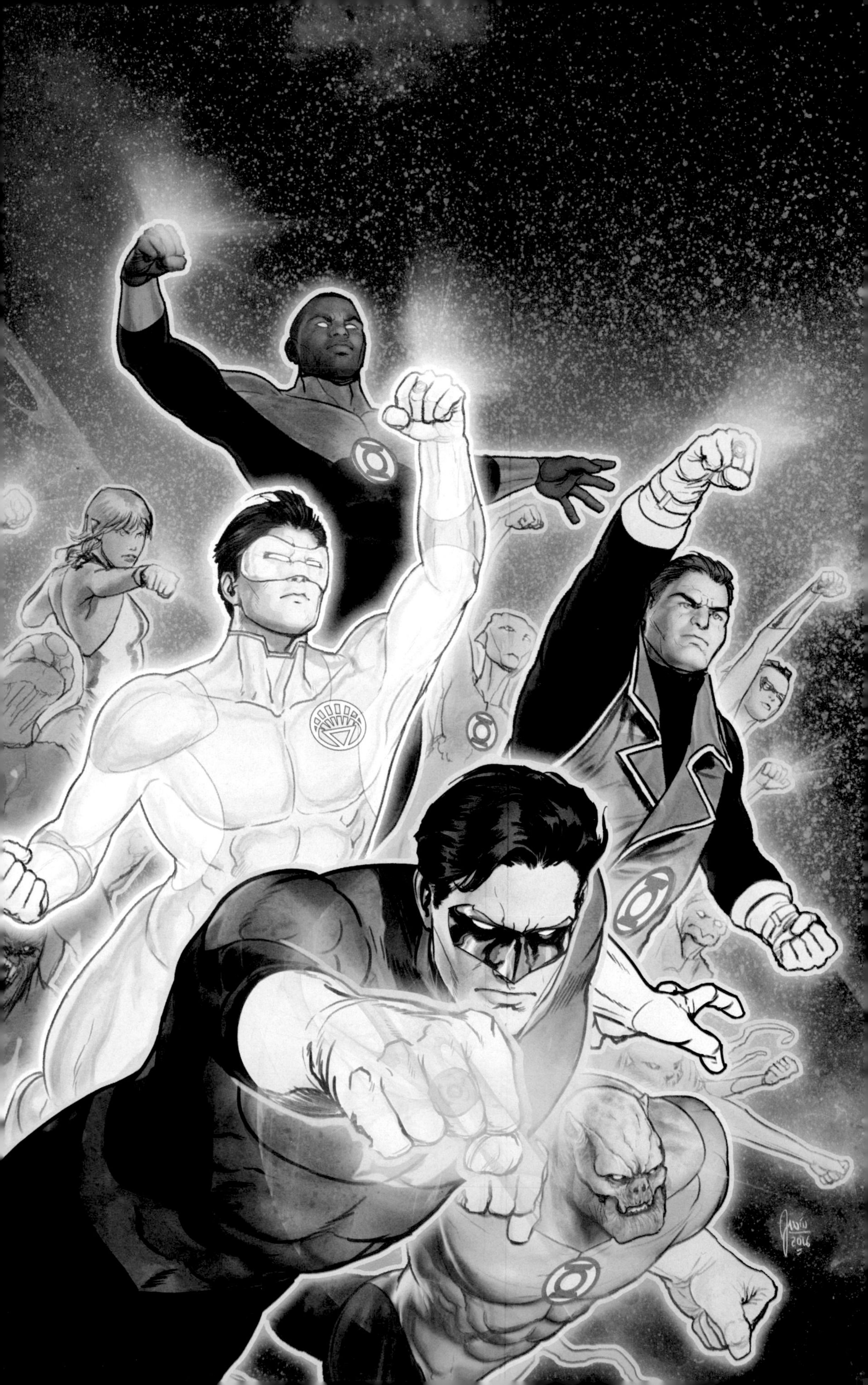

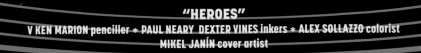

"HEROES"
V KEN MARION penciller ✴ **PAUL NEARY DEXTER VINES** inkers ✴ **ALEX SOLLAZZO** colorist
MIKEL JANÍN cover artist

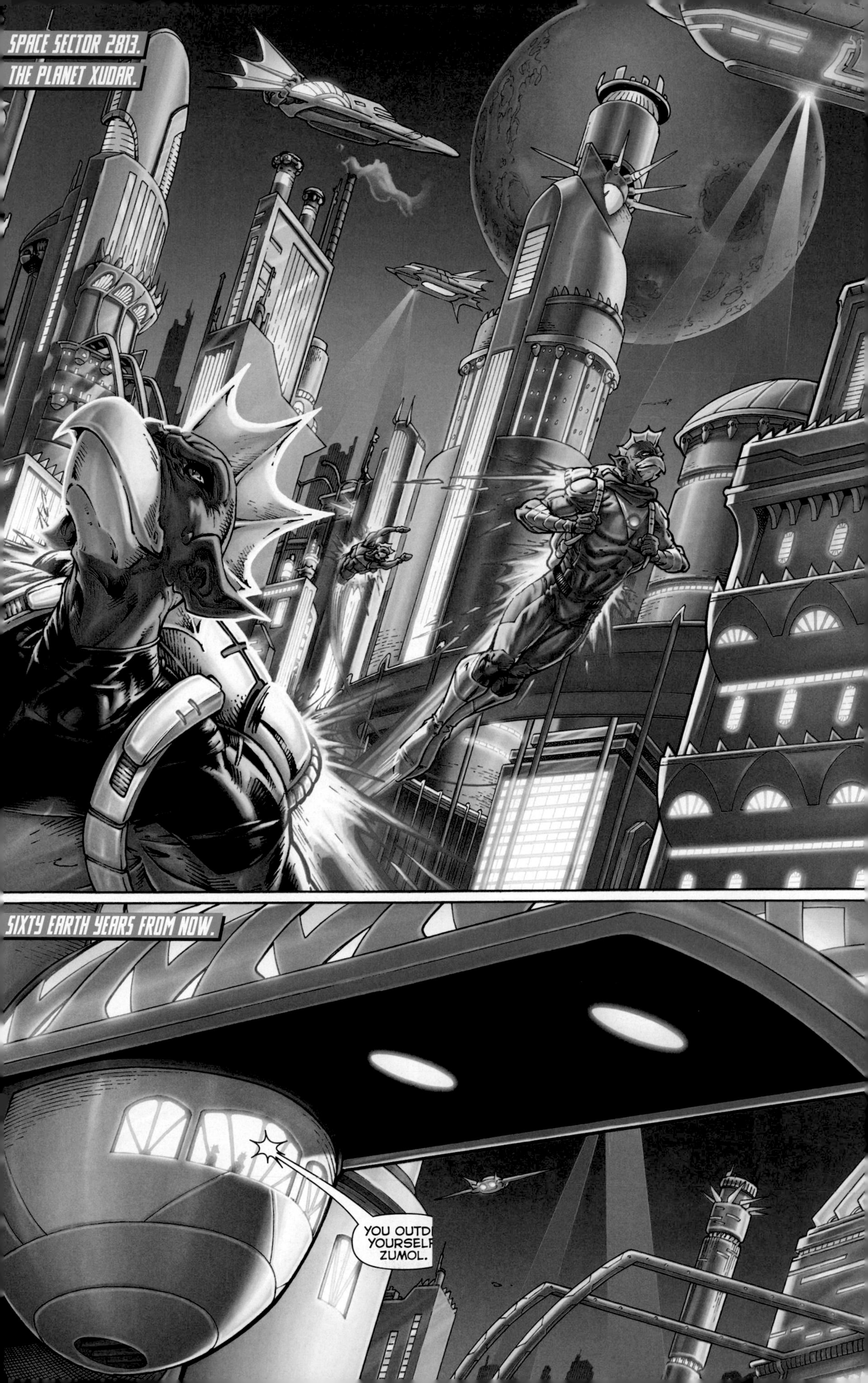
SPACE SECTOR 2813.
THE PLANET XUDAR.
SIXTY EARTH YEARS FROM NOW.
YOU OUTD YOURSELF ZUMOL.

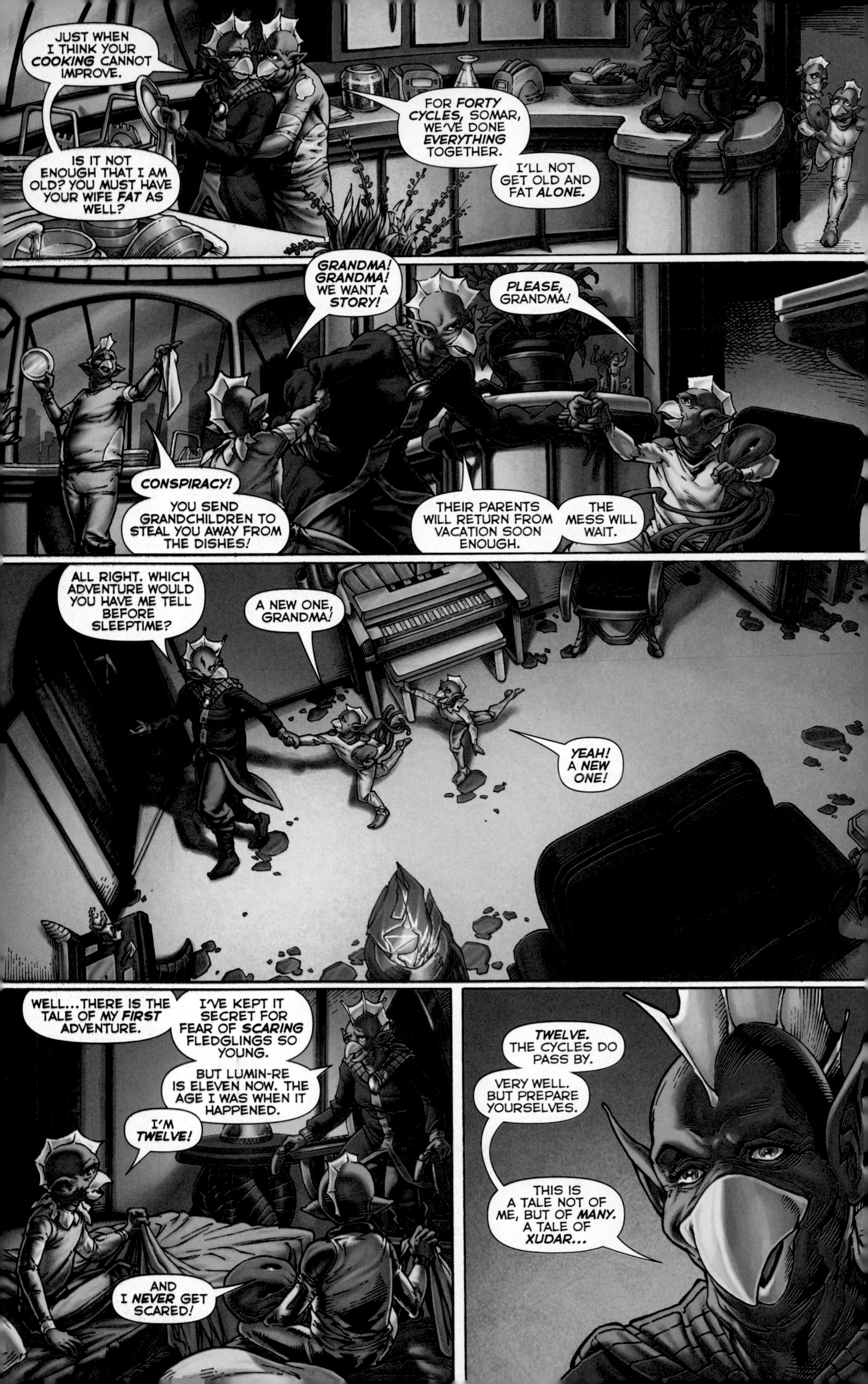
JUST WHEN I THINK YOUR COOKING CANNOT IMPROVE.
IS IT NOT ENOUGH THAT I AM OLD? YOU MUST HAVE YOUR WIFE FAT AS WELL?
FOR FORTY CYCLES, SOMAR, WE'VE DONE EVERYTHING TOGETHER.
I'LL NOT GET OLD AND FAT ALONE.
GRANDMA! GRANDMA! WE WANT A STORY!
PLEASE, GRANDMA!
CONSPIRACY!
YOU SEND GRANDCHILDREN TO STEAL YOU AWAY FROM THE DISHES!
THEIR PARENTS WILL RETURN FROM VACATION SOON ENOUGH.
THE MESS WILL WAIT.
ALL RIGHT. WHICH ADVENTURE WOULD YOU HAVE ME TELL BEFORE SLEEPTIME?
A NEW ONE, GRANDMA!
YEAH! A NEW ONE!
WELL...THERE IS THE TALE OF MY FIRST ADVENTURE.
I'VE KEPT IT SECRET FOR FEAR OF SCARING FLEDGLINGS SO YOUNG.
BUT LUMIN-RE IS ELEVEN NOW. THE AGE I WAS WHEN IT HAPPENED.
I'M TWELVE!
AND I NEVER GET SCARED!
TWELVE. THE CYCLES DO PASS BY.
VERY WELL. BUT PREPARE YOURSELVES.
THIS IS A TALE NOT OF ME, BUT OF MANY. A TALE OF XUDAR...

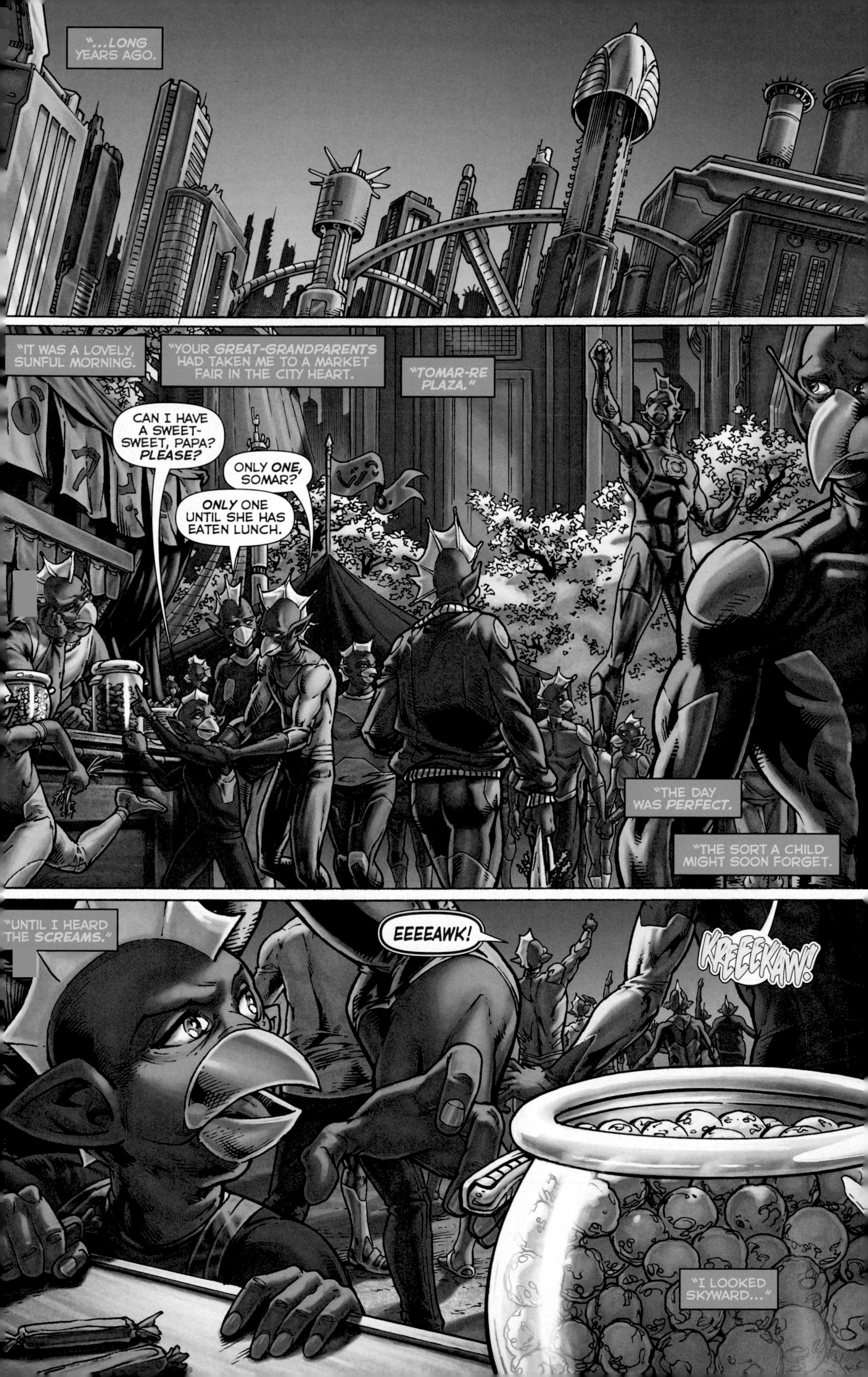
"...LONG YEARS AGO.
"IT WAS A LOVELY, SUNFUL MORNING.
"YOUR GREAT-GRANDPARENTS HAD TAKEN ME TO A MARKET FAIR IN THE CITY HEART.
"TOMAR-RE PLAZA."
CAN I HAVE A SWEET-SWEET, PAPA? PLEASE?
ONLY ONE, SOMAR?
ONLY ONE UNTIL SHE HAS EATEN LUNCH.
"THE DAY WAS PERFECT.
"THE SORT A CHILD MIGHT SOON FORGET.
"UNTIL I HEARD THE SCREAMS."
EEEEAWK!
KREEEKAW!
"I LOOKED SKYWARD..."

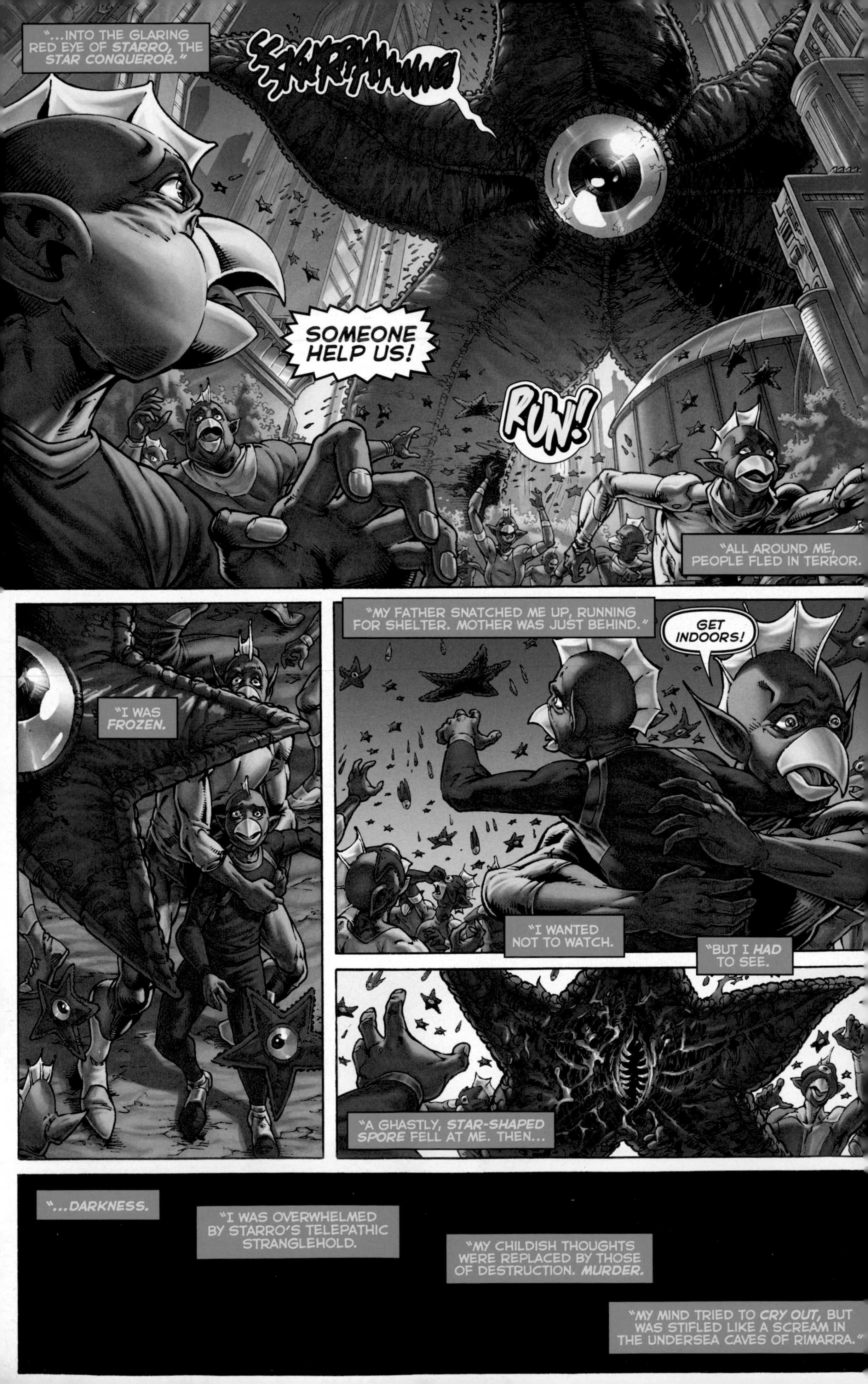
"...INTO THE GLARING RED EYE OF *STARRO*, THE *STAR CONQUEROR*."
SOMEONE HELP US!
RUN!
"ALL AROUND ME, PEOPLE FLED IN TERROR.
"I WAS *FROZEN.*
"MY FATHER SNATCHED ME UP, RUNNING FOR SHELTER. MOTHER WAS JUST BEHIND."
GET INDOORS!
"I WANTED NOT TO WATCH.
"BUT I *HAD* TO SEE.
"A GHASTLY, *STAR-SHAPED SPORE* FELL AT ME. THEN...
"...*DARKNESS.*
"I WAS OVERWHELMED BY STARRO'S TELEPATHIC STRANGLEHOLD.
"MY CHILDISH THOUGHTS WERE REPLACED BY THOSE OF DESTRUCTION. *MURDER.*
"MY MIND TRIED TO *CRY OUT*, BUT WAS STIFLED LIKE A SCREAM IN THE UNDERSEA CAVES OF RIMARRA."

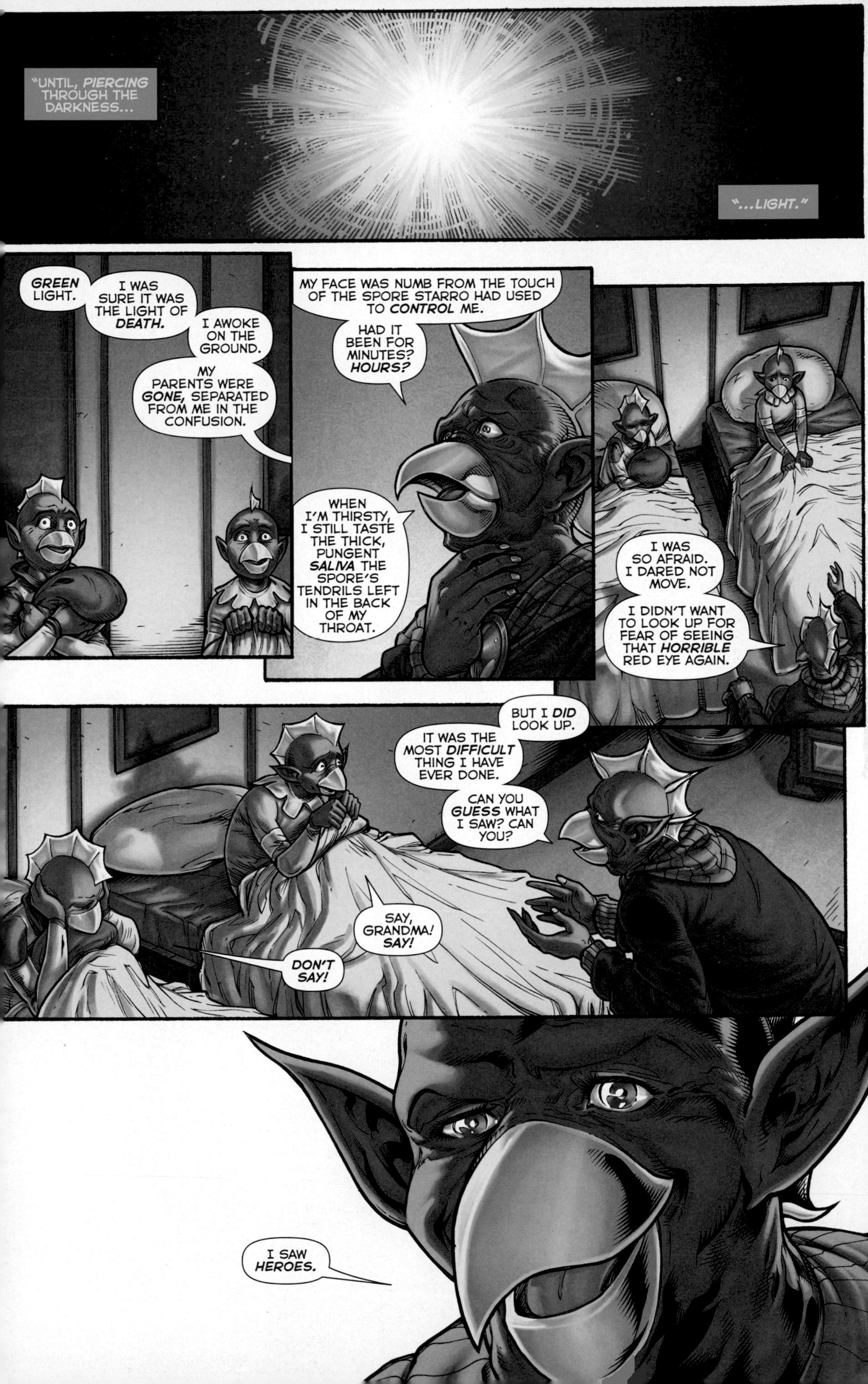
"UNTIL, PIERCING THROUGH THE DARKNESS...
"...LIGHT."
GREEN LIGHT.
I WAS SURE IT WAS THE LIGHT OF DEATH.
I AWOKE ON THE GROUND.
MY PARENTS WERE GONE, SEPARATED FROM ME IN THE CONFUSION.
MY FACE WAS NUMB FROM THE TOUCH OF THE SPORE STARRO HAD USED TO CONTROL ME.
HAD IT BEEN FOR MINUTES? HOURS?
WHEN I'M THIRSTY, I STILL TASTE THE THICK, PUNGENT SALIVA THE SPORE'S TENDRILS LEFT IN THE BACK OF MY THROAT.
I WAS SO AFRAID. I DARED NOT MOVE.
I DIDN'T WANT TO LOOK UP FOR FEAR OF SEEING THAT HORRIBLE RED EYE AGAIN.
BUT I DID LOOK UP.
IT WAS THE MOST DIFFICULT THING I HAVE EVER DONE.
CAN YOU GUESS WHAT I SAW? CAN YOU?
SAY, GRANDMA! SAY!
DON'T SAY!
I SAW HEROES.

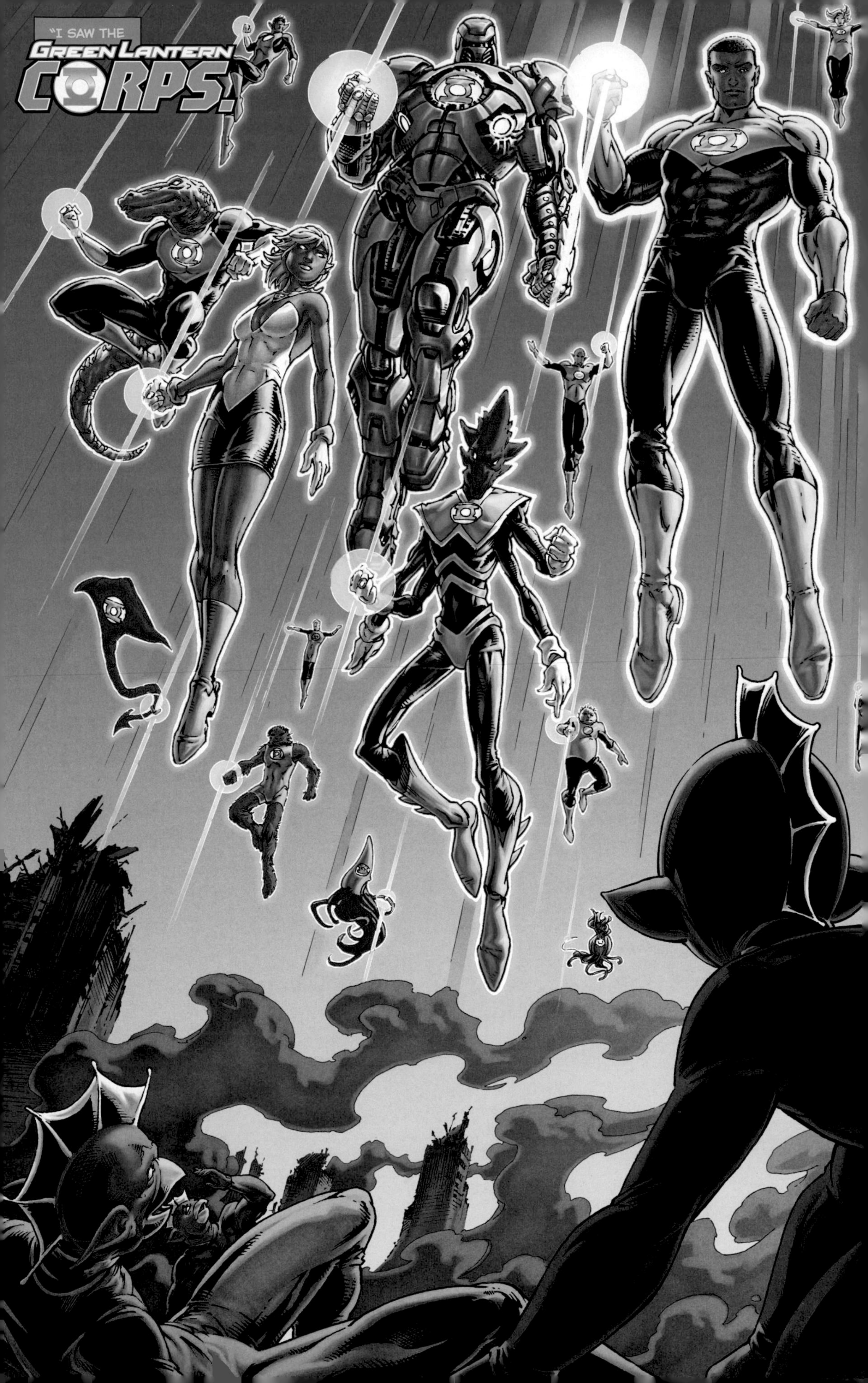
"I SAW THE
GREEN LANTERN
CORPS!

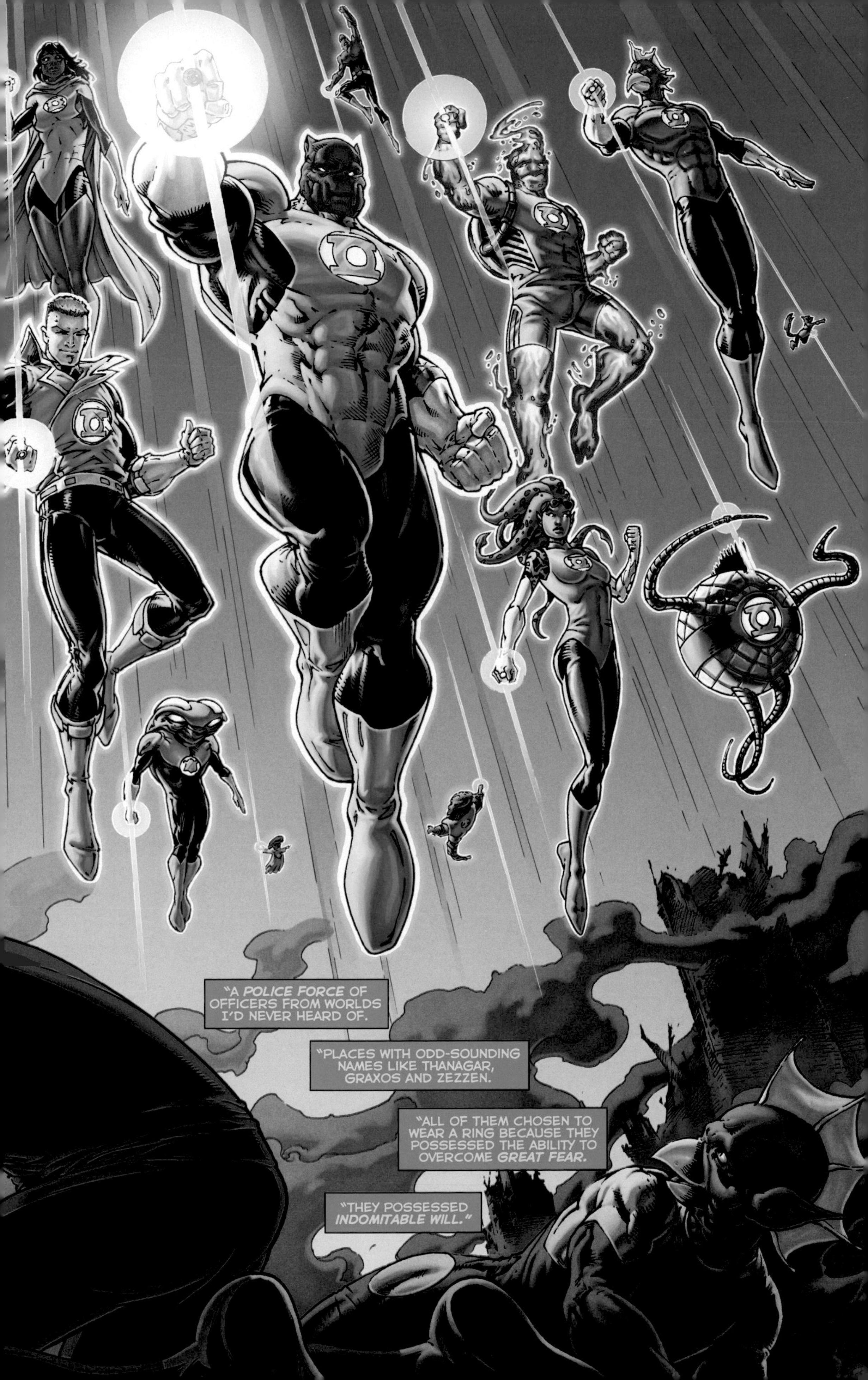
"A POLICE FORCE OF OFFICERS FROM WORLDS I'D NEVER HEARD OF.
"PLACES WITH ODD-SOUNDING NAMES LIKE THANAGAR, GRAXOS AND ZEZZEN.
"ALL OF THEM CHOSEN TO WEAR A RING BECAUSE THEY POSSESSED THE ABILITY TO OVERCOME GREAT FEAR.
"THEY POSSESSED INDOMITABLE WILL."

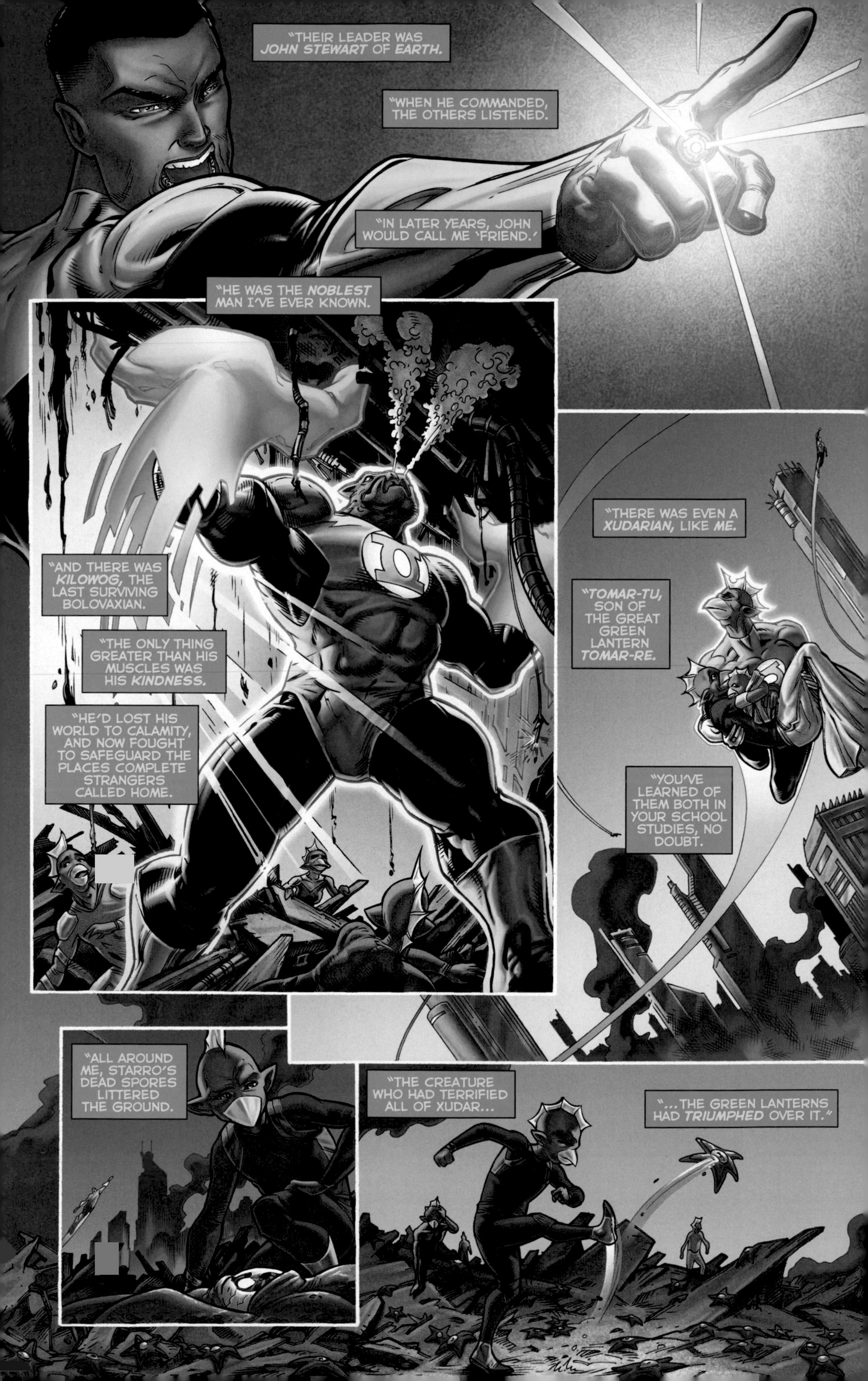
"THEIR LEADER WAS JOHN STEWART OF EARTH.
"WHEN HE COMMANDED, THE OTHERS LISTENED.
"IN LATER YEARS, JOHN WOULD CALL ME 'FRIEND.'
"HE WAS THE NOBLEST MAN I'VE EVER KNOWN.
"AND THERE WAS KILOWOG, THE LAST SURVIVING BOLOVAXIAN.
"THE ONLY THING GREATER THAN HIS MUSCLES WAS HIS KINDNESS.
"HE'D LOST HIS WORLD TO CALAMITY, AND NOW FOUGHT TO SAFEGUARD THE PLACES COMPLETE STRANGERS CALLED HOME.
"THERE WAS EVEN A XUDARIAN, LIKE ME.
"TOMAR-TU, SON OF THE GREAT GREEN LANTERN TOMAR-RE.
"YOU'VE LEARNED OF THEM BOTH IN YOUR SCHOOL STUDIES, NO DOUBT.
"ALL AROUND ME, STARRO'S DEAD SPORES LITTERED THE GROUND.
"THE CREATURE WHO HAD TERRIFIED ALL OF XUDAR...
"...THE GREEN LANTERNS HAD TRIUMPHED OVER IT."

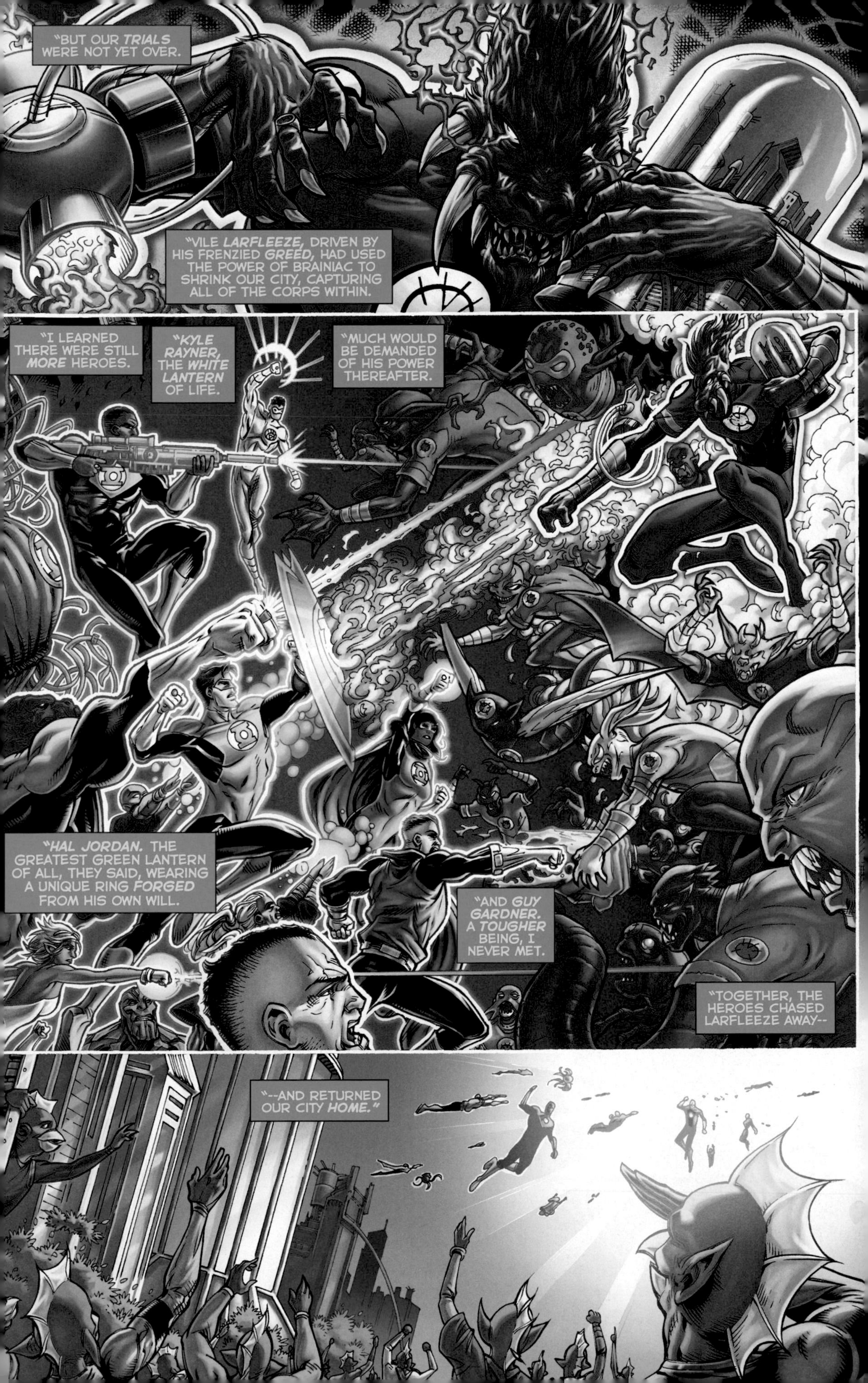
"BUT OUR *TRIALS* WERE NOT YET OVER.
"VILE *LARFLEEZE,* DRIVEN BY HIS FRENZIED *GREED,* HAD USED THE POWER OF BRAINIAC TO SHRINK OUR CITY, CAPTURING ALL OF THE CORPS WITHIN.
"I LEARNED THERE WERE STILL *MORE* HEROES.
"*KYLE RAYNER,* THE *WHITE LANTERN* OF LIFE.
"MUCH WOULD BE DEMANDED OF HIS POWER THEREAFTER.
"*HAL JORDAN.* THE GREATEST GREEN LANTERN OF ALL, THEY SAID, WEARING A UNIQUE RING *FORGED* FROM HIS OWN WILL.
"AND *GUY GARDNER.* A *TOUGHER* BEING, I NEVER MET.
"TOGETHER, THE HEROES CHASED LARFLEEZE AWAY--
"--AND RETURNED OUR CITY *HOME.*"

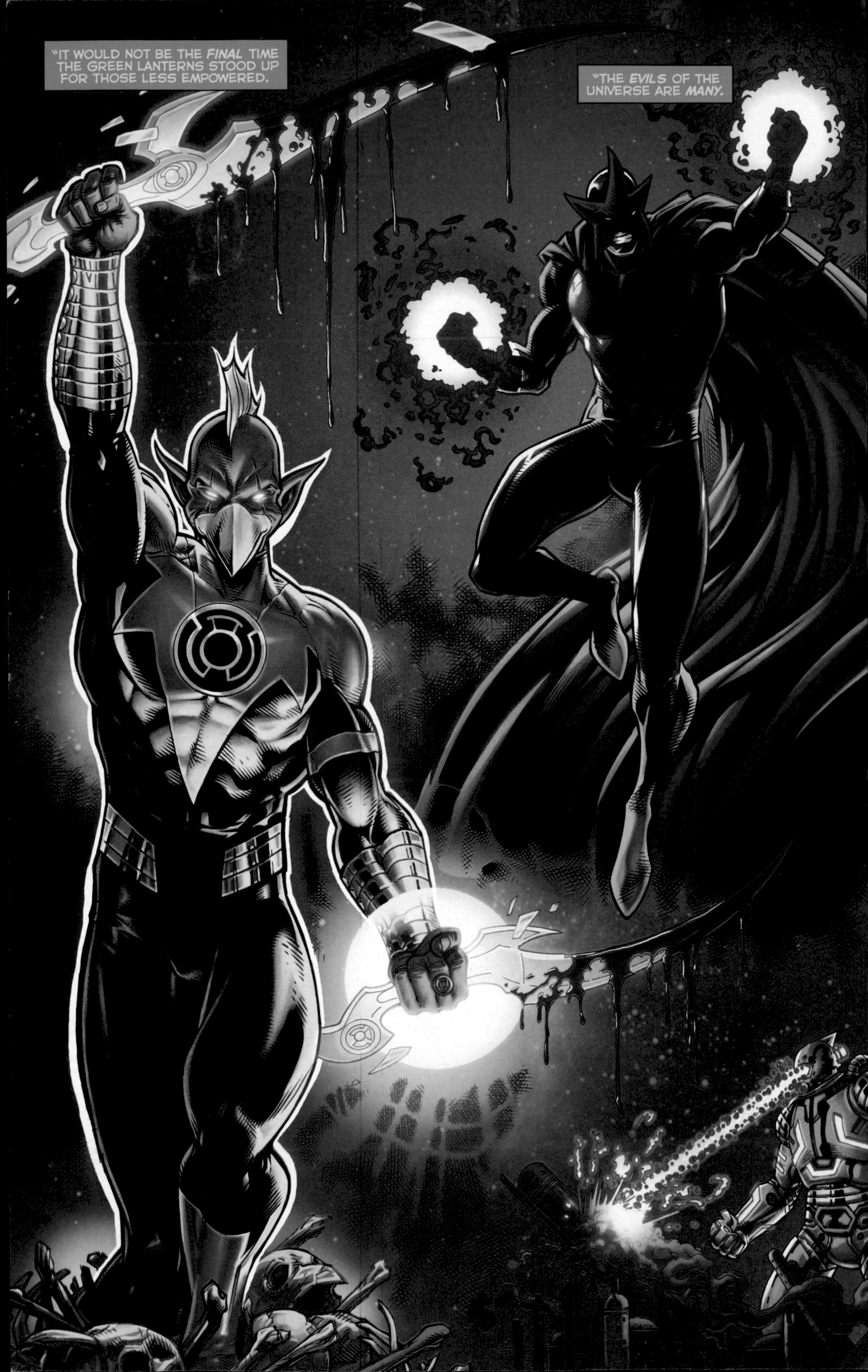
"IT WOULD NOT BE THE FINAL TIME THE GREEN LANTERNS STOOD UP FOR THOSE LESS EMPOWERED.
"THE EVILS OF THE UNIVERSE ARE MANY.

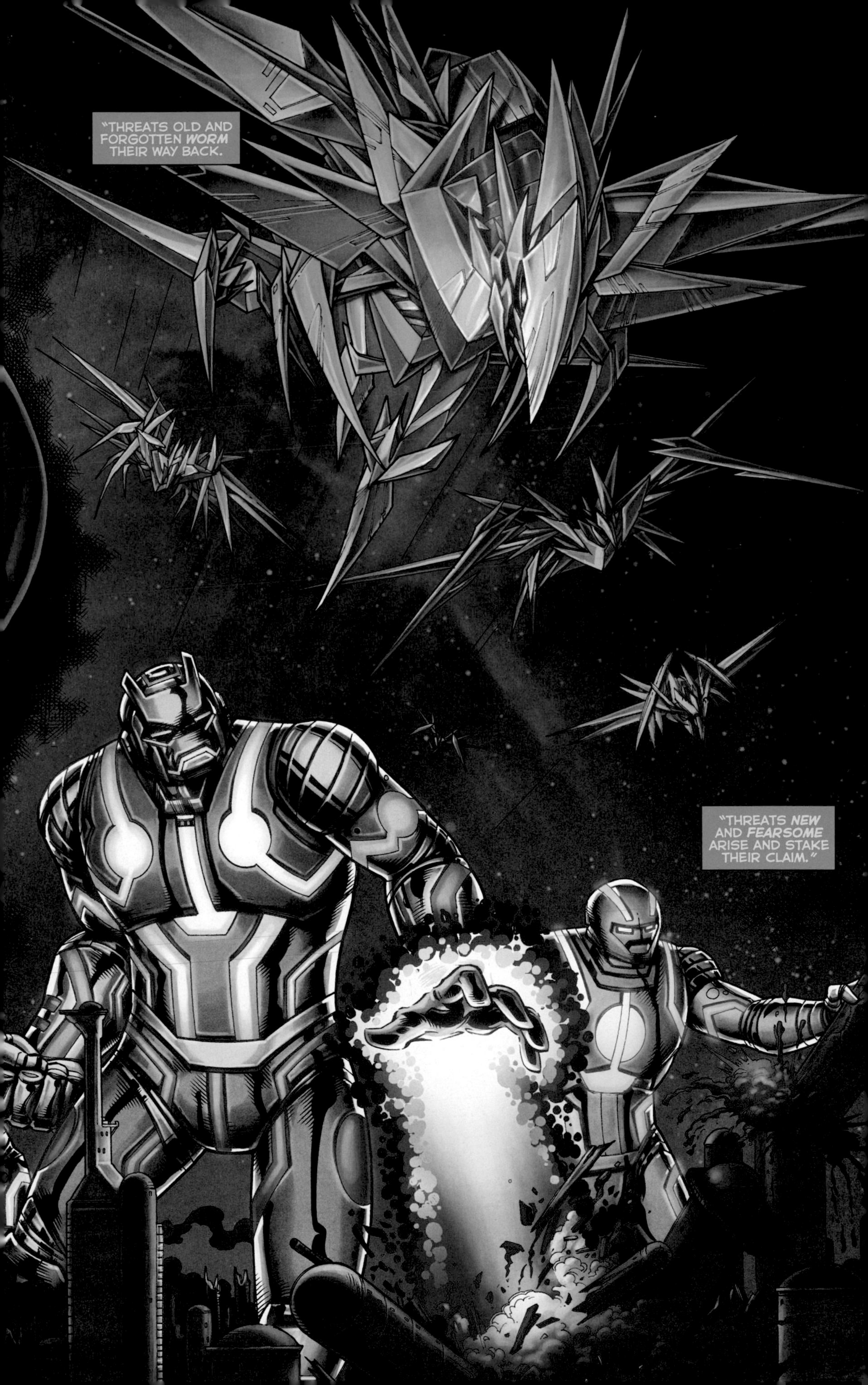
"THREATS OLD AND FORGOTTEN *WORM* THEIR WAY BACK.
"THREATS *NEW* AND *FEARSOME* ARISE AND STAKE THEIR CLAIM."

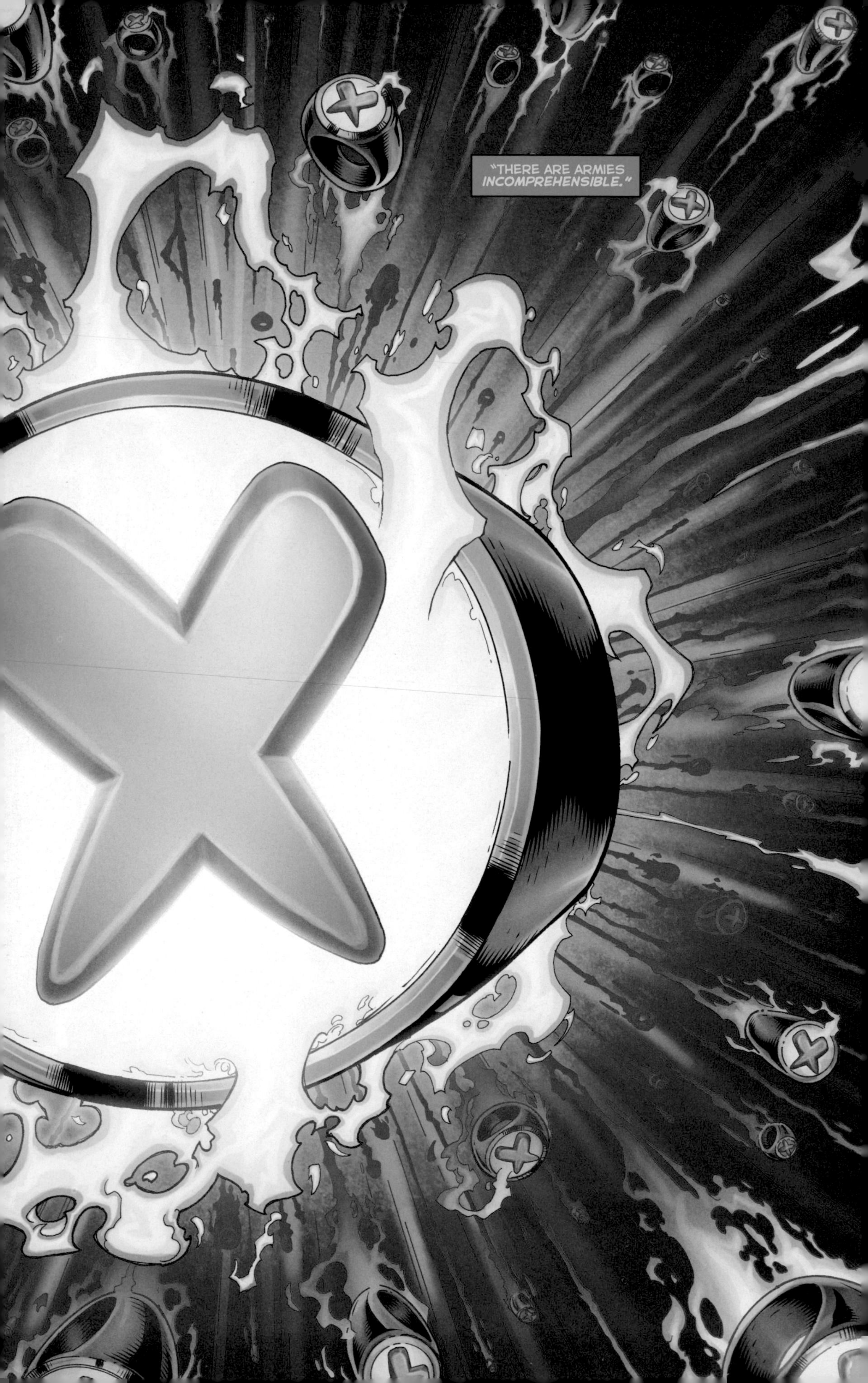
"THERE ARE ARMIES *INCOMPREHENSIBLE.*"

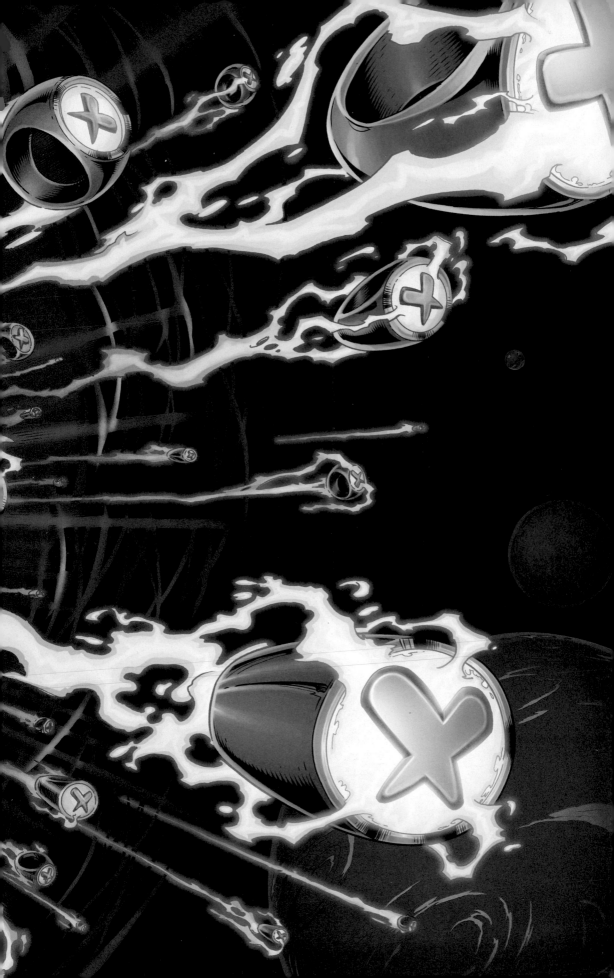

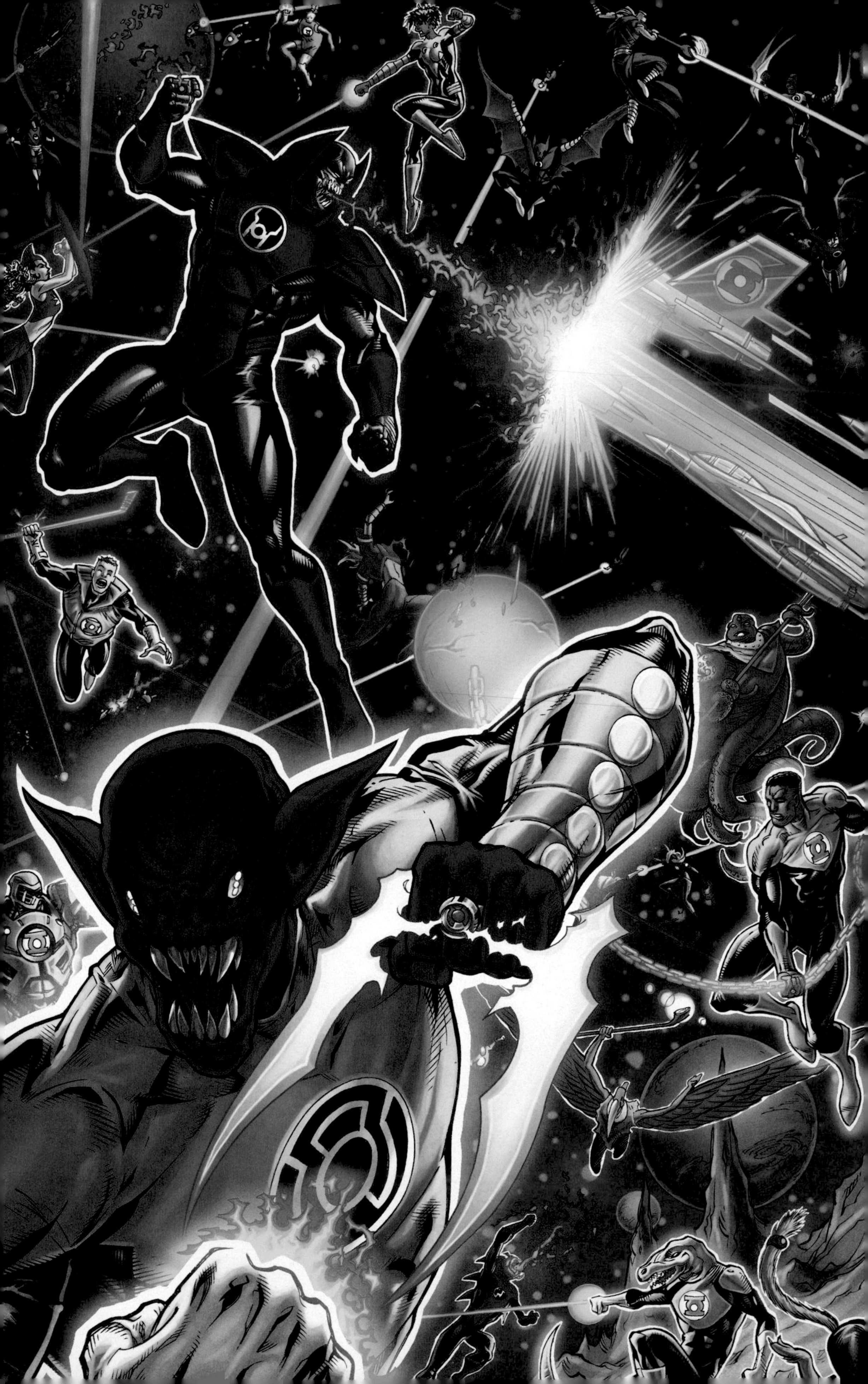

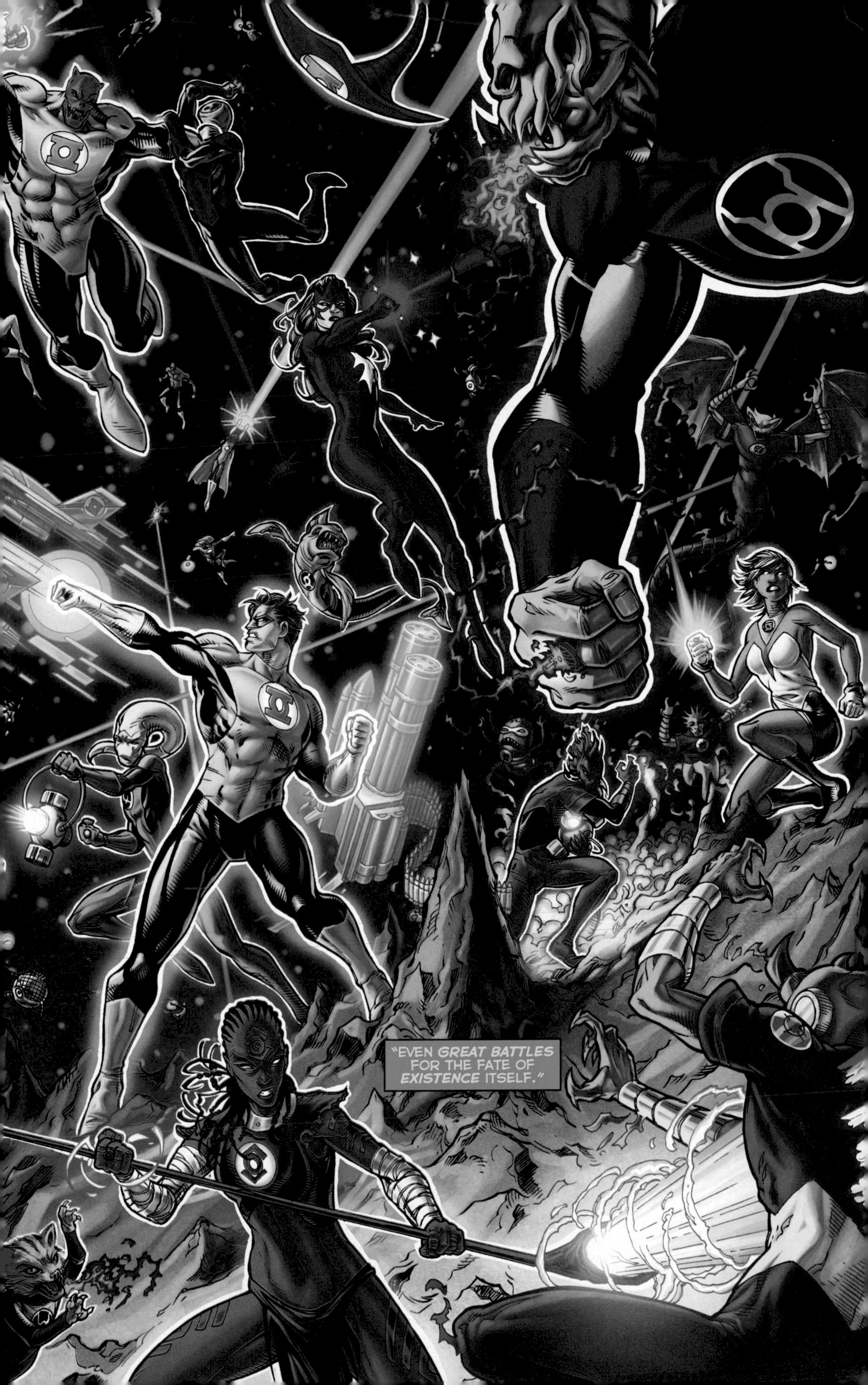
"EVEN GREAT BATTLES FOR THE FATE OF EXISTENCE ITSELF."

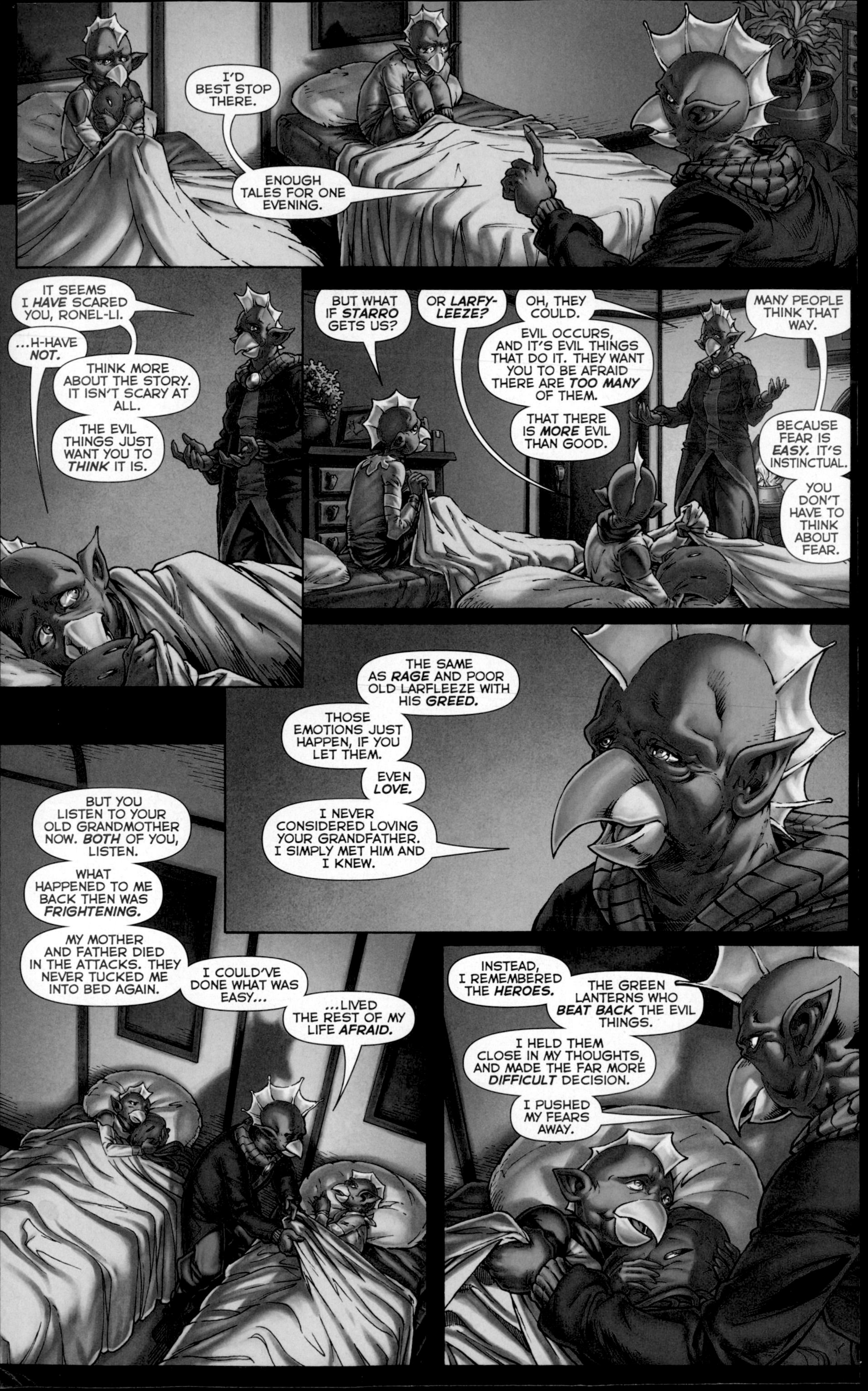
I'D BEST STOP THERE.
ENOUGH TALES FOR ONE EVENING.
IT SEEMS I HAVE SCARED YOU, RONEL-LI.
...H-HAVE NOT.
THINK MORE ABOUT THE STORY. IT ISN'T SCARY AT ALL.
THE EVIL THINGS JUST WANT YOU TO THINK IT IS.
BUT WHAT IF STARRO GETS US?
OR LARFY-LEEZE?
OH, THEY COULD.
EVIL OCCURS, AND IT'S EVIL THINGS THAT DO IT. THEY WANT YOU TO BE AFRAID THERE ARE TOO MANY OF THEM.
THAT THERE IS MORE EVIL THAN GOOD.
MANY PEOPLE THINK THAT WAY.
BECAUSE FEAR IS EASY. IT'S INSTINCTUAL.
YOU DON'T HAVE TO THINK ABOUT FEAR.
THE SAME AS RAGE AND POOR OLD LARFLEEZE WITH HIS GREED.
THOSE EMOTIONS JUST HAPPEN, IF YOU LET THEM.
EVEN LOVE.
I NEVER CONSIDERED LOVING YOUR GRANDFATHER. I SIMPLY MET HIM AND I KNEW.
BUT YOU LISTEN TO YOUR OLD GRANDMOTHER NOW. BOTH OF YOU, LISTEN.
WHAT HAPPENED TO ME BACK THEN WAS FRIGHTENING.
MY MOTHER AND FATHER DIED IN THE ATTACKS. THEY NEVER TUCKED ME INTO BED AGAIN.
I COULD'VE DONE WHAT WAS EASY...
...LIVED THE REST OF MY LIFE AFRAID.
INSTEAD, I REMEMBERED THE HEROES.
THE GREEN LANTERNS WHO BEAT BACK THE EVIL THINGS.
I HELD THEM CLOSE IN MY THOUGHTS, AND MADE THE FAR MORE DIFFICULT DECISION.
I PUSHED MY FEARS AWAY.

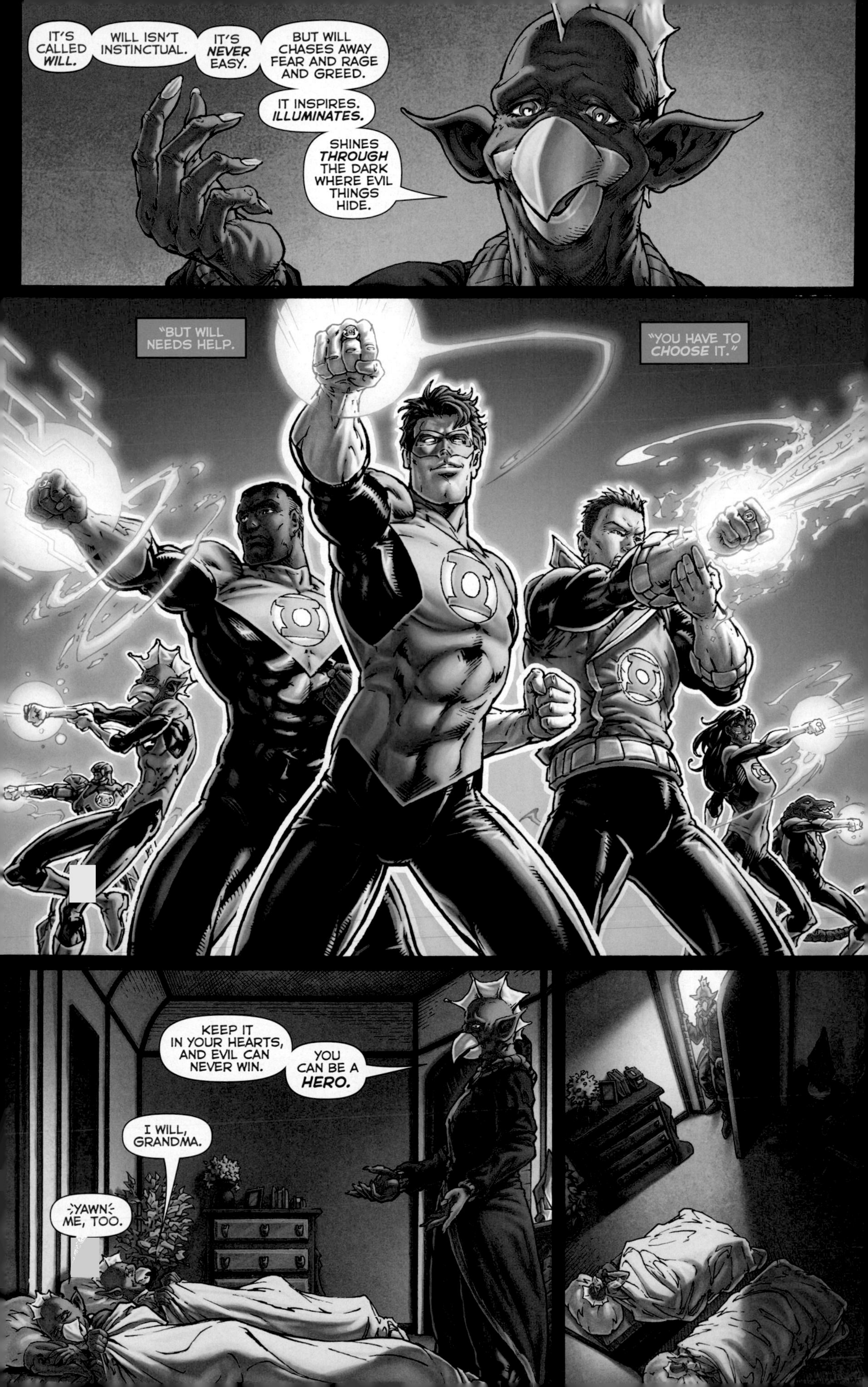
IT'S CALLED WILL.
WILL ISN'T INSTINCTUAL.
IT'S NEVER EASY.
BUT WILL CHASES AWAY FEAR AND RAGE AND GREED.
IT INSPIRES. ILLUMINATES.
SHINES THROUGH THE DARK WHERE EVIL THINGS HIDE.
"BUT WILL NEEDS HELP.
"YOU HAVE TO CHOOSE IT."
KEEP IT IN YOUR HEARTS, AND EVIL CAN NEVER WIN.
YOU CAN BE A HERO.
I WILL, GRANDMA.
YAWN
ME, TOO.

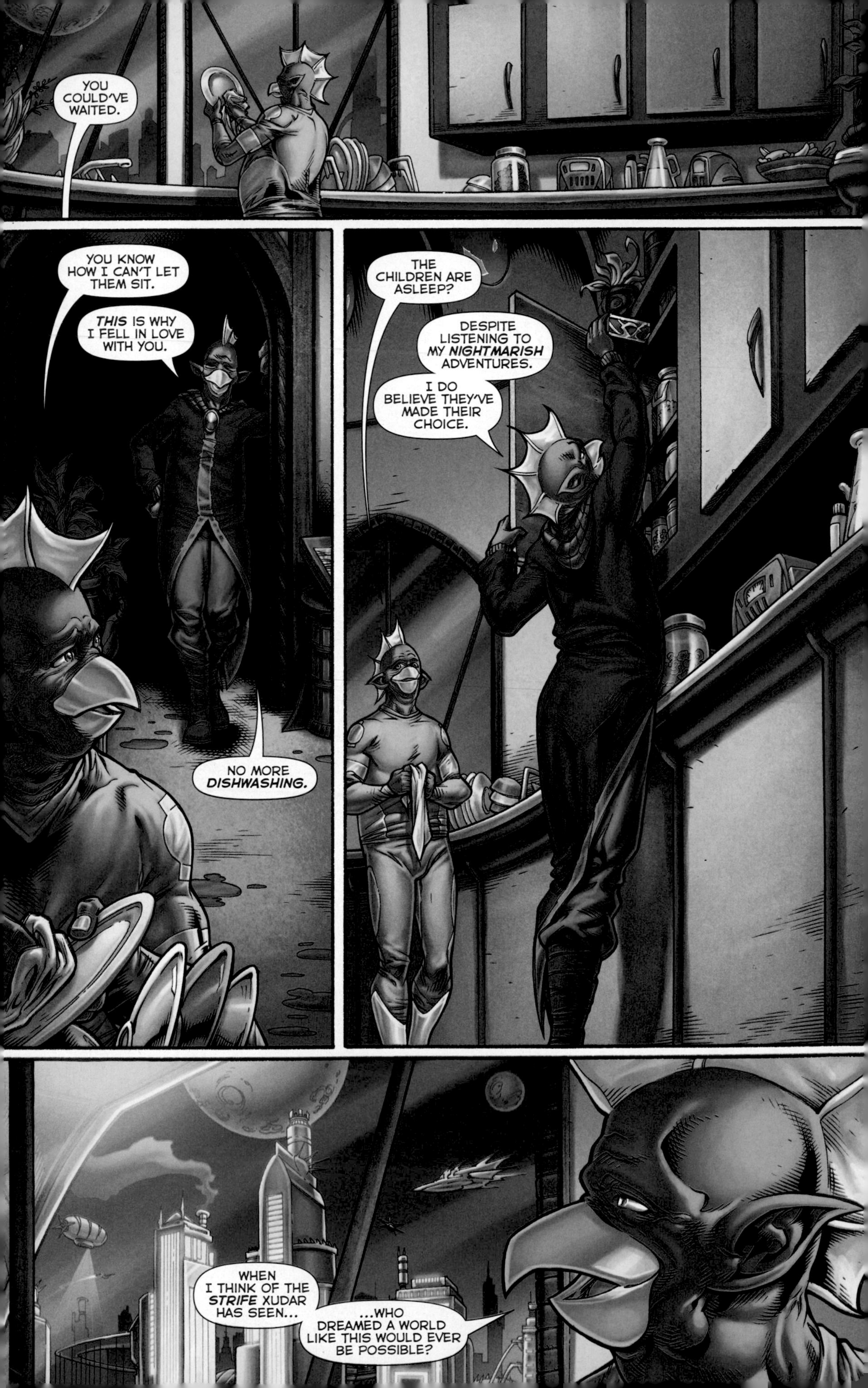
YOU COULD'VE WAITED.
YOU KNOW HOW I CAN'T LET THEM SIT.
THIS IS WHY I FELL IN LOVE WITH YOU.
NO MORE *DISHWASHING.*
THE CHILDREN ARE ASLEEP?
DESPITE LISTENING TO *MY NIGHTMARISH* ADVENTURES.
I DO BELIEVE THEY'VE MADE THEIR CHOICE.
WHEN I THINK OF THE *STRIFE* XUDAR HAS SEEN...
...WHO DREAMED A WORLD LIKE THIS WOULD EVER BE POSSIBLE?

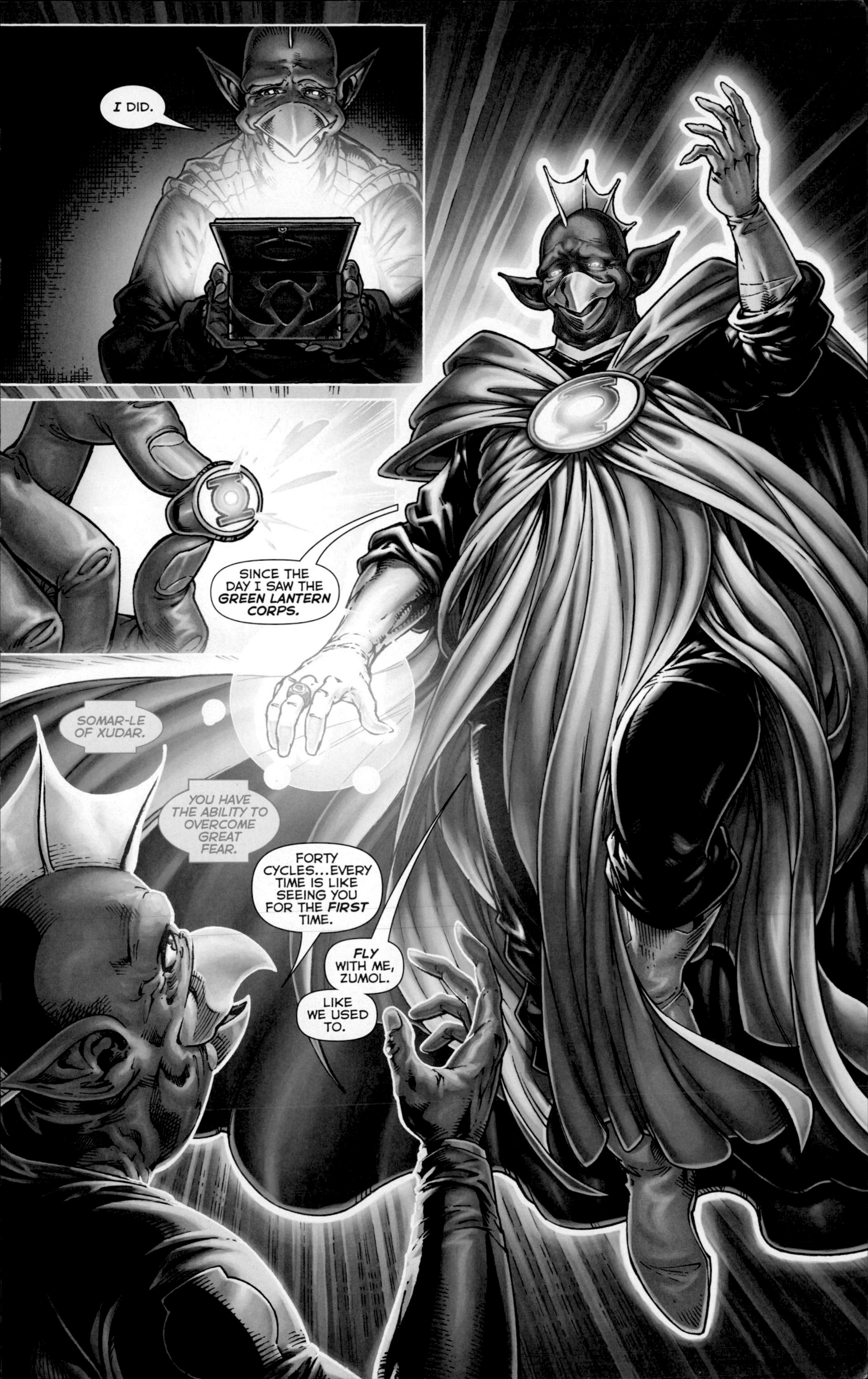
I DID.
SINCE THE DAY I SAW THE GREEN LANTERN CORPS.
SOMAR-LE OF XUDAR.
YOU HAVE THE ABILITY TO OVERCOME GREAT FEAR.
FORTY CYCLES...EVERY TIME IS LIKE SEEING YOU FOR THE FIRST TIME.
FLY WITH ME, ZUMOL.
LIKE WE USED TO.

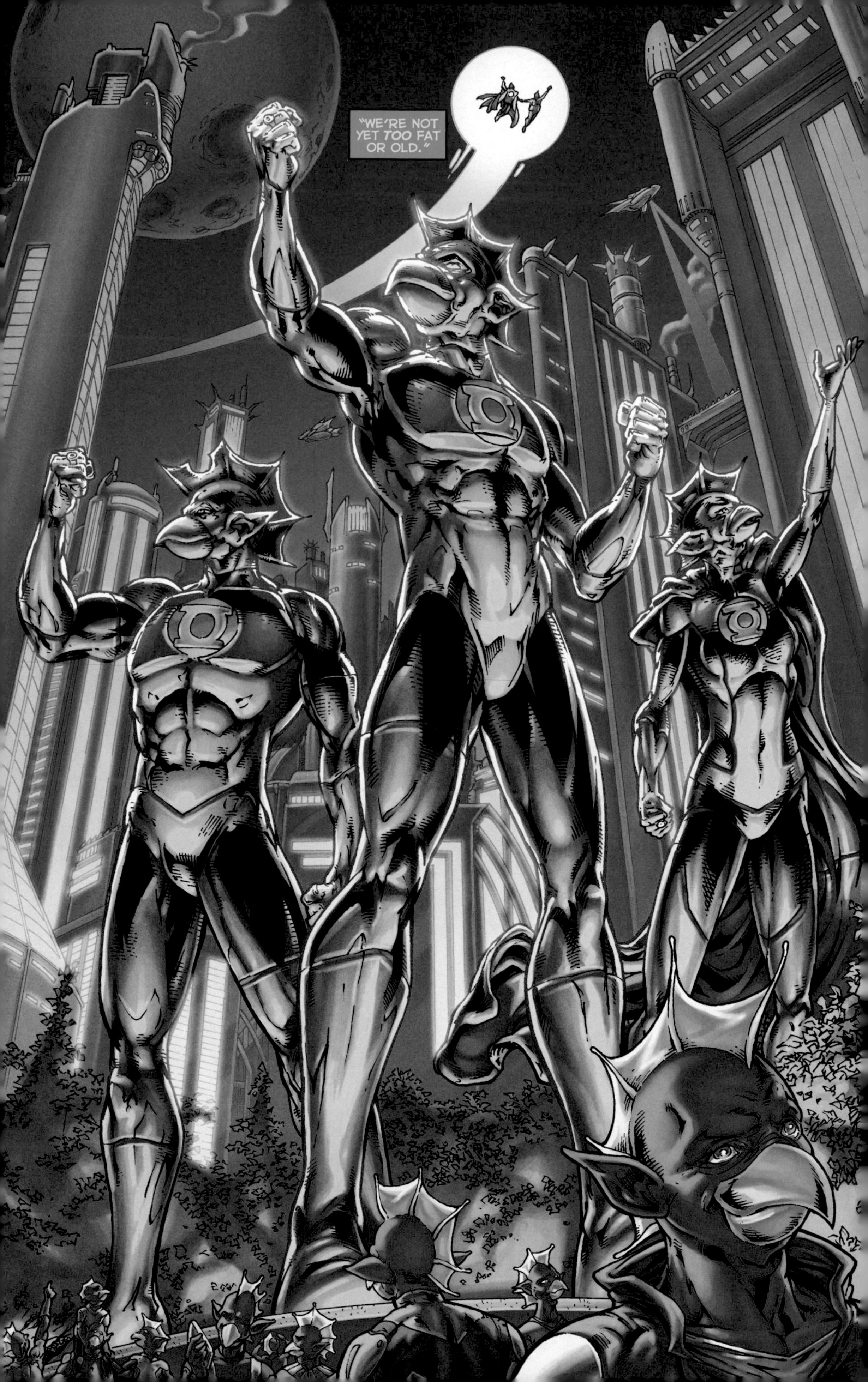
"WE'RE NOT YET *TOO* FAT OR OLD."

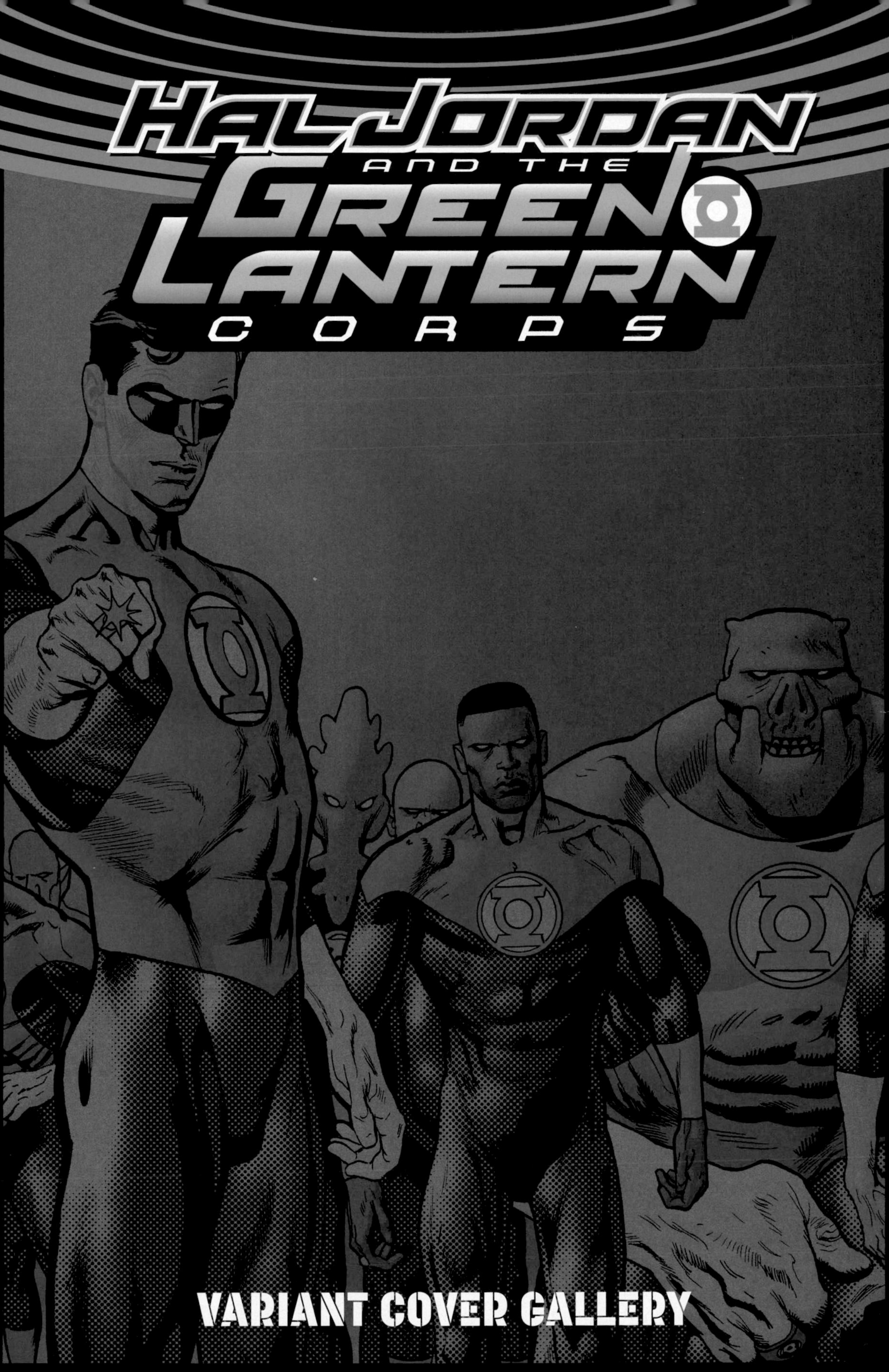
HAL JORDAN
AND THE
GREEN LANTERN
CORPS
VARIANT COVER GALLERY

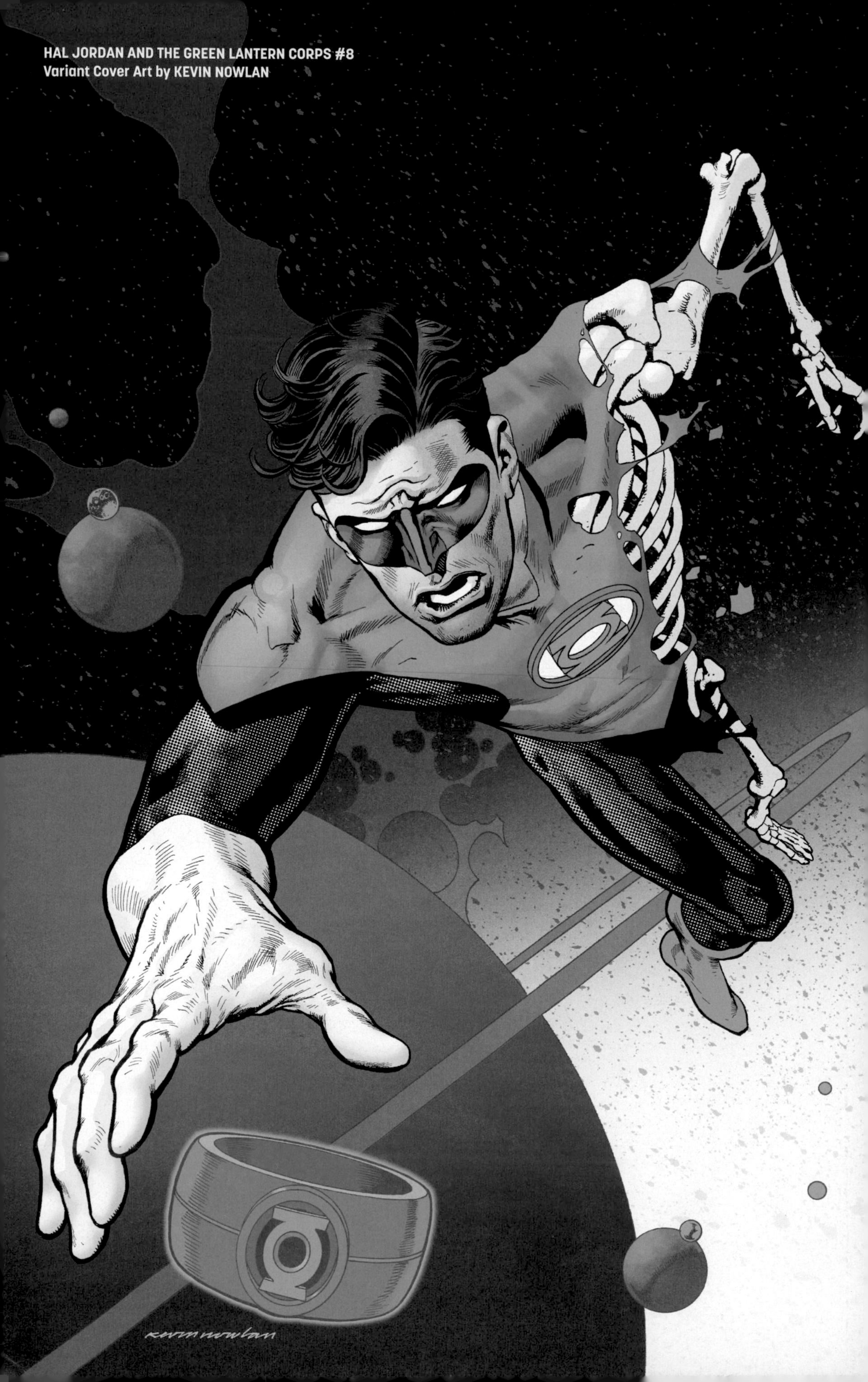

HAL JORDAN AND THE GREEN LANTERN CORPS #8
Variant Cover Art by KEVIN NOWLAN

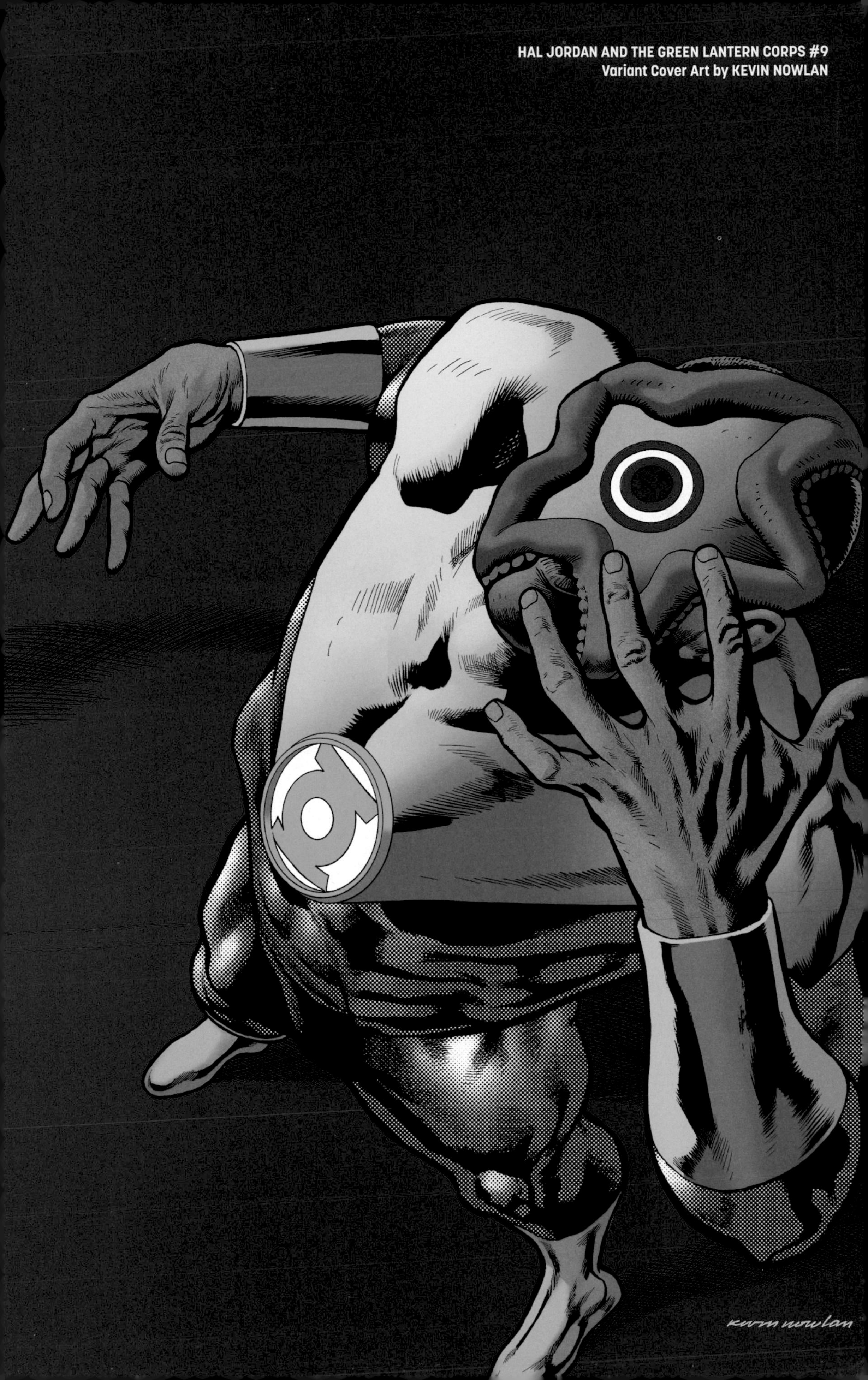
kevin nowlan

HAL JORDAN AND THE GREEN LANTERN CORPS #9
Variant Cover Art by KEVIN NOWLAN

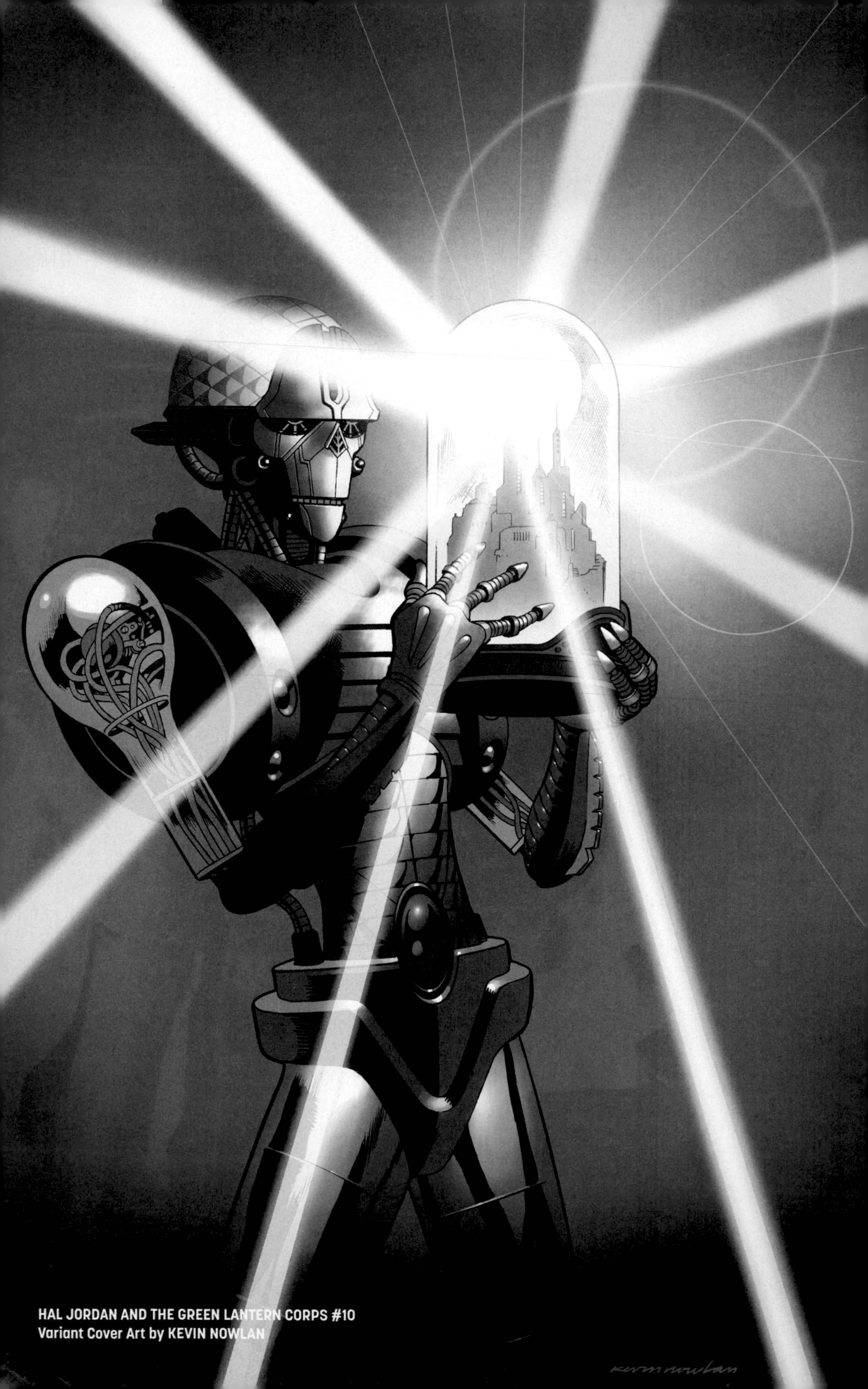

HAL JORDAN AND THE GREEN LANTERN CORPS #10
Variant Cover Art by KEVIN NOWLAN

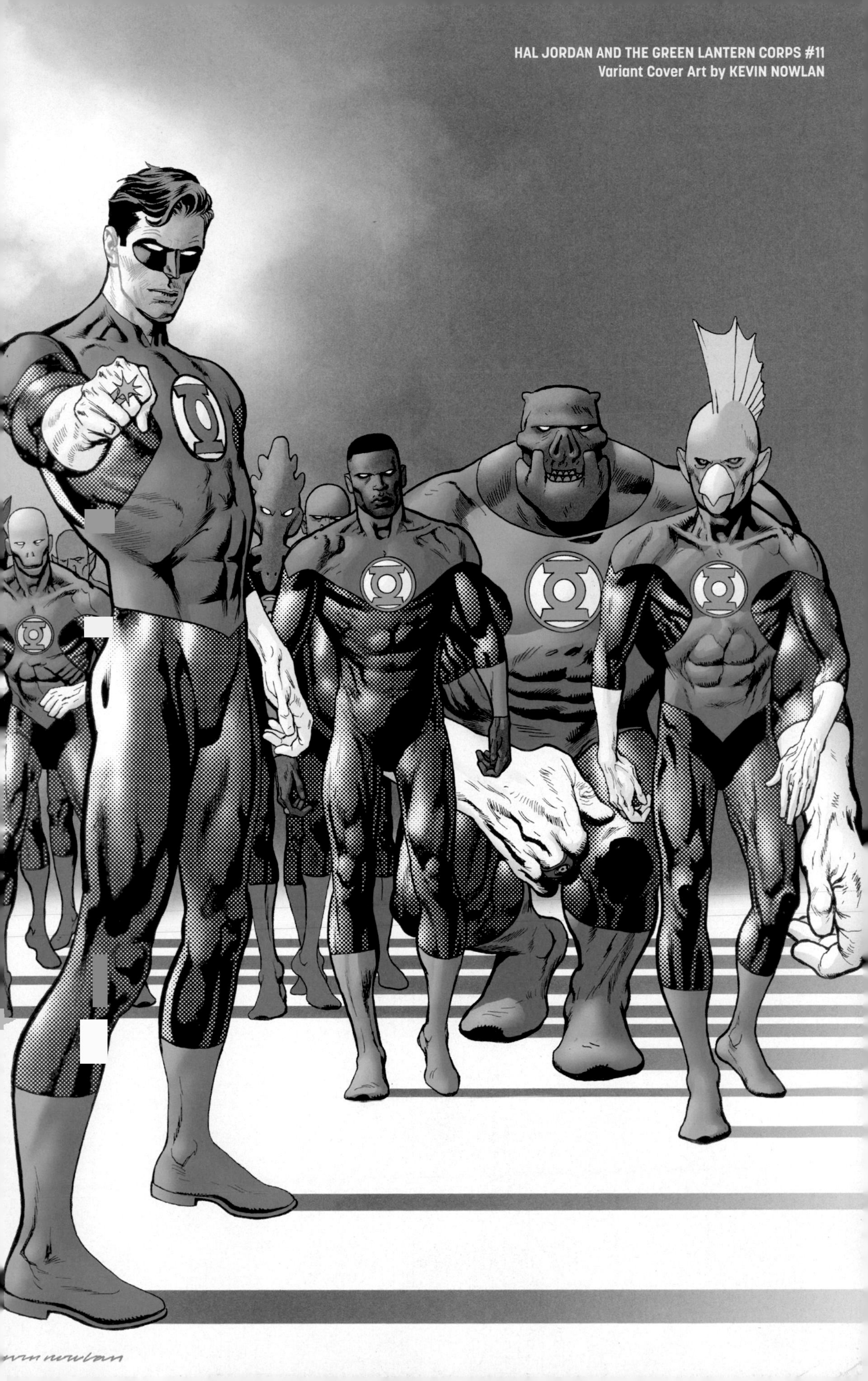

HAL JORDAN AND THE GREEN LANTERN CORPS #11
Variant Cover Art by KEVIN NOWLAN

HAL JORDAN AND THE GREEN LANTERN CORPS #12
Variant Cover Art by KEVIN NOWLAN

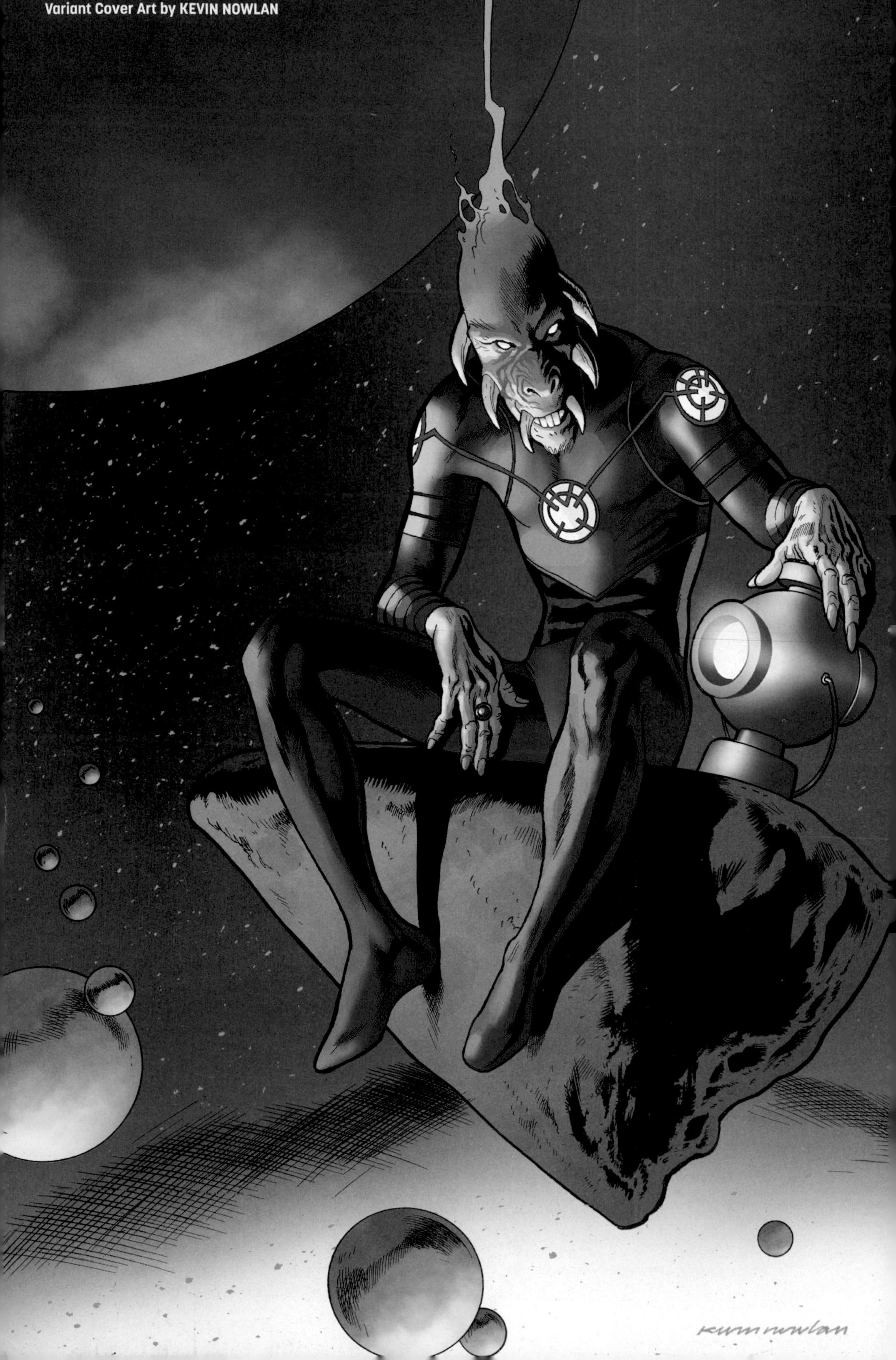

HAL JORDAN AND THE GREEN LANTERN CORPS #13
Variant Cover Art by KEVIN NOWLAN

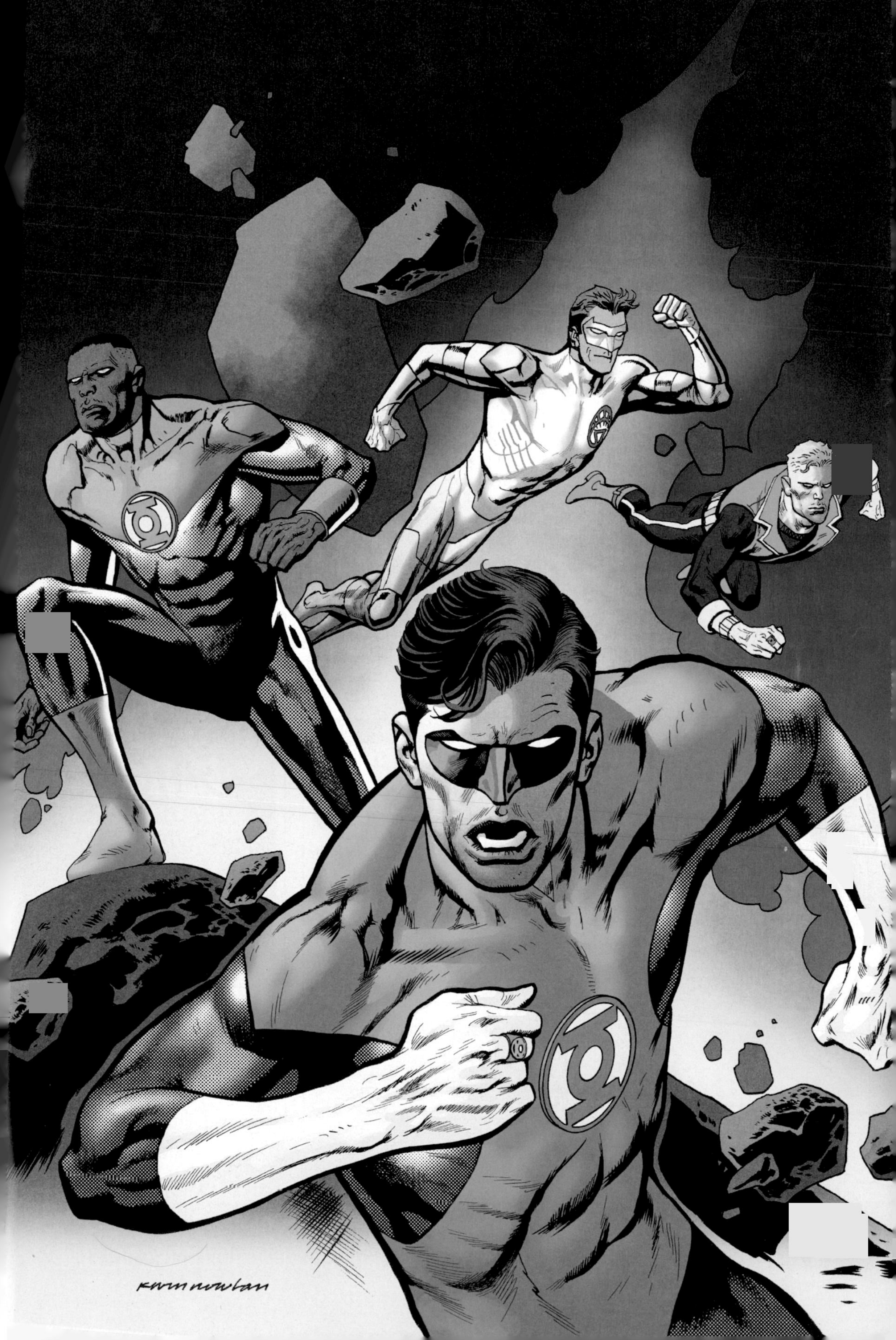
kevin nowlan

DC UNIVERSE REBIRTH

GREEN LANTERNS

VOL. 1: RAGE PLANET

SAM HUMPHRIES
with ETHAN VAN SCIVER

VOL. 1 RAGE PLANET

SAM HUMPHRIES ★ ROBSON ROCHA ★ ETHAN VAN SCIVER ★ ED BENES

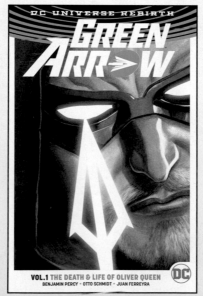

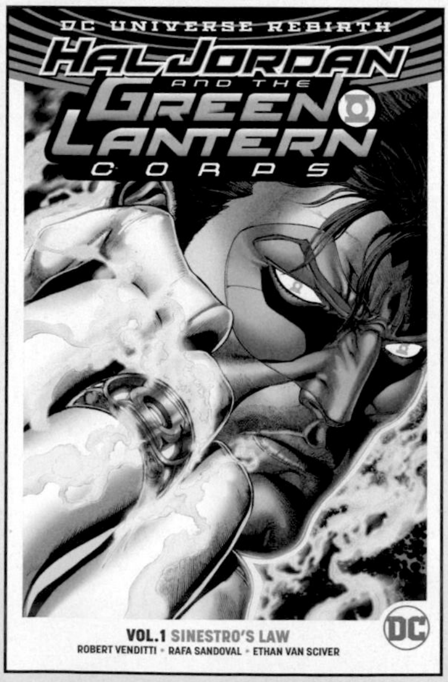

VOL. 1 SINESTRO'S LAW

ROBERT VENDITTI ★ RAFA SANDOVAL ★ ETHAN VAN SCIVER

VOL. 1 THE DEATH & LIFE OF OLIVER QUEEN

BENJAMIN PERCY ★ OTTO SCHMIDT ★ JUAN FERREYRA

VOL. 1 WHO IS ORACLE?

JULIE BENSON ★ SHAWNA BENSON ★ CLAIRE ROE

HAL JORDAN AND THE GREEN LANTERN CORPS VOL. 1: SINESTRO'S LAW

GREEN ARROW VOL. 1: THE DEATH & LIFE OF OLIVER QUEEN

BATGIRL AND THE BIRDS OF PREY VOL. 1: WHO IS ORACLE?